Presented to:

By:

On the
occasion of:

The Everyday Life Psalms and Proverbs

FEATURING NOTES *and* COMMENTARY
BY

JOYCE MEYER

New York • Nashville

The Everyday Life Psalms and Proverbs

FaithWords
Hachette Book Group
1290 Avenue of the Americas, New York, NY 10104
faithwords.com
twitter.com/faithwords

Originally published in hardcover by FaithWords in October 2006
under the title *The Everyday Life Bible*
First Edition: March 2018

FaithWords is a division of Hachette Book Group, Inc. The FaithWords name and
logo are trademarks of Hachette Book Group, Inc.

The publisher is not responsible for websites (or their content)
that are not owned by the publisher.

The Hachette Speakers Bureau provides a wide range of authors
for speaking events. To find out more, go to
www.hachettespeakersbureau.com or call (866) 376-6591.

The Holy Bible, Amplified Bible, copyright © 1954, 1958, 1962, 1964, 1965, 1987,
2015 by The Lockman Foundation, all rights reserved

This book was published with the assistance of Peachtree Publishing
Services, LLC (www.PeachtreePublishingServices.com).

ISBN: 9781546017882 (LeatherLuxe®)

Printed in China
RRD-S

10 9 8 7 6 5 4 3 2 1

FOREWORD

Scriptural Promise

"The grass withers, the flower fades,
But the word of our God stands forever."

Isaiah 40:8

The *Amplified* Bible has been produced with the conviction that the words of Scripture as originally penned in the Hebrew, Aramaic, and Greek were inspired by God. Since they are the eternal Word of God, the Holy Scriptures speak with fresh power to each generation, to give wisdom that leads to salvation, that people may serve Christ to the glory of God.

The Fourfold Aim of The Lockman Foundation

1. The publications shall be true to the original Hebrew, Aramaic, and Greek.
2. They shall be grammatically correct.
3. They shall be understandable to the people.
4. They shall give the Lord Jesus Christ His proper place, the place which the Word gives Him; therefore, no translation work will ever be personalized.

PREFACE

In 1958 The Lockman Foundation and Zondervan Publishing House issued the first edition of the *Amplified* New Testament. In 1962 and 1964 the two-volume *Amplified* Old Testament was released. In 1965 the complete *Amplified* Bible was published, and in 1987 the *Amplified* Bible, *Expanded Edition* was completed. Over fifty years have passed since the *Amplified* New Testament was translated and during that time there have been changes in both the style and usage of the English language; therefore, it seemed appropriate for The Lockman Foundation to revisit this well-loved translation of God's Word. Accordingly, Dr. Robert G. Lambeth, President of The Lockman Foundation, established a translation team and under his leadership the project was developed and completed.

The Lockman Foundation is now pleased to present the *Amplified* Bible of 2015. The English has been updated based on contemporary usage, a substantial number of new amplifications have been added to the Old Testament, and original amplifications have been updated, expanded, refined, or clarified where needed. The translation team has also added a significant number of new footnotes and references.

The result is a translation that is contemporary and firmly based on the foundation established by the *Amplified* Bible of 1965. That original translation project was envisioned and led by Frances Siewert (1881-1967), an amazing and gifted woman who devoted her life to serving the Lord and to making His Word available in an entirely new format. Her contribution to the spread of the Gospel through the *Amplified* Bible is impossible to quantify and her vision continues to speak to the hearts of people today.

The *Amplified* Bible of 2015 has been editorially recast so that a verse may be read either with or without amplification. The basic verse is the literal equivalent translation of the Hebrew,

Aramaic, or Greek text. The basic verse is then amplified in a way that permits the reader to have a greater understanding of the relationship between the crispness of contemporary English and the depth of meaning in the biblical languages.

EXPLANATION OF GENERAL FORMAT

Amplification is indicated within the English text by parentheses, brackets, and italicized conjunctions.

Parentheses in Roman type ( ) supply the definition in context of the preceding name, place, or word. When the *Amplified* Bible is read aloud the definition in context may be skipped over.

Parentheses in **bold** type () indicate a parenthetical phrase that is part of the original language and should be included when Scripture is read aloud.

Brackets in Roman type [ ] contain justified words, phrases, or brief commentary not fully expressed in the preceding English text, but which are validated by the meaning of the original Hebrew, Aramaic, or Greek, or are validated elsewhere by Scripture. The amplifications within brackets serve many purposes. They may expand the depth of meaning in the underlying Hebrew, Aramaic, or Greek word; they may clarify a theological word or concept; they may expand a teaching or principle; they may supply information that helps the reader grasp the context of the passage.

Brackets in **bold** type [] are footnoted and indicate text not found in early mss or found only in some early mss.

Italicized conjunctions: *and, or, nor* are not in the original text, but are used to connect additional English words indicated by the original Hebrew, Aramaic, or Greek.

Italicized words are not found in the original language, but implied by it.

Proper names of persons, places, or things are often used to replace pronouns. When pronouns are retained in the text they may be followed by a name placed in parentheses.

Pronouns referring to God, the Father; Jesus, the Son; and the Holy Spirit are always capitalized, so that the reader immediately recognizes Deity in the text.

Paragraphs are identified by **bold** verse numbers or **bold** letters. This allows paragraphs to be clearly identified without displaying the verses in paragraph format. The text can still be read or studied by paragraphs, but individual verses are much easier to find when each verse begins on a new line.

Small capital letters are used in the New Testament to indicate Old Testament quotations or obvious references to Old Testament texts. Variations of Old Testament wording are found in New Testament citations depending on whether the New Testa- ment writer translated from a Hebrew text, used existing Greek or Aramaic translations, or restated the material. It should be noted that modern rules for the indication of direct quotations were not used in biblical times; therefore, the ancient writer would use exact quotations or references to quotations without specific indication of such.

The proper name of God in the Old Testament is most significant and understandably so. The most common name for the Deity is God, a translation of the Hebrew word, *Elohim*. One of the titles for God is Lord, a translation of *Adonai*. There is yet another name which is particularly assigned to God as His special or proper name, that is, the four letters YHWH (Exodus 3:14 and Isaiah 42:8). This name has not been pronounced by the Jews because of reverence for the great sacredness of the divine name. Therefore, it has been consistently translated LORD. The only exception to this translation of YHWH is when it occurs in immediate proximity to the word *Lord*, that is, *Adonai*. In that case it is regularly translated GOD in order to avoid confusion. When the name of God appears within parentheses or brackets, the context of the verse determines which name and type style is used.

Verse references are placed in brackets at the end of some verses. If a verse contains more than one Scripture reference, the references are listed in biblical order.

Section headings are included in the text, but are not part of the original language.

ABBREVIATIONS AND SPECIAL MARKINGS

Aram	=	Aramaic
c	=	about
DSS	=	Dead Sea Scrolls
etc.	=	and so on
e.g.	=	for example
Gr	=	Greek translation of O.T. (Septuagint or LXX) or Greek text of N.T.
Heb	=	Hebrew text, usually Masoretic
i.e.,	=	that is
Lat	=	Latin
MT	=	Masoretic text
Syr	=	Syriac
Lit	=	A literal translation
Or	=	An alternate translation justified by the Hebrew, Aramaic, or Greek
ch, chs	=	chapter, chapters
cf	=	compare
f, ff	=	following verse or verses
mg	=	Refers to a marginal reading on another verse
ms, mss	=	manuscript, manuscripts
v, vv	=	verse, verses

THE LOCKMAN FOUNDATION

The Lockman Foundation wishes to express deepest gratitude to all those who have contributed to the development of the 2015 edition of the Amplified Bible. Throughout these years of translation many people have shared their time, talent, prayers and very best effort to bring this Bible translation to completion.

It is our prayer that each participant—whether scholar or staff, professor or proofreader, consultant or critical reader—will look at these pages of Scripture and know that each one's contribution is treasured . . . nothing is insignificant when dealing with God's Word.

To quote F. Dewey "Granddad" Lockman (1898–1974), "This work is a symphony, not a solo!" May each of you be specially blessed and always hold a special joy in your heart whenever you read the new Amplified Bible 2015. Thank you beloved.

Phoebe McAuley Lambeth
Coordinating Editor

A Personal Word from Joyce Meyer

For more than forty years, I have enjoyed and greatly benefit-ted from the *Amplified* Bible. It gives insights I have not found in other translations I have used. Because God has used the *Amplified* Bible in my life to open up many truths from His Word to me, I wanted to share the insight He has given me to help others. I prayed for many years to get permission from the publisher to produce a specialty Bible using this version and was thrilled when permission was finally granted.

God's Word is very precious to me. I can truly say that I love God's Word. It has changed me, and it has changed my life. I have also witnessed transformation in the lives of multitudes of people over the years through studying and believing God's Word. God's words are not ordinary words, as the words of people are. His words are filled with power. The power of God is actually inherent in His Word and it heals, delivers, comforts, saves, corrects, and encourages us.

When people are very discouraged, they can actually take God's Word as medicine for their souls. It encourages the discouraged, lifts up the lowly and downtrodden, heals the sick, saves the lost, fills the empty, and counsels those who need to make a decision.

Jesus is the Word of God Who took on human flesh and dwelt for a while among people (see John 1:14). When we read, study, meditate on, or confess the Word of God, we are fellowshipping with Jesus. We are actually taking Him as our nourishment and we find that only He can satisfy our souls. God's Word is our spiritual food and we need it regularly, just as we need natural food. The prophet Jeremiah said, "Your words were found and I ate them, and Your words became a joy to me and the delight of my heart" (Jeremiah 15:16).

God's Word is very important to Him. The Bible says in Psalm 138:2 that He has magnified together His name and His word. We should always respect and honor God's Word and give it a place of priority in our everyday lives. I truly believe that God's Word contains an answer to every problem and situation we encounter in life. It is certainly spiritual, but it is also very practical and has been given for our everyday lives. This is why, when we first produced the full edition of this Bible, using the *Amplified Classic* Bible, we called it *The Everyday Life Bible*. This Psalms and

Proverbs edition uses the most current *Amplified* Bible translation (2015). I believe that many people have connected the Bible only with church or some other spiritual activity when it really is a life-giving Book we can apply to our lives daily.

I also believe the Bible is largely a book about relationships. It offers in-depth information about our relationships with God, ourselves, and our fellow human beings. Much of the difficulty we face in life is the result of poor relationships. I have learned through God's Word how to receive His love, love myself in a balanced way, and let His love flow through me to others. I pray that this would be your goal because Jesus said that the thing we should concentrate on is loving God and loving others as we love ourselves (see Matthew 27:37–39).

Let me encourage you to be a "lifetime learner." Apply God's Word to situations in your life as you would apply medicine to an injury. If you are having a particular struggle such as anger, depression, or fear, go to God's Word and select passages that deal with these subjects (I have provided in the back of this book a topical index called "The Word for Your Everyday Life," which makes finding these passages easy for you). As you read these verses, slowly take them in, and roll them over and over in your mind. You will find a change taking place in your heart and life. I encourage you to love God's Word, for in it you will find resurrection power and contentment far greater than anything the world has to offer.

Now, I want to make sure you are aware of the special features *The Everyday Life Psalms and Proverbs* has to offer because I believe they will help tremendously as you live your life by the Word of God.

Book Introductions: At the beginning of the books of Psalms and Proverbs, you will find basic historical background information on that particular book, along with my thoughts on why each book is important and how it relates to practical living. You will also find "Everyday Life Principles," which summarize the key points and general themes of each book.

Everyday Life Articles: These articles are the longest, most thorough entries in the book. They correspond to specific verses or passages and provide great insight and advice on a variety of topics. I wrote many of them especially for *The Everyday Life Bible*, and I believe they will help you tremendously in your everyday life.

Life Points: If you have followed my teaching ministry for long, you may realize that I often use short, catchy, to-the-point phrases or "one-liners" to emphasize certain principles or truths. Life Points include many of these well-known phrases, as well and other nuggets of encouragement and exhortation.

Speak the Word: I believe that confessing God's Word is vital to a successful Christian life. Anywhere you see an entry titled, "Speak the Word," you will find a Scripture verse or passage adapted as a first-person confession or prayer. I encourage you to speak and pray these words as you come across them in this Bible and use them to teach you how to pray and confess other verses throughout God's Word.

Putting the Word to Work: We all need to apply the truths of God's Word to our lives. The "Putting the Word to Work" feature takes biblical principles and gives you opportunities to meditate on them, answer questions about them, and think about how you can specifically apply them to the situations in your life.

The Word for Your Everyday Life: Located in the back of this book, "The Word for Your Everyday Life" is a list of topics you are likely to face over the course of your life—perhaps many times. Under each topic heading, you will find Scripture references pertaining to that topic. Read those verses and passages, and you will discover biblical answers and guidance to help you overcome every challenge and live your life victoriously.

How to Receive Jesus as Your Personal Lord and Savior: The most important relationship of your life is a personal relationship with Jesus Christ. If you would like to receive Him as your Lord and Savior and enter into the greatest relationship you have ever known, please pray the prayer at the back of the book on the page titled, "How to Receive Jesus as Your Personal Lord and Savior."

Psalms

Author:
David, Asaph, the sons of Korah, Moses, and others

Date:
1000 BC–300 BC

Everyday Life Principles:
The Psalms are full of practical advice for you, and they are easy to read and to pray.

When you need encouragement, instruction, or comfort, read the Psalms.

Express your heart to God freely and fully, just as the psalmists did.

The Psalms are a collection of 150 songs and poems written over a period of many years.

Because they were originally intended and used as worship songs for congregations or individuals, many of the psalms address God directly, and they are very easy to read and to pray. They are filled not only with praise and worship to God, but with practical advice and great insight into the various emotions, victories, and struggles people face.

One thing I love about the Psalms is that the writers were very honest with God, and they communicated with Him from their hearts. Whether they were joyful, confident, depressed, angry, lonely, or afraid, they wrote about it. In the midst of expressing themselves freely and fully to Him, they also realized their need for God in fresh new ways and reaffirmed their trust in Him. Every emotion you or I could ever experience seems to be mentioned in the Psalms. No matter what you are going through, God wants to hear your heart.

Many people have a favorite Psalm. For most, it is probably Psalm 23; for others, it is Psalm 91; and for others it is Psalm 100. I would have to say that my personal favorite is Psalm 27.

I encourage you to read the Psalms and read them often. Let them remind you to always tell God what is in your heart and receive comfort, strength, and direction from Him. Let them also remind you to praise and worship God with all your heart.

BOOK ONE

PSALM 1

The Righteous and the Wicked Contrasted.

¹BLESSED [fortunate, prosperous, and favored by God] is the man who does not walk in the counsel of the wicked [following their advice and example],
Nor stand in the path of sinners,
Nor sit [down to rest] in the seat of scoffers (ridiculers).
²But his delight is in the law of the LORD,
And on His law [His precepts and teachings] he [habitually] meditates day and night. [Rom 13:8–10; Gal 3:1–29; 2 Tim 3:16]
³And he will be like a tree *firmly* planted [and fed] by streams of water,
Which yields its fruit in its season;
Its leaf does not wither;
And in whatever he does, he prospers [and comes to maturity]. [Jer 17:7, 8]

life point

Psalm 1 promises blessing and God's favor to those who delight in God's law (His precepts and teachings) and who meditate on His Word day and night. In other words, those who give God and His Word first place in their lives can expect to prosper in every way.

⁴The wicked [those who live in disobedience to God's law] are not so,
But they are like the chaff [worthless and without substance] which the wind blows away.
⁵Therefore the wicked will not stand [unpunished] in the judgment,
Nor sinners in the assembly of the righteous.
⁶For the LORD knows *and* fully approves the way of the righteous,
But the way of the wicked shall perish.

PSALM 2

The Reign of the LORD's Anointed.

¹WHY ARE the nations in an uproar [in turmoil against God],
And why do the people devise a vain *and* hopeless plot?
²The kings of the earth take their stand;
And the rulers take counsel together
Against the LORD and His Anointed (the Davidic King, the Messiah, the Christ), saying, [Acts 4:25–27]
³"Let us break apart their [divine] bands [of restraint]
And cast away their cords [of control] from us."

⁴He who sits [enthroned] in the heavens laughs [at their rebellion];
The [Sovereign] Lord scoffs at them [and in supreme contempt He mocks them].

⁵Then He will speak to them in
   His [profound] anger
And terrify them with His
   displeasure, saying,
⁶"Yet as for Me, I have
   anointed *and* firmly
   installed My King
Upon Zion, My holy
   mountain."

⁷"I will declare the decree of
   the LORD:
He said to Me, 'You are My Son;
This day [I proclaim] I have
   begotten You. [2 Sam 7:14;
   Heb 1:5; 3:5, 6; 2 Pet 1:17, 18]

life point

I once saw a movie in which a king
issued a royal decree. He wrote
down his command and then sent
forth riders on horseback throughout the country to "declare the
decree" to the citizens of that
kingdom. In the Scriptures we see
the issuing of such royal decrees in
Esther 8:8–14 and in Luke 2:1–3.

In Psalm 2:7, the psalmist wrote that
he would "declare the decree of
the Lord." What decree? The decree
in which the Lord declares that He
(Jesus) is God's only begotten Son
(see Hebrews 1:1–5).

The written Word of God is the
formal decree of the Lord, our King.
When we declare God's Word out
of our mouths, with hearts full of
faith, those faith-filled words go
forth to establish God's order in our
lives. When the royal decree is pronounced, things begin to change!

⁸'Ask of Me, and I will
   assuredly give [You]
   the nations as Your
   inheritance,
And the ends of the earth as
   Your possession.
⁹'You shall break them with a
   rod of iron;
You shall shatter them [in
   pieces] like earthenware.'"
   [Rev 12:5; 19:15]

¹⁰Now therefore, O kings, act
   wisely;
Be instructed *and* take
   warning, O leaders (judges,
   rulers) of the earth.
¹¹Worship the LORD *and* serve
   Him with reverence [with
   awe-inspired fear and
   submissive wonder];
Rejoice [yet do so] with
   trembling.
¹²Kiss (pay respect to) the Son,
   so that He does not become
   angry, and you perish in the
   way,
For His wrath may soon be
   kindled *and* set aflame.
How blessed [fortunate,
   prosperous, and favored by
   God] are all those who take
   refuge in Him!

PSALM 3

Morning Prayer of Trust
in God.

A Psalm of David. When he
fled from Absalom his son.

¹O LORD, how my enemies
   have increased!
Many are rising up against me.
²Many are saying of me,
   "There is no help [no salvation]
   for him in God."   *Selah.*

³But You, O LORD, are a shield for me,

My glory [and my honor], and the One who lifts my head.

hold your head high

Although there are "downers" in this life, there are also "lifters." In Psalm 3:1–3, the psalmist says that despite his distressing situation, he is not despairing or becoming depressed because his confidence is in the Lord, the One who lifts his head.

When we are depressed, it seems everything around us is falling apart. We lose strength; our heads and hands and hearts all begin to hang down. Even our eyes and our voices are lowered. We become downcast because we are looking at our problems rather than at the Lord.

No matter what is causing us to be downcast, the Lord encourages us throughout His Word to lift our heads and our hands and look to Him. We find one of these many examples in Genesis 13:14 when God told Abraham, who had been shortchanged by his nephew Lot, to "lift up" his eyes and look around him in all directions, for He was giving him all the land as far as he could see for his inheritance. In Psalm 24:7 the psalmist says, "Lift up your heads, O gates, and be lifted up, ancient doors, that the King of glory may come in." In 1 Timothy 2:8, the Apostle Paul encouraged people to pray, "lifting up holy hands."

These instructions are good for us to remember today. When people disappoint us, instead of becoming discouraged and depressed, God wants us to decide to lift up our heads and eyes and look at the possibilities, not the problems, around us, trusting Him to lead us into an even better situation—because He has one for us.

We may be tempted to say, "Oh, what's the use?" and just give up rather than moving in a new direction as Abraham did, but the Lord is constantly exhorting us to lift up our eyes and heads and hearts to take inventory of our blessings and not our problems. He encourages us to look at Him because God has plans to bless and increase us abundantly.

No matter how your life has turned out to this point, you have only two options. One is to give up and quit; the other is to keep going. If you decide to keep going, again you have only two choices. One is to live in depression and misery; the other is to live in hope and joy.

Choosing to live in hope and joy does not mean you will not face any more disappointments or discouraging situations; it just means you have decided not to let them get you down. Instead, you will lift up your eyes and hands and head and heart and look not at your problems, but at the Lord, Who has promised to see you through to abundance and victory.

[4] With my voice I was crying to
the LORD,
And He answered me from
His holy mountain.   *Selah.*
[5] I lay down and slept [safely];
I awakened, for the LORD
sustains me.
[6] I will not be intimidated *or*
afraid of the ten thousands
Who have set themselves
against me all around.

[7] Arise, O LORD; save me, O my
God!
For You have struck all my
enemies on the cheek;
You have shattered the teeth
of the wicked.
[8] Salvation belongs to the LORD;
May Your blessing be upon
Your people.   *Selah.*

PSALM 4

Evening Prayer of Trust in God.

To the Chief Musician; on
stringed instruments.
A Psalm of David.

[1] ANSWER ME when I call,
O God of my righteousness!
You have freed me when I was
hemmed in *and* relieved me
when I was in distress;

Be gracious to me and hear
[and respond to] my prayer.

[2] O sons of men, how long
will my honor *and* glory be
[turned into] shame?
How long will you [my enemies]
love worthless (vain, futile)
things and seek deception
and lies?   *Selah.*
[3] But know that the LORD has
set apart for Himself [and
dealt wonderfully with]
the godly man [the one of
honorable character and
moral courage—the one who
does right].
The LORD hears *and* responds
when I call to Him.

[4] Tremble [with anger or fear],
and do not sin;
Meditate in your heart upon
your bed and be still [reflect
on your sin and repent of
your rebellion]. [Eph 4:26]
                Selah.
[5] Offer righteous sacrifices;
Trust [confidently] in the LORD.

[6] Many are saying, "Oh, that we
might see some good!"
Lift up the light of Your face
upon us, O LORD.

speak the Word

Thank You, Lord, for hearing and responding to me
when I call to You.
−ADAPTED FROM PSALM 4:3

Thank You, God, that I can take refuge in You
and put my trust in You.
Thank You for covering me and sheltering me.
−ADAPTED FROM PSALM 5:11

⁷You have put joy in my heart,
More than [others know]
    when their wheat and
    new wine have yielded
    abundantly.
⁸In peace [and with a tranquil
    heart] I will both lie down
    and sleep,
For You alone, O Lᴏʀᴅ, make
    me dwell in safety *and*
    confident trust.

PSALM 5

Prayer for Protection from the Wicked.

To the Chief Musician; on
wind instruments. A Psalm
of David.

¹LISTEN TO my words,
    O Lᴏʀᴅ,
Consider my groaning *and*
    sighing.
²Heed the sound of my cry for
    help, my King and my God,
For to You I pray.
³In the morning, O Lᴏʀᴅ, You
    will hear my voice;
In the morning I will prepare
    [a prayer and a sacrifice]
    for You and watch *and* wait
    [for You to speak to my
    heart].

⁴For You are not a God
    who takes pleasure in
    wickedness;
No evil [person] dwells with
    You.
⁵The boastful *and* the
    arrogant will not stand in
    Your sight;
You hate all who do evil.
⁶You destroy those who tell
    lies;

The Lᴏʀᴅ detests *and* rejects
    the bloodthirsty and
    deceitful man.
⁷But as for me, I will enter
    Your house through the
    abundance of Your steadfast
    love *and* tender mercy;
At Your holy temple I will bow
    [obediently] in reverence for
    You.

⁸O Lᴏʀᴅ, lead me in Your
    righteousness because of
    my enemies;
Make Your way straight
    (direct, right) before me.
⁹For there is nothing
    trustworthy *or* reliable *or*
    truthful in what they say;
Their heart is destruction
    [just a treacherous chasm, a
    yawning gulf of lies].
Their throat is an open grave;
They [glibly] flatter with their
    [silken] tongue. [Rom 3:13]
¹⁰Hold them guilty, O God;
Let them fall by their own
    designs *and* councils!
Cast them out because of
    the abundance of their
    transgressions,
For they are mutinous *and*
    have rebelled against You.

¹¹But let all who take refuge
    and put their trust in You
    rejoice,
Let them ever sing for joy;
Because You cover *and* shelter
    them,
Let those who love Your name
    be joyful *and* exult in You.
¹²For You, O Lᴏʀᴅ, bless the
    righteous man [the one who
    is in right standing with
    You];

You surround him with favor
as with a shield.

PSALM 6

Prayer for Mercy in Time of Trouble.

To the Chief Musician; on
stringed instruments, set
[possibly] an octave below.
A Psalm of David.

¹ O LORD, do not rebuke *or*
punish me in Your anger,
Nor discipline me in Your wrath.
² Have mercy on me *and* be
gracious to me, O LORD, for I
am weak (faint, frail);
Heal me, O LORD, for my
bones are dismayed *and*
anguished.
³ My soul [as well as my body]
is greatly dismayed.
But as for You, O LORD—how
long [until You act on my
behalf]?

⁴ Return, O LORD, rescue my soul;
Save me because of Your
[unfailing] steadfast love *and*
mercy.
⁵ For in death there is no
mention of You;
In Sheol (the nether world,
the place of the dead) who
will praise You *and* give You
thanks?

⁶ I am weary with my groaning;
Every night I soak my bed
with tears,
I drench my couch with my
weeping.
⁷ My eye grows dim with grief;
It grows old because of all my
enemies.

⁸ Depart from me, all you who do
evil,
For the LORD has heard the
voice of my weeping. [Matt
7:23; Luke 13:27]
⁹ The LORD has heard my
supplication [my plea for
grace];
The LORD receives my prayer.
¹⁰ Let all my enemies be ashamed
and greatly horrified;
Let them turn back, let them
suddenly be ashamed [of
what they have done].

PSALM 7

The LORD Implored to Defend the Psalmist against the Wicked.

An Ode of David, [perhaps in a
wild, irregular, enthusiastic
strain,] which he sang
to the LORD concerning
the words of Cush, a
Benjamite.

¹ O LORD my God, in You I
take refuge;
Save me and rescue me
from all those who pursue
me,
² So that my enemy will not
tear me like a lion,

speak the Word

*God, I thank You for hearing my supplication
and receiving my prayer.*
—ADAPTED FROM PSALM 6:9

when God tests your emotions

In Psalm 7:9 we read that God "tries" our hearts and minds, our emotions (Revelation 2:23 conveys a similar message). What does *the* word *try* mean in this context? It means "to test until purified."

A few years ago, as I was praying, I felt God let me know that He was going to "test my emotions." I had never heard of anything like that, and had not yet discovered the scriptures about this in the Bible.

About six months later, I became an emotional wreck. I cried for no reason. Everything hurt my feelings. There were times when I went to bed praying, feeling as sweet as could be, then I woke up the next morning in a really cranky mood, as if I had stayed up all night eating nails! I thought, *What is the problem here? What's going on?* Then the Lord reminded me of what He had spoken to me earlier: "I am going to test your emotions." As He led me to Psalm 7:9 and Revelation 2:23, He caused me to understand that He was doing a work in my emotional life for my own good. He was going to teach me how to be stable and continue walking in the fruit of the Holy Spirit (see Galatians 5:22, 23) regardless of how I felt.

No matter who you are, there will be periods of time when you feel more emotional than usual. You may wake up one morning and feel like breaking down and crying for no reason. You may feel sad or depressed; you may feel that nobody cares about you; or you might feel sorry for yourself. During those times you must learn how to manage your emotions and not allow them to manage you. At these times your feelings will probably get hurt very easily. The slightest thing might make you angry. Emotions are very fickle! They can be one way one day and entirely different the next day. God has to teach us not to live by our feelings, or we will never enjoy victorious living and we will not give God the glory He deserves.

What should you do when you start feeling that your emotions are being tested? (1) Do not allow yourself to fall under condemnation. (2) Do not even try to figure out what is happening. (3) Instead, simply say, "This is one of those times when my emotions are being tried. I'm going to trust God and learn to control them."

How are you and I ever going to learn to control ourselves emotionally unless God allows us to go through some trying times? Remember, the Bible says that God will never allow any more to come upon us than we are able to bear (see 1 Corinthians 10:13). If the Lord does not allow such testing times to come upon us, we will never grow, and we will never learn how to deal with Satan when he brings things against us—which will happen sooner or later.

Trying times are learning times. They are testing times, and I always say, "Pass your test this time so you will not have to take it again."

Dragging me away while
    there is no one to rescue
    [me].

³O Lᴏʀᴅ my God, if I have done
    this,
If there is injustice in my
    hands,
⁴If I have done evil to him
    who was at peace with me,
Or without cause robbed him
    who was my enemy,
⁵Let the enemy pursue me and
    overtake me;
And let him trample my life to
    the ground
And lay my honor in the dust.
                    Selah.

⁶Arise, O Lᴏʀᴅ, in Your anger;
Lift up Yourself against the
    rage of my enemies;
Rise up for me; You have
    commanded judgment *and*
    vindication.
⁷Let the assembly of the
    nations be gathered around
    You,
And return on high over
    them.

Have you ever looked into the vast,
starry sky at night and felt very
small in comparison? Consider the
greatness of God as you observe
His creation all around you, and
remember that you are a master-
piece of God's creation, made in
His very image! Take a moment to
praise God for His excellence and
thank Him for crowning you with
glory and honor.

⁸The Lᴏʀᴅ judges the
    peoples;
Judge me, O Lᴏʀᴅ, *and*
    grant me justice
    according to my
    righteousness and
    according to the
    integrity within me.
⁹Oh, let the wickedness
    of the wicked come
    to an end, but establish
    the righteous [those in
    right standing with You];
For the righteous God tries
    the hearts and minds.
    [Rev 2:23]
¹⁰My shield *and* my defense
    depend on God,
Who saves the upright in
    heart.
¹¹God is a righteous judge,
And a God who is indignant
    every day.

¹²If a man does not repent,
    God will sharpen His
    sword;
He has strung *and* bent His
    [mighty] bow and made it
    ready.
¹³He has also prepared
    [other] deadly weapons for
    Himself;
He makes His arrows fiery
    shafts [aimed at the
    unrepentant].
¹⁴Behold, the [wicked and
    irreverent] man is
    pregnant with sin,
And he conceives mischief
    and gives birth to lies.
¹⁵He has dug a pit and
    hollowed it out,
And has fallen into the
    [very] pit which he made
    [as a trap].

¹⁶His mischief will return on
his own head,
And his violence will come
down on the top of his head
[like loose dirt].

¹⁷I will give thanks to the
LORD according to His
righteousness *and* justice,
And I will sing praise to the
name of the LORD Most High.

PSALM 8

The LORD's Glory and Man's Dignity.

To the Chief Musician; set to a
Philistine lute [or perhaps to a
particular Hittite tune].
A Psalm of David.

¹O LORD, our Lord,
How majestic *and* glorious *and*
excellent is Your name in all
the earth!
You have displayed Your
splendor above the heavens.
²Out of the mouths of infants
and nursing babes You have
established strength
Because of Your adversaries,
That You might silence
the enemy *and* make the
revengeful cease. [Matt
21:15, 16]

life point

You have been singled out by God, Who has placed His crown of glory and honor, or favor and excellence, upon your head, according to Psalm 8:5. You may not see your crown, but it is there—just like the robe of righteousness in which you are dressed. You may not see with your physical eyes your robe of righteousness or the crown of God's favor, but they exist in the spiritual realm (see Isaiah 61:10). We need to remember that the natural man cannot perceive the things of God because they are spiritually discerned (see 1 Corinthians 2:14).

Even though the Bible *says* we have been crowned with glory and honor, often we do not act as though we are. One reason we do not tap into God's blessings is that we do not believe we deserve them. Another reason is that we have not been taught that God's blessings can be ours and consequently have not activated our faith in this area. So we wander through life, taking whatever the devil throws at us without ever resisting him and claiming what is rightfully ours.

If you will reread Psalm 8:6, you will see that God has put all things under our feet; He has given us dominion over the works of His hands. To me, those words do not indicate that we are supposed to allow our problems or the devil and his demons to intimidate, dominate, and oppress us. If we will receive by faith the blessing of glory and honor with which the Lord our God has crowned us, not only will our faces shine forth with the glory of the Lord, but we will enjoy respect, esteem, favor, and a good reputation.

³When I see *and* consider
   Your heavens, the work
   of Your fingers,
The moon and the stars,
   which You have
   established,
⁴What is man that You are
   mindful of him,
And the son of
   [earthborn] man that
   You care for him?
⁵Yet You have made
   him a little lower than
   God,
And You have crowned
   him with glory and
   honor.
⁶You made him to have
   dominion over the works
   of Your hands;
You have put all things
   under his feet,
   [1 Cor 15:27; Eph 1:22, 23;
   Heb 2:6–8]
⁷All sheep and oxen,
And also the beasts of the
   field,
⁸The birds of the air, and the
   fish of the sea,
Whatever passes through
   the paths of the seas.

⁹O Lᴏʀᴅ, our Lord,
   How majestic *and*
   glorious *and* excellent
   is Your name in all the
   earth!

PSALM 9

A Psalm of Thanksgiving for God's Justice.

To the Chief Musician;
on Muth-labben. A Psalm
of David.

¹I WILL give thanks *and*
   praise the Lᴏʀᴅ, with all
   my heart;
I will tell aloud all Your
   wonders *and* marvelous
   deeds.
²I will rejoice and exult in you;
I will sing praise to Your
   name, O Most High.

³When my enemies turn back,
   They stumble and perish
   before You.
⁴For You have maintained my
   right and my cause;
You have sat on the throne
   judging righteously.
⁵You have rebuked the nations,
   You have destroyed the
   wicked *and* unrepentant;
You have wiped out their
   name forever and ever.
⁶The enemy has been cut
   off *and* has vanished in
   everlasting ruins,
You have uprooted their
   cities;
The very memory of them has
   perished.

speak the Word

I will thank You and praise You, Lord, with all my heart,
and I will tell people about the wonderful and marvelous things
You have done.
I will rejoice and exult in You.
−ADAPTED FROM PSALM 9:1, 2

⁷But the LORD will remain *and*
   sit enthroned forever;
He has prepared *and*
   established His
   throne for judgment.
   [Heb 1:11]
⁸And He will judge the world
   in righteousness;
He will execute judgment for
   the nations with fairness
   (equity). [Acts 17:31]
⁹The LORD also will be a refuge
   and a stronghold for the
   oppressed,
A refuge in times of trouble;
¹⁰And those who know
   Your name [who have
   experienced Your precious
   mercy] will put their
   confident trust in You,
For You, O LORD, have not
   abandoned those who seek
   You. [Ps 42:1]

¹¹Sing praises to the LORD, who
   dwells in Zion;
Declare among the peoples
   His [great and wondrous]
   deeds.
¹²For He who avenges blood
   [unjustly shed] remembers
   them (His people);
He does not forget the cry of
   the afflicted *and* abused.
¹³Have mercy on me *and* be
   gracious to me, O LORD;
See how I am afflicted by
   those who hate me,
You who lift me up from the
   gates of death,
¹⁴That I may tell aloud all Your
   praises,
That in the gates of the
   daughter of Zion (Jerusalem)
I may rejoice in Your salvation
   and Your help.

¹⁵The nations have sunk down
   in the pit which they have
   made;
In the net which they hid,
   their own foot has been
   caught.
¹⁶The LORD has made Himself
   known;
He executes judgment;
The wicked are trapped
   by the work of their own
   hands.
      Higgaion (meditation) Selah.

¹⁷The wicked will turn to Sheol
   (the nether world, the place
   of the dead),
Even all the nations who forget
   God.
¹⁸For the poor will not always be
   forgotten,
Nor the hope of the burdened
   perish forever.
¹⁹Arise, O LORD, do not let man
   prevail;
Let the nations be judged
   before You.
²⁰Put them in [reverent] fear of
   You, O LORD,
So that the nations may know
   they are but [frail and
   mortal] men.   *Selah.*

PSALM 10

A Prayer for the Overthrow
of the Wicked.

¹WHY DO You stand far away,
   O LORD?
Why do You hide [Yourself,
   veiling Your eyes] in times
   of trouble?
²In pride *and* arrogance the
   wicked hotly pursue *and*
   persecute the afflicted;

Let them be caught in the plots which they have devised.

³For the wicked boasts *and* sings the praises of his heart's desire,
And the greedy man curses and spurns [and even despises] the LORD.
⁴The wicked, in the haughtiness of his face, will not seek *nor* inquire for *Him;*
All his thoughts are, "There is no God [so there is no accountability or punishment]."

⁵His ways prosper at all times;
Your judgments [LORD] are on high, out of his sight [so he never thinks about them];
As for all his enemies, he sneers at them.
⁶He says to himself, "I will not be moved;
For throughout all generations I will not be in adversity [for nothing bad will happen to me]."
⁷His mouth is full of curses and deceit (fraud) and oppression;
Under his tongue is mischief and wickedness [injustice and sin].
⁸He lurks in ambush in the villages;
In hiding places he kills the innocent;
He lies in wait for the unfortunate [the unhappy, the poor, the helpless].
⁹He lurks in a hiding place like a lion in his lair;
He lies in wait to catch the afflicted;

He catches the afflicted when he draws him into his net.
¹⁰He crushes [his prey] and crouches;
And the unfortunate fall by his mighty *claws.*
¹¹He says to himself, "God has [quite] forgotten;
He has hidden His face; He will never see my deed."

¹²Arise, O LORD! O God, lift up Your hand [in judgment];
Do not forget the suffering.
¹³Why has the wicked spurned *and* shown disrespect to God?
He has said to himself, "You will not require me to account."
¹⁴You have seen it, for You have noted mischief and vexation (irritation) to take it into Your hand.
The unfortunate commits *himself* to You;
You are the helper of the fatherless.
¹⁵Break the arm of the wicked and the evildoer,
Seek out his wickedness until You find no more.

¹⁶The LORD is King forever and ever;
The nations will perish from His land.
¹⁷O LORD, You have heard the desire of the humble *and* oppressed;
You will strengthen their heart, You will incline Your ear to hear,
¹⁸To vindicate *and* obtain justice for the fatherless and the oppressed,

So that man who is of the earth
will no longer terrify them.

PSALM 11

The LORD a Refuge and Defense.

To the Chief Musician.
A Psalm of David.

¹ IN THE LORD I take refuge
[and put my trust];
How can you say to me, "Flee
like a bird to your mountain;
² For look, the wicked are
bending the bow;
They take aim with their
arrow on the string
To shoot [by stealth] in
darkness at the upright in
heart.
³ "If the foundations [of a godly
society] are destroyed,
What can the righteous do?"

⁴ The LORD is in His holy temple;
the LORD's throne is in heaven.
His eyes see, His eyelids test
the children of men. [Acts
7:49; Rev 4:2]
⁵ The LORD tests the righteous
and the wicked,
And His soul hates the
[malevolent] one who loves
violence. [James 1:12]
⁶ Upon the wicked (godless) He
will rain coals of fire;
Fire and brimstone and a
dreadful scorching wind
will be the portion of their
cup [of doom].
⁷ For the LORD is [absolutely]
righteous, He loves
righteousness (virtue,
morality, justice);

The upright shall see His
face.

PSALM 12

God, a Helper against the Treacherous.

To the Chief Musician; set
an octave below. A Psalm
of David.

¹ SAVE *AND* help *and* rescue,
LORD, for godly people cease
to be,
For the faithful vanish from
among the sons of men.
² They speak deceitful *and*
worthless words to one
another;
With flattering lips and a
double heart they speak.
³ May the LORD cut off all
flattering lips,
The tongue that speaks great
things [in boasting];
⁴ Who have said, "With our
tongue we will prevail;
Our lips are our own; who is
lord *and* master over us?"
⁵ "Because of the devastation of
the afflicted, because of the
groaning of the needy,
Now I will arise," says the
LORD; "I will place him in
the safety for which he
longs."

⁶ The words *and* promises of
the LORD are pure words,
Like silver refined in an
earthen furnace, purified
seven times.
⁷ You, O LORD, will preserve *and*
keep them;
You will protect him from this
[evil] generation forever.

⁸ The wicked strut about [in
   pompous self-importance]
   on every side,
As vileness is exalted *and*
   baseness is prized among
   the sons of men.

PSALM 13

Prayer for Help in Trouble.

To the Chief Musician.
A Psalm of David.

the importance of faithfulness

In Psalm 12:1 David asked the Lord for help because people were not being godly or faithful. Being faithful is as important today as it was then.

It is hard to find people who will be really faithful—people who will stick with you when they find out you are not perfect. The Bible says, "A friend loves at all times, and a brother is born for adversity" (Proverbs 17:17). In other words, a true friend is a person who is born to stick with you in your hard and not-so-nice times. I believe one of the saddest things in our society today is that we do not have this kind of loyalty and commitment. Many people miss out on so much because they are not faithful to see things through to the finish. Even sadder is that most of them will never even realize what incredible blessings they have missed.

David continues to say in the next verse of this psalm that people were speaking worthless, untrue words with deceitful, double hearts. We need single-minded men and women who can set their hearts on something and stick with it without being double-minded and speaking empty words. Double-hearted people believe one thing one day and something else the next. One day they like you and the next day they do not. They may be for you today, but against you tomorrow.

The Bible gives us many examples of faithful people. One of them was Moses, who was faithful in all the house of God (see Numbers 12:7). That means he was faithful to do exactly the duties God gave him to do day after day, month after month, year after year, even when he did not feel like being faithful. Moses was so faithful that even when his sister and brother, Miriam and Aaron, spoke against him, he loved them and remained faithful to them. He had so much faithfulness in his character that even when the people in his life did not treat him well, he remained the same way.

The Bible tells us that God remains faithful even when we are faithless (see 2 Timothy 2:13). That is the way God wants us to be. If everybody else is faithless, then we remain faithful. If you feel as though you are the only one who is being nice, the only one who apologizes or tries to do the right thing, keep on doing it. Determine in your heart to stay loyal to God and to keep bearing the fruit of faithfulness.

¹HOW LONG, O Lord? Will
  You forget me forever?
How long will You hide Your
  face from me?
²How long must I take counsel
  in my soul,
Having sorrow in my heart day
  after day?
How long will my enemy exalt
  himself *and* triumph over
  me?

³Consider and answer me,
  O Lord my God;
Give light (life) to my eyes, or I
  will sleep the *sleep of* death,
⁴And my enemy will say, "I
  have overcome him,"
And my adversaries will
  rejoice when I am shaken.

⁵But I have trusted *and* relied
  on *and* been confident in
  Your lovingkindness *and*
  faithfulness;
My heart shall rejoice *and*
  delight in Your salvation.
⁶I will sing to the Lord,
Because He has dealt
  bountifully with me.

PSALM 14

Folly and Wickedness of Men.

To the Chief Musician.
A Psalm of David.

¹THE [SPIRITUALLY
  ignorant] fool has said in
  his heart, "There is no God."
They are corrupt, they have
  committed repulsive *and*
  unspeakable deeds;
There is no one who does
  good. [Rom 3:10]

²The Lord has looked down
  from heaven upon the
  children of men
To see if there are any who
  understand (act wisely),
Who [truly] seek after God,
  [longing for His wisdom
  and guidance].
³They have all turned aside,
  together they have become
  corrupt;
There is no one who does
  good, not even one. [Rom
  3:11, 12]

⁴Have all the workers of
  wickedness *and* injustice no
  knowledge,
Who eat up my people as they
  eat bread,
And do not call upon the Lord?
⁵There they tremble with great
  fear,
For God is with the
  [consistently] righteous
  generation.
⁶You [evildoers] shamefully
  plan against the poor,
But the Lord is his safe
  refuge.

⁷Oh, that the salvation of Israel
  would come out of Zion!
When the Lord restores His
  captive people,
Then Jacob will rejoice, Israel
  will be glad. [Rom 11:25–27]

PSALM 15

Description of a Citizen of Zion.

A Psalm of David.

¹O LORD, who may lodge [as a
  guest] in Your tent?

Who may dwell [continually]
　on Your holy hill?
² He who walks with integrity
　and strength of character,
　and works righteousness,
And speaks *and* holds truth in
　his heart.
³ He does not slander with his
　tongue,
Nor does evil to his neighbor,
Nor takes up a reproach
　against his friend;
⁴ In his eyes an evil person is
　despised,
But he honors those who fear
　the Lord [and obediently
　worship Him with awe-
　inspired reverence and
　submissive wonder].
He keeps his word even to his
　own disadvantage and does
　not change it [for his own
　benefit];
⁵ He does not put out his money
　at interest [to a fellow
　Israelite],
And does not take a bribe
　against the innocent.
He who does these things
　will never be shaken.
　[Ex 22:25, 26]

PSALM 16

The Lord, the Psalmist's
Portion in Life and Deliverer
in Death.

A Mikhtam of David
[probably intended to record
memorable thoughts].

¹ KEEP *AND* protect me,
　O God, for in You I have
　placed my trust *and* found
　refuge.

² I said to the Lord, "You are my
　Lord;
I have no good besides You."
³ As for the saints (godly
　people) who are in the land,
They are the majestic *and* the
　noble *and* the excellent ones
　in whom is all my delight.
⁴ The sorrows [pain and
　suffering] of those who
　have chosen another *god*
　will be multiplied [because
　of their idolatry];
I will not pour out their drink
　offerings of blood,
Nor will I take their names
　upon my lips.

⁵ The Lord is the portion of my
　inheritance, my cup [He is
　all I need];
You support my lot.
⁶ The [boundary] lines [of the
　land] have fallen for me in
　pleasant places;
Indeed, my heritage is
　beautiful to me.

⁷ I will bless the Lord who has
　counseled me;
Indeed, my heart (mind)
　instructs me in the night.
⁸ I have set the Lord continually
　before me;
Because He is at my right
　hand, I will not be shaken.
⁹ Therefore my heart is glad
　and my glory [my innermost
　self] rejoices;
My body too will dwell
　[confidently] in safety,
¹⁰ For You will not abandon me
　to Sheol (the nether world,
　the place of the dead),

Nor will You allow Your Holy
One to undergo decay. [Acts
13:35]
[11] You will show me the path of
life;
In Your presence is fullness
of joy;
In Your right hand there are
pleasures forevermore.
[Acts 2:25–28, 31]

PSALM 17

Prayer for Protection
against Oppressors.

A Prayer of David.

[1] HEAR THE just (righteous)
cause, O Lord; listen to my
loud [piercing] cry;
Listen to my prayer, that
comes from guileless lips.
[2] Let my verdict of vindication
come from Your presence;
May Your eyes look with
equity *and* behold things
that are just.
[3] You have tried my heart;
You have visited me in the
night;
You have tested me and You
find nothing [evil in me];
I intend that my mouth will
not transgress.

life point

We must learn to seek God's face
and not just His hand. Seeking God
for Who He is, not just for what He
can do for us, assures us "fullness of
joy" (Psalm 16:11) and is vital to our
victory as believers.

[4] Concerning the deeds of men,
by the word of Your lips
I have kept away from the
paths of the violent.
[5] My steps have held closely to
Your paths;
My feet have not staggered.

[6] I have called upon You, for
You, O God, will answer me;
Incline Your ear to me, hear
my speech.
[7] Wondrously show Your
[marvelous and amazing]
lovingkindness,
O Savior of those who take
refuge at Your right hand
From those who rise up
against them.
[8] Keep me [in Your affectionate
care, protect me] as the
apple of Your eye;
Hide me in the [protective]
shadow of Your wings
[9] From the wicked who despoil
and deal violently with me,
My deadly enemies who
surround me.
[10] They have closed their
unfeeling *heart* [to kindness
and compassion];
With their mouths they
speak proudly *and* make
presumptuous claims.
[11] They track us down *and* have
now surrounded us in our
steps;
They set their eyes to force us
to the ground,
[12] He is like a lion eager to tear
[his prey],
And like a young lion lurking
in hiding places.

[13] Arise, O Lord, confront him,
cast him down;

Save my soul from the wicked
with Your sword,
¹⁴From men with Your hand,
O Lord,
From men of the world [these
moths of the night] whose
portion [of enjoyment] is in
this life—idle and vain,
And whose belly You fill with
Your treasure;
They are satisfied with
children,
And they leave what they
have left [of wealth] to their
children.
¹⁵As for me, I shall see Your
face in righteousness;
I will be [fully] satisfied when
I awake [to find myself]
seeing Your likeness.

PSALM 18

David Praises the Lord
for Rescuing Him.

To the Chief Musician.
A Psalm of David, the servant
of the Lord, who spoke
the words of this song
to the Lord on the day when
the Lord rescued him from
the hand of all his enemies
and from the hand of Saul.
And he said:

¹"I LOVE You [fervently and
devotedly], O Lord, my
strength."
²The Lord is my rock, my
fortress, and the One who
rescues me;
My God, my rock *and* strength
in whom I trust *and* take
refuge;
My shield, and the horn of
my salvation, my high
tower—my stronghold.
[Heb 2:13]

life point

Psalm 17:15 is one of my favorite
verses because it teaches us how to
wake up in the morning feeling satisfied in the Lord. Earlier in my life,
I had many unhappy days because
the minute I awoke each morning,
I began to think about the wrong
things. But since I have learned
the importance of seeking God's
presence and not just His presents,
I am a different person. I wake up
with a thankful heart, and God has
taught me to think of others and
not just myself. Fellowshipping with
God early in the morning is one sure
way to begin enjoying every day of
your life.

speak the Word

*Lord, I declare that You are my Rock and Strength, my Fortress,
and the One who rescues me. You are my Shield,
the Horn of my salvation,
and my High Tower—my Stronghold!*
−ADAPTED FROM PSALM 18:2

³I call upon the Lord, who is
worthy to be praised;
And I am saved from my
enemies. [Rev 5:12]

⁴The cords of death
surrounded me,
And the streams of
ungodliness *and* torrents of
destruction terrified me.
⁵The cords of Sheol (the nether
world, the place of the dead)
surrounded me;
The snares of death
confronted me.
⁶In my distress [when I
seemed surrounded] I
called upon the Lord
And cried to my God for help;
He heard my voice from His
temple,
And my cry for help came
before Him, into His *very*
ears.

⁷Then the earth shook and
quaked,
The foundations of the
mountains trembled;
They were shaken because
He was indignant *and*
angry.
⁸Smoke went up from His
nostrils,
And fire from His mouth
devoured;
Coals were kindled by it.
⁹He bowed the heavens also
and came down;
And thick darkness was
under His feet.
¹⁰And He rode upon a cherub
(storm) and flew;
And He sped on the wings of
the wind.

¹¹He made darkness His hiding
place (covering); His
pavilion (canopy) around
Him,
The darkness of the waters,
the thick clouds of the skies.
¹²Out of the brightness before
Him passed His thick
clouds,
Hailstones and coals of fire.
¹³The Lord also thundered in
the heavens,
And the Most High uttered
His voice,
Hailstones and coals of fire.
¹⁴He sent out His arrows and
scattered them;
And *He sent* an abundance
of lightning flashes and
confused *and* routed them
[in defeat].
¹⁵Then the stream beds of the
waters appeared,
And the foundations of the
world were laid bare
At Your rebuke, O Lord,
At the blast of the breath of
Your nostrils.

¹⁶He reached from on high,
He took me;
He drew me out of many
waters.
¹⁷He rescued me from my
strong enemy,
And from those who hated
me, for they were too strong
for me.
¹⁸They confronted me in the
day of my disaster,
But the Lord was my support.
¹⁹He brought me out into a
broad place;
He rescued me because He
was pleased with me *and*
delighted in me.

²⁰ The Lord dealt with
me according to my
righteousness (moral
character, spiritual
integrity);
According to the cleanness
of my hands He has
rewarded me.
²¹ For I have kept the ways of
the Lord,
And have not wickedly
departed from my God.
²² For all His ordinances were
before me,
And I did not put away His
statutes from me.
²³ I was blameless before Him,
And I kept myself free from
my sin.
²⁴ Therefore the Lord has
rewarded me according
to my righteousness
(moral character, spiritual
integrity),
According to the cleanness of
my hands in His sight.

²⁵ With the kind (merciful,
faithful, loyal) You show
Yourself kind,
With the blameless You show
Yourself blameless,
²⁶ With the pure You show
Yourself pure,
And with the crooked You
show Yourself astute.
²⁷ For You save an afflicted *and*
humble people,

But bring down those
[arrogant fools] with
haughty eyes.
²⁸ For You cause my lamp to be
lighted *and* to shine;
The Lord my God illumines
my darkness.
²⁹ For by You I can crush a troop,
And by my God I can leap
over a wall.

³⁰ As for God, His way is
blameless.
The word of the Lord is tested
[it is perfect, it is faultless];
He is a shield to all who take
refuge in Him.
³¹ For who is God, but the Lord?
Or who is a rock, except our God,
³² The God who encircles me
with strength
And makes my way
blameless?
³³ He makes my feet like hinds'
feet [able to stand firmly
and tread safely on paths of
testing and trouble];
He sets me [securely] upon
my high places.
³⁴ He trains my hands for war,
So that my arms can bend a
bow of bronze.
³⁵ You have also given me the
shield of Your salvation,
And Your right hand upholds
and sustains me;
Your gentleness [Your
gracious response when I
pray] makes me great.

speak the Word

*God, I know that Your way is blameless; Your word is tested. It is
perfect and faultless. You are a shield to all who take refuge in You.*
–ADAPTED FROM PSALM 18:30

36 You enlarge the path beneath
me *and* make my steps
secure,
So that my feet will not slip.

37 I pursued my enemies and
overtook them;
And I did not turn back until
they were consumed.
38 I shattered them so that they
were not able to rise;
They fell [wounded] under
my feet.
39 For You have encircled me
with strength for the battle;
You have subdued under
me those who rose up
against me.
40 You have also made my
enemies turn their backs to
me [in defeat],
And I silenced *and* destroyed
those who hated me.
41 They cried for help, but there
was no one to save them—
Even to the LORD [they cried],
but He did not answer them.
42 Then I beat them fine as the
dust before the wind;
I emptied them out as the dirt
of the streets.

43 You have rescued me from the
contentions of the people;
You have placed me as the
head of the nations;
A people whom I have not
known serve me.
44 As soon as they hear me, they
respond *and* obey me;
Foreigners feign obedience
to me.
45 Foreigners lose heart,
And come trembling out of
their strongholds.

46 The LORD lives, blessed be my
rock;
And may the God of my
salvation be exalted,
47 The God who avenges me,
And subdues peoples
(nations) under me.
48 He rescues me from my
enemies;
Yes, You lift me up above those
who rise up against me;
You deliver me from the man
of violence.
49 Therefore will I give thanks
and praise You, O LORD,
among the nations,
And sing praises to Your
name. [Rom 15:9]
50 He gives great triumphs to His
king,
And shows steadfast love *and*
mercy to His anointed,
To David and his
descendants forever.
[2 Sam 22:2–51]

putting the Word to work

Our everyday lives are governed
by man-made laws that are for our
benefit—obeying the speed limit,
stopping at red lights, etc. Are you
equally aware of the benefits of living by God's perfect Law? Wisdom,
joy, righteousness, rewards—all
these things and more are benefits
that come from living according to
God's Law. Spend time studying
God's Word each day, and ask Him
to help you live by it, so you can
glorify Him and enjoy His blessings.

PSALM 19

The Works and the Word of God.

To the Chief Musician.
A Psalm of David.

[1] THE HEAVENS are telling of the glory of God;
And the expanse [of heaven] is declaring the work of His hands. [Rom 1:20, 21]

enjoy God's handiwork

God speaks to everyone through His handiwork. Even people living outside God's will perceive right from wrong and the reality of God, because Psalm 19:1–4 tells us that nature itself testifies of God's power and divine plan.

I encourage you to take time to look at what God has created. The main message God speaks to us through nature is that *He is*. This is an important revelation because the Bible says that before we can get anywhere with God, we must first believe He is: "But without faith it is impossible to [walk with God and] please Him, for whoever comes [near] to God must [necessarily] believe that God exists and that He rewards those who [earnestly and diligently] seek Him" (Hebrews 11:6). We *can* believe God because the Bible says He has given every person a degree of faith to believe in Him (see Romans 12:3).

The very first words of the Bible give our first lesson of faith: "In the beginning God . . ." (Genesis 1:1). Many people acknowledge that God exists, but they have not learned to relate to Him on a day-to-day level. Through grace, God tries to reach us every day, and He places reminders of Himself everywhere. He leaves clues of Himself all around us, clues that bellow out clearly, "I am here. You do not have to live in fear; you do not have to worry, I am here." God wants to be involved in every aspect of your life. If He has taken time to keep all your tears in a bottle and count the very hairs on your head, then surely He cares about everything else.

Jesus said to think about "the lilies and wildflowers of the field" (see Matthew 6:28) and the birds of the air (see Luke 12:24). Meditating on how God adorns the fields and provides for the birds can remind us that He cares even more for us. A nice walk outdoors is a great opportunity to take a short vacation from the pressures of daily living and look at the trees, the birds, the flowers, and the children playing. Let me encourage you to take time to appreciate God's awesome handiwork today and to thank Him that He *is*.

Life is sometimes very complicated, but we can purposefully learn to enjoy the simple yet powerful and beautiful things God has created!

²Day after day pours forth
speech,
And night after night reveals
knowledge.
³There is no speech, nor are
there [spoken] words [from
the stars];
Their voice is not heard.
⁴Yet their voice [in quiet
evidence] has gone out
through all the earth,
Their words to the end of the
world.
In them *and* in the heavens
He has made a tent for the
sun, [Rom 10:18]
⁵Which is as a bridegroom
coming out of his chamber;
It rejoices as a strong man to
run his course.
⁶The sun's rising is from one
end of the heavens,
And its circuit to the other
end of them;
And there is nothing hidden
from its heat.

life point

In Psalm 19:14, the psalmist prays:
"Let the words of my mouth and the
meditation of my heart be acceptable and pleasing in Your sight,
O LORD, my [firm, immovable] rock
and my Redeemer." Notice that he
mentions both the mind and the
mouth. This is because the two work
together. We need to make sure
that meditations (our thoughts) are
pleasing to God so that our words
will be acceptable to Him as well.

⁷The law of the LORD is perfect
(flawless), restoring *and*
refreshing the soul;
The statutes of the LORD are
reliable *and* trustworthy,
making wise the simple.
⁸The precepts of the LORD are
right, bringing joy to the
heart;
The commandment of the
LORD is pure, enlightening
the eyes.
⁹The fear of the LORD is clean,
enduring forever;
The judgments of the LORD
are true, they are righteous
altogether.
¹⁰They are more desirable than
gold, yes, than much fine
gold;
Sweeter also than honey
and the drippings of the
honeycomb.
¹¹Moreover, by them Your
servant is warned
[reminded, illuminated, and
instructed];
In keeping them there is great
reward.
¹²Who can understand his
errors *or* omissions? Acquit
me of hidden (unconscious,
unintended) *faults.*
¹³Also keep back Your servant
from presumptuous
(deliberate, willful) *sins;*
Let them not rule *and* have
control over me.
Then I will be blameless
(complete),
And I shall be acquitted of
great transgression.
¹⁴Let the words of my mouth
and the meditation of my
heart

Be acceptable *and* pleasing in
  Your sight,
O Lᴏʀᴅ, my [firm, immovable]
  rock and my Redeemer.

PSALM 20

Prayer for Victory
over Enemies.

To the Chief Musician.
A Psalm of David.

¹ MAY THE Lᴏʀᴅ answer you
  (David) in the day of trouble!
May the name of the God of
  Jacob set you *securely* on high
  [and defend you in battle]!
² May He send you help from
  the sanctuary (His dwelling
  place)
And support *and* strengthen
  you from Zion!
³ May He remember all your
  meal offerings
And accept your burnt
  offering.   *Selah.*

⁴ May He grant you your heart's
  desire
And fulfill all your plans.
⁵ We will sing joyously over
  your victory,
And in the name of our God
  we will set up our banners.
May the Lᴏʀᴅ fulfill all your
  petitions.

⁶ Now I know that the Lᴏʀᴅ
  saves His anointed;
He will answer him from His
  holy heaven
With the saving strength of
  His right hand.
⁷ Some *trust* in chariots and
  some in horses,

But we will remember *and*
  trust in the name of the
  Lᴏʀᴅ our God.
⁸ They have bowed down and
  fallen,
But we have risen and stood
  upright.
⁹ O Lᴏʀᴅ, save [the king];
May the King answer us in
  the day we call.

PSALM 21

Praise for Help.

To the Chief Musician.
A Psalm of David.

¹ O LORD the king will delight
  in Your strength,
And in Your salvation how
  greatly will he rejoice!
² You have given him his
  heart's desire,
And You have not withheld
  the request of his lips. *Selah.*
³ For You meet him with
  blessings of good things;
You set a crown of pure gold
  on his head.
⁴ He asked life of You,
And You gave it to him,
Long life forever and evermore.
⁵ His glory is great because of
  Your victory;
Splendor and majesty You
  bestow upon him.
⁶ For You make him most blessed
  [and a blessing] forever;
You make him joyful with the
  joy of Your presence. [Gen
  12:2]
⁷ For the king [confidently]
  trusts in the Lᴏʀᴅ,

And through the lovingkindness (faithfulness, goodness) of the Most High he will never be shaken.

8 Your hand will reach out *and* defeat all your enemies; Your right hand will reach those who hate you.

9 You will make them as [if in] a blazing oven in the time of your anger; The LORD will swallow them up in His wrath, And the fire will devour them.

10 Their offspring You will destroy from the earth, And their descendants from the sons of men.

11 For they planned evil against You; They devised a [malevolent] plot And they will not succeed.

12 For You will make them turn their backs [in defeat]; You will aim Your bowstring [of divine justice] at their faces.

13 Be exalted, LORD, in Your strength; We will sing and praise Your power.

PSALM 22

A Cry of Anguish and a Song of Praise.

To the Chief Musician; set to [the tune of] Aijeleth Hashshahar (The Doe of the Dawn). A Psalm of David.

1 MY GOD, my God, why have You forsaken me? Why are You so far from helping me, and from the words of my groaning? [Matt 27:46]

life point

God is enthroned in the praises of His people (see Psalm 22:3). That means He is comfortable in the midst of our sweet praises, but He is not comfortable in the midst of our sour attitudes.

I encourage you to take an inventory of your inner life because it is the dwelling place of God. When God dwelled in the portable tabernacle that the children of Israel carried through the wilderness, they understood that the inner court was a holy place. But now in the mystery of God's plan, we are like a portable tabernacle; we move from place to place, and God dwells inside us. There is still an outer court, a holy place, and a most holy place. The outer court is our body, the holy place is our soul, and the most holy place is our spirit.

When we examine our inner lives, we are looking at holy ground where the Spirit of God wants to make His home. God is much more interested in our inner lives than in our outer lives, and we need to be more concerned about what goes on *inside* us than about our external behavior. Praise, worship, and honor God in your inner life. When your "insides" are right, your "outsides" will follow!

2 O my God, I call out by day,
   but You do not answer;
And by night, but I find no
   rest *nor* quiet.
3 But You are holy,
 O You who are enthroned
   in [the holy place where]
   the praises of Israel [are
   offered].
4 In You our fathers trusted
   [leaned on, relied on, and
   were confident];
 They trusted and You rescued
   them.
5 They cried out to You and
   were delivered;
 They trusted in You and
   were not disappointed *or*
   ashamed.

6 But I am [treated as] a
   worm [insignificant and
   powerless] and not a man;
 I am the scorn of men and
   despised by the people.
   [Matt 27:39–44]
7 All who see me laugh at me
   and mock me;
 They [insultingly] open their
   lips, they shake their head,
   saying, [Matt 27:43]
8 "He trusted *and* committed
   himself to the LORD, let Him
   save him.
 Let Him rescue him, because
   He delights in him." [Matt
   27:39, 43; Mark 15:29, 30;
   Luke 23:35]

9 Yet You are He who pulled me
   out of the womb;
 You made me trust when on
   my mother's breasts.
10 I was cast upon You from
   birth;

From my mother's womb You
   have been my God.

11 Do not be far from me, for
   trouble is near;
And there is no one to help.
12 Many [enemies like] bulls
   have surrounded me;
 Strong *bulls* of Bashan have
   encircled me. [Ezek 39:18;
   Amos 4:1]
13 They open wide their mouths
   against me,
 Like a ravening and a roaring
   lion.
14 I am poured out like water,
 And all my bones are out of
   joint.
 My heart is like wax;
 It is melted [by anguish]
   within me.
15 My strength is dried up
   like a fragment of clay
   pottery;
 And my [dry] tongue clings to
   my jaws;
 And You have laid me
   in the dust of death.
   [John 19:28]
16 For [a pack of] dogs have
   surrounded me;
 A gang of evildoers has
   encircled me,
 They pierced my hands
   and my feet. [Is 53:7;
   John 19:37]
17 I can count all my bones;
 They look, they stare at me.
   [Luke 23:27, 35]
18 They divide my clothing
   among them
 And cast lots for my garment.
   [John 19:23, 24]
19 But You, O LORD, do not be far
   from me;

O You my help, come quickly
    to my assistance.
²⁰Rescue my life from the sword,
    My only *life* from the paw of
    the dog (the executioner).
²¹Save me from the lion's
    mouth;
From the horns of the wild
    oxen You answer me.

²²I will tell of Your name to my
    countrymen;
In the midst of the
    congregation I will praise
    You. [John 20:17; Rom 8:29;
    Heb 2:12]
²³You who fear the LORD [with
    awe-inspired reverence],
    praise Him!
All you descendants of Jacob,
    honor Him.
Fear Him [with submissive
    wonder], all you
    descendants of Israel.
²⁴For He has not despised nor
    detested the suffering of the
    afflicted;
Nor has He hidden His face
    from him;
But when he cried to Him for
    help, He listened.

²⁵My praise will be of You in
    the great assembly.
I will pay my vows [made in
    the time of trouble] before
    those who [reverently] fear
    Him.
²⁶The afflicted will eat and be
    satisfied;
Those who [diligently] seek
    Him *and* require Him [as
    their greatest need] will
    praise the LORD.
May your hearts live
    forever!

²⁷All the ends of the earth will
    remember and turn to the
    LORD,
And all the families of the
    nations will bow down *and*
    worship before You,
²⁸For the kingship *and* the
    kingdom are the LORD's
And He rules over the
    nations.
²⁹All the prosperous of
    the earth will eat and
    worship;
All those who go down
    to the dust (the dead)
    will bow before Him,

life point

The last part of the beloved Psalm 23 describes the condition in which the Lord wants us to be continually. He wants us to be protected, guided, and comforted. He wants to set a table of blessings before us in the very face of our enemies. He wants to anoint us with the oil of joy instead of mourning. He wants our cup of blessings to overflow continually in thanksgiving and praise to Him for His goodness, mercy, and unfailing love toward us. And He wants us to live, moment by moment, in His presence.

All these things are part of His good plan for each of us. Regardless of how far we may have fallen, He wants to raise us up and restore us to that right and perfect plan He has for our lives.

Even he who cannot keep his
soul alive.
³⁰Posterity will serve Him;
They will tell of the Lord to
the next generation.
³¹They will come and declare
His righteousness
To a people yet to be
born—that He has done
it [and that it is finished].
[John 19:30]

PSALM 23

The LORD, the Psalmist's Shepherd.

A Psalm of David.

¹THE LORD is my Shepherd
[to feed, to guide and to
shield me], [Ezek 34:11–31]
I shall not want.
²He lets me lie down in green
pastures;

God restores and leads

The twenty-third Psalm is so comforting. In it the psalmist David tells us
the Lord leads, feeds, guides, and shields us. He causes us to lie down
and rest, and He "refreshes and restores" (Psalm 23:3) our lives. I like
the way the Amplified Bible translates this verse, but I also like the way
the beautiful old King James Version renders it: "He restoreth my soul."
The soul is comprised of the mind, the will, and the emotions.

With our souls, we process our circumstances, we entertain our
thoughts, we feel and express emotions, and we make decisions. What
a wonderful promise—that God will restore our souls! The word *restore*
means "to bring back into existence or use" or "to bring back to an
original state or condition." The word is often used in a situation when a
dethroned ruler is put back on his throne. *Restore* also means, "to make
restitution, to cause to return, or to refresh."

When David says God will restore our souls and our lives, I believe he
means that God will return us to the state or condition we were in before
we strayed from following the good plan God had predestined for us
before our birth, or before Satan attacked us to draw us out of God's
plan for our lives.

We can take confidence that God will lead us in the path of righteousness, uprightness, and right standing with Him. I believe David is saying here that God individually leads each of us in the path that is right
for us, a path that restores us in every way to the good places God has
for us.

God has a path predestined for your restoration. If you will allow Him
to do so, He will guide you by His Holy Spirit along the unique way that
leads to restoration and to being able to fulfill the great purposes He has
for your life.

He leads me beside the still
and quiet waters. [Rev 7:17]
³ He refreshes *and* restores my
soul (life);
He leads me in the paths of
righteousness
for His name's sake.

⁴ Even though I walk through
the [sunless] *valley of the
shadow of death,
I fear no evil, for You are with
me;
Your rod [to protect] and
Your staff [to guide], they
comfort *and* console me.
⁵ You prepare a table before
me in the presence of my
enemies.
You have anointed *and*
refreshed my head with oil;
My cup overflows.
⁶ Surely goodness and mercy *and*
unfailing love shall follow me
all the days of my life,

putting the Word to work

At some point in our lives, all of us will walk through the valley of the shadow of death, either facing our own death, the death of a loved one or some other extraordinarily difficult time (see Psalm 23:4). Are you or is someone you love walking through that valley right now? Remember, where there is a shadow, there must be light—and the Light of the world, Jesus, has promised to be with you always. Ask Him right now to comfort and guide you, and know that He is walking with you in every situation.

And I shall dwell forever
[throughout all my days]
in the house *and* in the
presence of the LORD.

PSALM 24

The King of Glory Entering Zion.

A Psalm of David.

¹ THE EARTH is the LORD's,
and the fullness of it,
The world, and those who
dwell in it. [1 Cor 10:26]
² For He has founded it upon
the seas
And established it upon the
streams *and* the rivers.
³ Who may ascend onto the
mountain of the LORD?
And who may stand in His
holy place?
⁴ He who has clean hands and
a pure heart,
Who has not lifted up his soul
to what is false,
Nor has sworn [oaths]
deceitfully. [Matt 5:8]
⁵ He shall receive a blessing
from the LORD,
And righteousness from the
God of his salvation.
⁶ This is the generation
(description) of those
who diligently seek Him
and require Him as their
greatest need,
Who seek Your face, even [as
did] Jacob. [Ps 42:1]   *Selah.*

⁷ Lift up your heads, O gates,
And be lifted up, ancient
doors,
That the King of glory may
come in.

8 Who is the King of glory?
The LORD strong and mighty,
The LORD mighty in battle.
9 Lift up your heads, O gates,
And lift them up, ancient doors,
That the King of glory may
come in.
10 Who is [He then] this King of
glory?
The LORD of hosts,
He is the King of glory [who
rules over all creation with
His heavenly armies]. *Selah.*

PSALM 25

Prayer for Protection, Guidance and Pardon.

A Psalm of David.

1 TO YOU, O LORD, I lift up my soul.
2 O my God, in You I [have
unwavering] trust [and I
rely on You with steadfast
confidence],
Do not let me be ashamed
or my hope in You be
disappointed;
Do not let my enemies
triumph over me.
3 Indeed, none of those who
[expectantly] wait for You
will be ashamed;
Those who turn away from
what is right *and* deal
treacherously without
cause will be ashamed
(humiliated, embarrassed).

4 Let me know Your ways,
O LORD;
Teach me Your paths.
5 Guide me in Your truth and
teach me,
For You are the God of my
salvation;
For You [and only You] I wait
[expectantly] all the day
long.
6 Remember, O LORD, Your
[tender] compassion and
Your lovingkindnesses,
For they have been from of
old.
7 Do not remember the
sins of my youth or my
transgressions;
According to Your
lovingkindness remember
me,
For Your goodness' sake,
O LORD.

8 Good and upright is the LORD;
Therefore He instructs
sinners in the way.
9 He leads the humble in
justice,
And He teaches the humble His
way.
10 All the paths of the LORD
are lovingkindness *and*
goodness and truth *and*
faithfulness
To those who keep His
covenant and His
testimonies.

speak the Word

*God, I pray that You would let me know Your ways and teach me
Your paths. I am asking You to guide me in Your truth. You are my
salvation, and I am waiting expectantly on You.*
–ADAPTED FROM PSALM 25:4, 5

¹¹For Your name's sake,
   O Lᴏʀᴅ,
 Pardon my wickedness
   and my guilt, for they are
   great.

¹²Who is the man who fears the
   Lᴏʀᴅ [with awe-inspired
   reverence and worships
   Him with submissive
   wonder]?

at ease

In order to live victorious lives, we need to be comfortable spiritually. That may sound strange to you, so let me share a story to explain what I mean.

In 1980, I had a job as the pastor's secretary at my church in St. Louis. After working one day, I got fired. Do you know why? Because I was not supposed to be a secretary; therefore, God would not bless me in that job.

You see, my desire to be a secretary was *my* idea, not God's; it was something *I* wanted to do, not something God wanted me to do. The job was not a "fit" for me; it was not comfortable for me, and I did not have grace to do it. It was not part of God's purpose for my life, and He would not allow me to stay in that job because He had other plans for me.

Trying to do things that are not part of God's plan for our lives is like trying to force our feet into shoes that are too small. I have been guilty of wanting to buy shoes that are slightly too tight, but I do not do that anymore. I have learned that tight shoes are not comfortable, and I want my feet to be comfortable.

During those days, I wanted to be comfortable spiritually too. I wanted to be relaxed in spirit; I wanted my inner life to be at ease, as though I were walking around in my most comfortable shoes. I wanted to be relaxed in my relationship with God and to feel at home in His presence. I also wanted to be comfortable around other people and not be afraid of their disapproval. All those things that I wanted I now enjoy because I have learned to follow God's plan rather than my own.

Do you feel the same way? Are you tired of being uncomfortable and being in places that do not fit God's call on your life? Are you tired of being spiritually uncomfortable, insecure, or anxious all the time?

I have good news for you. Psalm 25:12, 13 tell us that we can "dwell in prosperity and goodness," which is another way of saying we can be at ease, if we fear God, worship Him, and do what He has planned for us without trying to force our own agendas or striving to do what *we* want to do. God loves you, and He has awesome plans for your life. Surrender to His plans and His way—and you will find yourself at ease.

He will teach him [through His word] in the way he should choose.

13 His soul will dwell in prosperity *and* goodness, And his descendants will inherit the land.

14 The secret [of the wise counsel] of the LORD is for those who fear Him, And He will let them know His covenant *and* reveal to them [through His word] its [deep, inner] meaning. [John 7:17; 15:15]

15 My eyes are continually toward the LORD, For He will bring my feet out of the net.

16 Turn to me [LORD] and be gracious to me, For I am alone and afflicted.

17 The troubles of my heart are multiplied; Bring me out of my distresses.

18 Look upon my affliction and my trouble, And forgive all my sins.

19 Look upon my enemies, for they are many; They hate me with cruel *and* violent hatred.

20 Guard my soul and rescue me; Do not let me be ashamed *or* disappointed, For I have taken refuge in You.

21 Let integrity and uprightness protect me, For I wait [expectantly] for You.

22 O God, redeem Israel, Out of all his troubles.

PSALM 26

Protestation of Integrity and Prayer for Protection.

A Psalm of David.

1 VINDICATE ME, O LORD, for I have walked in my integrity; I have [relied on and] trusted [confidently] in the LORD without wavering *and* I shall not slip.

2 Examine me, O LORD, and try me; Test my heart and my mind.

3 For Your lovingkindness is before my eyes, And I have walked [faithfully] in Your truth.

4 I do not sit with deceitful *or* unethical *or* worthless men, Nor seek companionship with pretenders (self-righteous hypocrites).

5 I hate the company of evildoers, And will not sit with the wicked.

6 I will wash my hands in innocence, And I will go about Your altar, O LORD,

7 That I may proclaim with the voice of thanksgiving And declare all Your wonders.

8 O LORD, I love the habitation of Your house

And the place where Your
glory dwells.
⁹ Do not sweep my soul away
with sinners,
Nor [sweep away] my
life with men of
bloodshed,
¹⁰ In whose hands is a wicked
scheme,

And whose right hand is full
of bribes.
¹¹ But as for me, I shall walk in
my integrity;
Redeem me and be merciful
and gracious to me.
¹² My foot stands on a level
place;
In the congregations I will
bless the LORD.

seek the "one thing"

If you could ask for only one thing, what would it be? In Psalm 27:4, David said there was only one thing that he sought after—to dwell in God's presence. More than anything else, David wanted to know God, to see God as He really is and to be with Him. Truly, to know God is the highest calling we have.

Unfortunately, we can get so distracted with the busy details of our lives that we neglect the most important thing—spending time with God. Luke 10:38–42 illustrates this point well as it relates the story of busy Martha. When Jesus visited her home, she became preoccupied with serving, but her sister Mary stopped all work and sat at His feet. Jesus told Martha that only one thing was really important, and Mary had chosen it. Mary had decided she was not going to miss the opportunity to listen to the Master. I suppose Martha intended to work Jesus into her schedule somewhere, but Mary was willing to stop what she was doing and work her schedule around Him.

How foolish we are to spend our lives seeking those things that cannot satisfy while we ignore God, the "One Thing" Who can give us great joy, peace, satisfaction, and contentment. The world is filled with empty people who are trying to satisfy the void in their lives with the latest-model car, a promotion at work, a human relationship, a vacation, or some other thing. Their efforts to find fulfillment in those things never work. It is sad that so many people waste their entire lives and never realize it. They never know the joy of seeking the "One Thing" they really need. Each one of us has a God-shaped hole inside, and nothing can fill it except God Himself. No matter what else we try to fill it with, we will remain empty and frustrated.

If God is on your list of things to seek, but not at the top, I encourage you to move everything around and put it all *after* Him. If you will put Him first in everything you do, you will be so blessed. Investing your life in God is the very best thing you can do.

PSALM 27

A Psalm of Fearless Trust in God.

A Psalm of David.

¹ THE LORD is my light and
my salvation—
Whom shall I fear?
The LORD is the refuge *and*
fortress of my life—
Whom shall I dread?
² When the wicked came
against me to eat up my
flesh,
My adversaries and my
enemies, they stumbled and
fell.
³ Though an army encamp
against me,
My heart will not fear;
Though war arise against
me,
Even in this I am confident.

⁴ One thing I have asked
of the LORD, and that
I will seek:
That I may dwell in the
house of the LORD [in His
presence] all the days of my
life,
To gaze upon the beauty [the
delightful loveliness and
majestic grandeur] of the
LORD
And to meditate in His
temple. [Ps 16:11; 18:6; 65:4;
Luke 2:37]
⁵ For in the day of trouble
He will hide me in His
shelter;
In the secret place of His tent
He will hide me;
He will lift me up on
a rock.

⁶ And now my head will be
lifted up above my enemies
around me,
In His tent I will offer
sacrifices with shouts
of joy;
I will sing, yes, I will sing
praises to the LORD.

⁷ Hear, O LORD, when I cry
aloud;
Be gracious *and*
compassionate to me and
answer me.
⁸ *When You said,* "Seek
My face [in prayer,
require My presence
as your greatest need],"
my heart said to You,
"Your face, O LORD,
I will seek [on the
authority of Your
word]."
⁹ Do not hide Your face from
me,
Do not turn Your servant
away in anger;
You have been my help;
Do not abandon me nor
leave me,
O God of my salvation!
¹⁰ Although my father and
my mother have
abandoned me,
Yet the LORD will take me
up [adopt me as His child].
[Ps 22:10]

¹¹ Teach me Your way,
O LORD,
And lead me on a level
path
Because of my enemies
[who lie in wait].
¹² Do not give me up to the will
of my adversaries,

For false witnesses have come
   against me;
They breathe out violence.
[13] *I would have despaired* had I
   not believed that I would
   see the goodness of the
   LORD
In the land of the living.
[14] Wait for *and* confidently expect
   the LORD;
Be strong and let your heart
   take courage;
Yes, wait for *and* confidently
   expect the LORD.

PSALM 28

A Prayer for Help, and Praise for Its Answer.

A Psalm of David.

[1] TO YOU I call, O LORD,
   My rock, do not be deaf to me,
   For if You are silent to me,
   I will become like those who
      go down to the pit (grave).
[2] Hear the voice of my
   supplication (specific
   requests, humble entreaties)
   as I cry to You for help,

the land of the living

In Psalm 27:13, David asked, "What in the world would have happened to me? What kind of condition would I be in? What pit would I be in, had I not believed I would see the Lord's goodness in the land of the living?"

We spend a lot of time talking about what heaven will be like. That is great, but we are here on earth right now. We need to know something good is going to happen to us now. David said that he believed he would see God's goodness while he was alive, not just after he went to heaven.

I am looking forward to heaven, but I do not believe that God put us on earth to try to muddle through life until we get to heaven so we can finally have some joy. In John 10:10, Jesus says, "The thief comes only in order to steal and kill and destroy. I came that they may have and enjoy life, and have it in abundance [to the full, till it overflows]." God wants us to have abundant life right now, and one of the worst things we can do is fail to live lives that we enjoy. I have decided to enjoy my life while I am "in the land of the living." I want to have so much fun that the devil gets frustrated at my joy.

Let me encourage you to be like David and to believe that you will see and experience God's goodness not just in the "sweet by-and-by," but here on earth, every day, in the ordinary activities of your life. No matter what you are going through, put your hope in God's goodness and expect Him to move in your situation. Be brave and of good courage; let your heart be stout and enduring. Wait for and hope for and expect the Lord where you live today—in the land of the living.

As I lift up my hands
and heart toward Your
innermost sanctuary (Holy
of Holies).
3 Do not drag me away with the
wicked
And with those who do evil,
Who speak peace with their
neighbors,
While malice *and* mischief
are in their hearts.
4 Repay them according to their
work and according to the
evil of their practices;
Repay them according to the
deeds of their hands;
Repay them what they
deserve. [2 Tim 4:14;
Rev 18:6]
5 Because they have no regard
for the works of the LORD
Nor the deeds of His hands,
He will tear them down and
not rebuild them.

6 Blessed be the LORD,
Because He has heard the
voice of my supplication.
7 The LORD is my strength and
my [impenetrable] shield;
My heart trusts [with
unwavering confidence] in
Him, and I am helped;
Therefore my heart greatly
rejoices,
And with my song I shall
thank Him *and* praise Him.
8 The LORD is their [unyielding]
strength,

And He is the fortress of
salvation to His anointed.
9 Save Your people and bless
Your inheritance;
Be their shepherd also, and
carry them forever.

PSALM 29

The Voice of the LORD
in the Storm.

A Psalm of David.

1 ASCRIBE TO the LORD, O sons
of the mighty,
Ascribe to the LORD glory and
strength.
2 Ascribe to the LORD the glory
due His name;
Worship the LORD in the
beauty *and* majesty of His
holiness [as the creator and
source of holiness].

3 The voice of the LORD is upon
the waters;
The God of glory thunders;
The LORD is over many waters.
4 The voice of the LORD is
powerful;
The voice of the LORD is full of
majesty.
5 The voice of the LORD breaks
the cedars;
Yes, the LORD breaks in pieces
the cedars of Lebanon.
6 He makes Lebanon skip like a
calf,
And Sirion (Mount Hermon)
like a young, wild ox.

speak the Word

Lord, You are my Strength and my impenetrable Shield.
My heart trusts in You with unwavering confidence.
–ADAPTED FROM PSALM 28:7

⁷The voice of the LORD rakes
flames of fire (lightning).
⁸The voice of the LORD shakes
the wilderness;
The LORD shakes the
wilderness of Kadesh.
⁹The voice of the LORD
makes the doe labor *and*
give birth
And strips the forests bare;
And in His temple all are
saying, "Glory!"

¹⁰The LORD sat *as King* at the
flood;
Yes, the LORD sits as King
forever.
¹¹The LORD will give
[unyielding and
impenetrable] strength
to His people;
The LORD will bless His
people with peace.

PSALM 30

Thanksgiving for Deliverance from Death.

A Psalm; a Song at
the Dedication of the House
(Temple). *A Psalm* of David.

¹I WILL extol *and* praise You,
O LORD, for You have lifted
me up,
And have not let my enemies
rejoice over me.

²O LORD my God,
I cried to You for help, and
You have healed me.
³O LORD, You have brought
my life up from Sheol (the
nether world, the place of
the dead);
You have kept me alive, so
that I would not go down to
the pit (grave).
⁴Sing to the LORD, O you His
godly ones,
And give thanks at the
mention of His holy *name*.
⁵For His anger is but for a
moment,
His favor is for a lifetime.
Weeping may endure for a
night,
But a shout of joy comes
in the morning.
[2 Cor 4:17]

⁶As for me, in my prosperity
I said,
"I shall never be moved."
⁷By Your favor *and* grace,
O LORD, you have
made my mountain
stand strong;
You hid Your face, and I was
horrified.
⁸I called to You, O LORD,
And to the Lord I made
supplication (specific
request).

speak the Word

*Thank You, God, that Your anger lasts but for
a moment, but Your favor
is for a lifetime. Thank You that weeping
may endure for only a night
and that a shout of joy comes in the morning.*
—ADAPTED FROM PSALM 30:5

9 "What profit is there in my
blood (death), if I go down
to the pit (grave)?
Will the dust praise You? Will
it declare Your faithfulness
[to man]?

10 "Hear, O Lord, be gracious *and*
show favor to me;
O Lord, be my helper."
11 You have turned my mourning
into dancing for me;
You have taken off my
sackcloth and clothed me
with joy,
12 That my soul may sing praise
to You and not be silent.
O Lord my God, I will give
thanks to You forever.

PSALM 31

A Psalm of Complaint and
of Praise.

To the Chief Musician.
A Psalm of David.

1 IN YOU, O Lord, I have placed
my trust *and* taken refuge;
Let me never be ashamed;
In Your righteousness
rescue me.
2 Incline Your ear to me, deliver
me quickly;
Be my rock of refuge,
And a strong fortress to
save me.
3 Yes, You are my rock and my
fortress;
For Your name's sake You will
lead me and guide me.
4 You will draw me out of the
net that they have secretly
laid for me,
For You are my strength *and*
my stronghold.

5 Into Your hand I commit my
spirit;
You have redeemed me,
O Lord, the God of truth *and*
faithfulness. [Luke 23:46;
Acts 7:59]

6 I hate those who pay regard
to vain (empty, worthless)
idols;
But I trust in the Lord
[and rely on Him with
unwavering confidence].
7 I will rejoice and be glad in
Your steadfast love,
Because You have seen my
affliction;
You have taken note of my
life's distresses,
8 And You have not given me
into the hand of the enemy;
You have set my feet in a
broad place.

9 Be gracious *and*
compassionate to me,
O Lord, for I am in trouble;
My eye is clouded *and*
weakened by grief, my soul
and my body also.
10 For my life is spent with sorrow
And my years with sighing;
My strength has failed
because of my iniquity,
And even my body has wasted
away.
11 Because of all my enemies I
have become a reproach *and*
disgrace,
Especially to my neighbors,
And an object of dread to my
acquaintances;
Those who see me on the
street run from me.
12 I am forgotten like a dead
man, out of mind;

I am like a broken vessel.

13 For I have heard the slander
and whispering of many,
Terror is on every side;
While they schemed together
against me,
They plotted to take away my
life. [Jer 20:10]

14 But as for me, I trust
[confidently] in You *and*
Your greatness, O LORD;
I said, "You are my God."

15 My times are in Your hands;
Rescue me from the hand
of my enemies and from
those who pursue *and*
persecute me.

16 Make Your face shine upon
Your servant;
Save me in Your
lovingkindness.

17 Let me not be put to shame,
O LORD, for I call on You;
Let the wicked (godless) be
put to shame, let them be
silent in Sheol (the nether
world, the place of the
dead).

18 Let the lying lips be mute,
Which speak insolently *and*
arrogantly against the
[consistently] righteous
With pride and contempt.

19 How great is Your goodness,
Which You have stored up for
those who [reverently] fear
You,
Which You have prepared for
those who take refuge in
You,
Before the sons of man!

20 In the secret place of
Your presence You hide
them from the plots *and*
conspiracies of man;

You keep them secretly in a
shelter (pavilion) from the
strife of tongues.

21 Blessed be the LORD,
For He has shown His
marvelous favor *and*
lovingkindness to me [when
I was assailed] in a besieged
city.

22 As for me, I said in my alarm,
"I am cut off from Your eyes."
Nevertheless You heard the
voice of my supplications
(specific requests)
When I cried to You [for help].

23 O love the LORD, all you His
godly ones!
The LORD preserves the
faithful [those with moral
and spiritual integrity]
And fully repays the [self-
righteousness of the]
arrogant.

24 Be strong and let your hearts
take courage,
All you who wait for *and*
confidently expect the LORD.

PSALM 32

Blessedness of Forgiveness
and of Trust in God.

A Psalm of David. A skillful
song, *or* a didactic *or*
reflective poem.

1 BLESSED [FORTUNATE,
prosperous, favored by God]
is he whose transgression is
forgiven,
And whose sin is covered.

2 Blessed is the man to whom
the LORD does not impute
wickedness,
And in whose spirit there is
no deceit. [Rom 4:7, 8]

³When I kept silent *about my sin,* my body wasted away Through my groaning all the day long.

⁴For day and night Your hand [of displeasure] was heavy upon me;

everyday Christianity

God is good. All the time! Psalm 31:19 says that He stores up goodness for those who reverently fear Him. Notice also that this verse mentions the importance of trusting God "before the sons of man." This phrase says to me that if I refuse to be what some might call a "closet Christian," but instead be open and live my Christianity before all people, God will store up His goodness for me.

A number of people today profess to be Christians, but they do not want to admit it or live the principles of their faith outside their Christian circles. They are "Sunday morning" Christians, but on Monday morning they act no differently than unbelievers do. I call them "Sunday morning saints and Monday morning sinners."

I was once that way! I used to do all the "right" things in the right Christian circles, but I was not demonstrating vital faith elsewhere. I was on the church board, my husband was an elder in the church, our children went to Christian schools, our social life revolved around church, and we had a set of Christian bumper stickers for our cars. However, in my neighborhood, a person could not tell the difference between my behavior and the behavior of an unsaved person. At work, a person could not tell from my words or behavior that I was any different from my unsaved coworkers. Perhaps there was some difference, but not enough to notice! I was not taking the strong stand that I should have taken for God.

This is true for many of us. Because we are afraid of being rejected, isolated, or laughed at, we are afraid to take a stand and say, "I really don't want to hear a dirty joke. I'm a Christian, and I don't like to hear people take the Lord's name in vain. I'm not really interested in going to movies that leave wrong images in my mind or running to the bar every night after work for happy hour. That's not what I'm about. My life and my relationship with God are too important to me." That is what the Scripture means when it says, "Those who take refuge in You, before the sons of man" will be blessed. We must care more about our reputation in heaven than our reputation among people on earth. Stand strong for God, and never be ashamed or embarrassed to live the Christian life openly and boldly before other people.

My energy (vitality, strength)
   was drained away as
   with the burning heat of
   summer.   *Selah.*
⁵I acknowledged my sin to You,
   And I did not hide my
   wickedness;
   I said, "I will confess [all] my
   transgressions to the LORD";
   And You forgave the guilt of
   my sin.   *Selah.*
⁶Therefore, let everyone who
   is godly pray to You [for
   forgiveness] in a time when
   You [are near and] may be
   found;
   Surely when the great waters
   [of trial and distressing
   times] overflow they will
   not reach [the spirit in]
   him.

life point

**Psalm 32:9 encourages us not to be
like horses or mules, which need bits
and bridles in order to follow their
masters. Either a horse follows the
pull of the bridle, which controls the
bit in his mouth, or he experiences
great pain by resisting it. The same
principle applies to us and to our relationship with the Holy Spirit. He is
our bridle and the bit in our mouths.
He should be controlling the reins of
our lives. If we follow His prompt-
ings, we will end up at the right
places and stay out of the wrong
places. But if we do not follow Him,
we will end up with a lot of pain.
Determine today that you will let
Him guide you and that you will not
resist His leading in your life.**

⁷You are my hiding place;
   You, LORD, protect me from
   trouble;
   You surround me with songs
   and shouts of deliverance.
                              Selah.

⁸I will instruct you and teach
   you in the way you should go;
   I will counsel you [who are
   willing to learn] with My
   eye upon you.
⁹Do not be like the horse or
   like the mule which have no
   understanding,
   Whose trappings include
   bridle and rein to hold them
   in check,
   Otherwise they will not come
   near to you.
¹⁰Many are the sorrows of the
   wicked,
   But he who trusts in
   and relies on the LORD
   shall be surrounded
   with compassion *and*
   lovingkindness.
¹¹Be glad in the LORD and
   rejoice, you righteous [who
   actively seek right standing
   with Him];
   Shout for joy, all you upright
   in heart.

PSALM 33

Praise to the Creator and
Preserver.

¹REJOICE IN the LORD, you
   righteous ones;
   Praise is becoming *and*
   appropriate for those who
   are upright [in heart—those
   with moral integrity and
   godly character].

2 Give thanks to the Lord with
the lyre;
Sing praises to Him with the
harp of ten strings.
3 Sing to Him a new song;
Play skillfully [on the strings]
with a loud *and* joyful sound.
4 For the word of the Lord is
right;
And all His work is done in
faithfulness.
5 He loves righteousness and
justice;
The earth is full of the
lovingkindness of the Lord.

6 By the word of the Lord were
the heavens made,
And all their host by the
breath of His mouth. [Gen
1:1–3; Job 38:4–11; Heb 11:3;
2 Pet 3:5]
7 He gathers the waters of
the sea together as in a
wineskin;
He puts the deeps in
storehouses.
8 Let all the earth fear *and*
worship the Lord;
Let all the inhabitants of the
world stand in awe of Him.
9 For He spoke, and it was done;
He commanded, and it stood
fast.
10 The Lord nullifies the counsel
of the nations;
He makes the thoughts
and plans of the people
ineffective.

11 The counsel of the Lord
stands forever,
The thoughts *and* plans
of His heart through all
generations.
12 Blessed [fortunate,
prosperous, and favored by
God] is the nation whose
God is the Lord,
The people whom He
has chosen as His own
inheritance. [Deut 32:8, 9]

13 The Lord looks [down] from
heaven;
He sees all the sons of man;
14 From His dwelling place He
looks closely
Upon all the inhabitants of
the earth—
15 He who fashions the hearts of
them all,
Who considers *and*
understands all that they do.
16 The king is not saved by the
great size of his army;
A warrior is not rescued by
his great strength.
17 A horse is a false hope for
victory;
Nor does it deliver anyone by
its great strength.

18 Behold, the eye of the Lord is
upon those who fear Him
[and worship Him with
awe-inspired reverence and
obedience],

speak the Word

*God, I declare that Your word is right and that all
Your work is done in faithfulness.*
–ADAPTED FROM PSALM 33:4

at *all* times

Notice that the psalmist says he will bless the Lord "at all times," not just when it is convenient or it feels good (Psalm 34:1). Let me share with you a story that really emphasized this point for me.

One of my favorite things to do when I have finished a conference is to go to a restaurant, sit down, and have a good meal. I work hard, and that is one way I relax. One time, we called a restaurant and asked for a reservation. They sounded like they had taken our reservation, but when we got there, we found out they had not. The place was jam-packed, and we waited about forty-five minutes for a table. I felt irritation rise in me, but I told myself, *Joyce, you just finished preaching and telling people how to behave in hard times, so just practice what you preach.* (It is amazing how sometimes when you talk about what you believe, Satan will come around and test you on it!)

Finally we were seated and began ordering. The waitress came with our beverages on a large tray. The place was so crowded that she accidentally bumped the tray and dumped all the beverages on my husband, Dave. He had on a very nice suit, and it was soaked in water, coffee, iced tea, and soda pop. At that point he could have blown up. But Dave was so nice to the waitress about the whole ordeal. He said to her, "Don't worry about it. It was a mistake. I understand. I used to work at a restaurant, and one time I dumped malts inside a customer's car. He had on a really nice suit and was taking his date out. I know how you feel. Don't worry about it." Then he went to the manager and said, "I don't want her to get in trouble. The place is overly crowded. She is doing a good job. It was not her fault." He went to the extreme to be nice.

Soon the waitress came back with the second tray of beverages, and it was obvious she had been crying. She said to us, "I feel so bad that I dumped all those drinks on you." Then she looked right at me and said, "I think I'm just nervous because you're here. I watch you on television every day."

In my heart I said, "Oh, thank You, God, thank You, thank You, thank You, that we didn't act badly about this!" What would it have done to her—what would it have said to her about God, about leaders, about television evangelists—if she had heard me preach every day on television and then seen Dave and me throw a fit over her spilling the beverages on him?

Did I feel like blowing up? To be honest, yes. The Bible never says that our temptation to sin dies or goes away. It says that since Christ died for our sin we should consider ourselves dead to sin. And sometimes that means learning to bless Him at *all times*—especially when things are not going our way.

On those who hope
[confidently] in His
compassion *and*
lovingkindness,
¹⁹ To rescue their lives from
death
And keep them alive in famine.
²⁰ We wait [expectantly] for the
LORD;
He is our help and our shield.
²¹ For in Him our heart rejoices,
Because we trust [lean on,
rely on, and are confident]
in His holy name.
²² Let Your [steadfast]
lovingkindness, O LORD, be
upon us,
In proportion as we have
hoped in You.

PSALM 34

The LORD, a Provider and
the One Who Rescues Me.

A Psalm of David; when
he pretended to be insane
before Abimelech, who drove
him out, and he went away.

¹ I WILL bless the LORD at all
times;
His praise shall continually
be in my mouth.

² My soul makes its boast in the
LORD;
The humble *and* downtrodden
will hear it and rejoice.
³ O magnify the LORD with me,
And let us lift up His name
together.

⁴ I sought the LORD [on the
authority of His word], and
He answered me,
And delivered me from all my
fears. [Ps 73:25; Matt 7:7]
⁵ They looked to Him and were
radiant;
Their faces will never blush
in shame *or* confusion.
⁶ This poor man cried, and the
LORD heard him
And saved him from all his
troubles.
⁷ The angel of the LORD
encamps around those
who fear Him [with
awe-inspired reverence
and worship Him with
obedience],
And He rescues [each of]
them. [2 Kin 6:8–23;
Ps 18:1; 145:20]

life point

Psalm 34:7 teaches us that "the angel of the LORD encamps around those who fear Him" Do you want your angels to go to work in your life? Then start worshiping God, because the Bible says that the angel of the Lord camps around those who revere and worship Him to rescue them.

putting the Word to work

Psalm 34:8 encourages us to "taste and see" that the Lord is good. Think for a moment about your favorite food. Can you imagine how it tastes and the pleasure it brings? How infinitely greater is the pleasure of knowing the goodness of God! Let the sweetness of His praise be on your lips continually!

⁸O taste and see that the LORD [our God] is good;
How blessed [fortunate, prosperous, and favored by God] is the man who takes refuge in Him. [1 Pet 2:2, 3]
⁹O [reverently] fear the LORD, you His saints (believers, holy ones);
For to those who fear Him there is no want.
¹⁰The young lions lack [food] and grow hungry,
But they who seek the LORD will not lack any good thing.
¹¹Come, you children, listen to me;
I will teach you to fear the LORD [with awe-inspired reverence and worship Him with obedience].
¹²Who is the man who desires life
And loves many days, that he may see good?
¹³Keep your tongue from evil
And your lips from speaking deceit.
¹⁴Turn away from evil and do good;
Seek peace and pursue it.

¹⁵The eyes of the LORD are toward the righteous [those with moral courage and spiritual integrity]
And His ears are open to their cry.
¹⁶The face of the LORD is against those who do evil,
To cut off the memory of them from the earth. [1 Pet 3:10–12]
¹⁷When *the righteous* cry [for help], the LORD hears

And rescues them from all their distress *and* troubles.
¹⁸The LORD is near to the heartbroken
And He saves those who are crushed in spirit (contrite in heart, truly sorry for their sin).
¹⁹Many hardships *and* perplexing circumstances confront the righteous,
But the LORD rescues him from them all.
²⁰He keeps all his bones;
Not one of them is broken. [John 19:33, 36]
²¹Evil will cause the death of the wicked,
And those who hate the righteous will be held guilty *and* will be condemned.
²²The LORD redeems the soul of His servants,
And none of those who take refuge in Him will be condemned.

PSALM 35

Prayer for Rescue from Enemies.

A Psalm of David.

¹CONTEND, O LORD, with those who contend with me;
Fight against those who fight against me.
²Take hold of shield and buckler (small shield),
And stand up for my help.
³Draw also the spear and javelin to meet those who pursue me.
Say to my soul, "I am your salvation."

⁴Let those be ashamed and
   dishonored who seek my
   life;
 Let those be turned back [in
   defeat] and humiliated who
   plot evil against me.
⁵Let them be [blown away]
   like chaff before the
   wind [worthless, without
   substance],
 With the angel of the LORD
   driving them on.
⁶Let their way be dark and
   slippery,
 With the angel of the LORD
   pursuing *and* harassing
   them.
⁷For without cause they hid
   their net for me;
 Without cause they dug a pit
   [of destruction] for my life.
⁸Let destruction come upon my
   enemy by surprise;
 Let the net he hid for me
   catch him;
 Into that very destruction let
   him fall.

⁹Then my soul shall rejoice in
   the LORD;
 It shall rejoice in His
   salvation.
¹⁰All my bones will say, "LORD,
   who is like You,
 Who rescues the afflicted
   from him who is too strong
   for him [to resist alone],
 And the afflicted and the
   needy from him who robs
   him?"
¹¹Malicious witnesses rise up;
 They ask me of things that I
   do not know.
¹²They repay me evil for good,
 To the sorrow of my soul.

¹³But as for me, when they
   were sick, my clothing
   was sackcloth (mourning
   garment);
 I humbled my soul with fasting,
 And I prayed with my head
   bowed on my chest.
¹⁴I behaved as if grieving for
   my friend or my brother;
 I bowed down in mourning,
   as one who sorrows for his
   mother.
¹⁵But in my stumbling they
   rejoiced and gathered
   together [against me];
 The slanderers whom I did not
   know gathered against me;
 They slandered *and* reviled
   me without ceasing.
¹⁶Like godless jesters at a feast,
 They gnashed at me with
   their teeth [in malice].

¹⁷LORD, how long will You look
   on [without action]?
 Rescue my life from their
   destructions,
 My only *life* from the young
   lions.
¹⁸I will give You thanks in the
   great congregation;
 I will praise You among a
   mighty people.
¹⁹Do not let those who are
   wrongfully my enemies
   rejoice over me;
 Nor let those who hate me
   without cause wink their
   eye [maliciously]. [John
   15:24, 25]
²⁰For they do not speak peace,
 But they devise deceitful
   words [half-truths and lies]
   against those who are quiet
   in the land.

21 They open their mouths wide
    against me;
  They say, "Aha, aha, our eyes
    have seen it!"

22 You have seen this, O Lᴏʀᴅ;
    do not keep silent.
  O Lord, do not be far
    from me.
23 Wake Yourself up, and arise
    to my right
  And to my cause, my God and
    my Lord.
24 Judge me, O Lᴏʀᴅ my God,
    according to
  Your righteousness *and*
    justice;
  And do not let them rejoice
    over me.
25 Do not let them say in their
    heart, "Aha, that is what we
    wanted!"
  Do not let them say, "We have
    swallowed him up *and*
    destroyed him."
26 Let those be ashamed
    and humiliated together
    who rejoice at my
    distress;
  Let those be clothed with
    shame and dishonor
    who magnify themselves
    over me.

27 Let them shout for joy and
    rejoice, who favor my
    vindication *and* want what
    is right for me;

Let them say continually, "Let
  the Lᴏʀᴅ be magnified, who
  delights *and* takes pleasure
  in the prosperity of His
  servant."
28 And my tongue shall declare
    Your righteousness
    (justice),
  And Your praise all the day
    long.

PSALM 36

Wickedness of Men and Lovingkindness of God.

To the Chief Musician.
A Psalm of David the
servant of the Lᴏʀᴅ.

1 TRANSGRESSION SPEAKS
  [like an oracle] to the
  wicked (godless) [deep]
  within his heart;
  There is no fear (dread) of
    God before his eyes. [Rom
    3:18]
2 For he flatters *and* deceives
    himself in his own eyes
  Thinking that his sinfulness
    will not be discovered and
    hated [by God].
3 The words of his mouth are
    wicked and deceitful;
  He has ceased to be wise *and*
    to do good.
4 He plans wrongdoing on his
    bed;

speak the Word

Thank You, Lord, that Your loving-kindness and graciousness
extend to the skies and Your faithfulness to the clouds.
Your righteousness is like the mountains and Your judgments
are like the great deep.
—ᴀᴅᴀᴘᴛᴇᴅ ғʀᴏᴍ Pꜱᴀʟᴍ 36:5, 6

He sets himself on a path that
is not good;
He does not reject *or* despise
evil.

5 Your lovingkindness *and*
graciousness, O Lord,
extend to the skies,
Your faithfulness [reaches] to
the clouds.
6 Your righteousness is like the
mountains of God,
Your judgments are like the
great deep.
O Lord, You preserve man and
beast.
7 How precious is Your
lovingkindness, O God!
The children of men take
refuge in the shadow of
Your wings.
8 They drink their fill of the
abundance of Your house;
And You allow them to drink
from the river of Your
delights.
9 For with You is the fountain
of life [the fountain of life-
giving water];
In Your light we see light.
[John 4:10, 14]

10 O continue Your
lovingkindness to those
who know You,
And Your righteousness
(salvation) to the upright in
heart.
11 Do not let the foot of the
proud [person] overtake
me,

And do not let the hand of the
wicked drive me away.
12 There those who [are
perverse and] do evil have
fallen;
They have been thrust down
and cannot rise.

PSALM 37

Security of Those Who Trust
in the Lord, and Insecurity
of the Wicked.

A Psalm of David.

1 DO NOT worry because of
evildoers,
Nor be envious toward
wrongdoers;
2 For they will wither quickly
like the grass,
And fade like the green herb.
3 Trust [rely on and have
confidence] in the Lord and
do good;
Dwell in the land and feed
[securely] on His faithfulness.
4 Delight yourself in the Lord,
And He will give you the
desires *and* petitions of your
heart.
5 Commit your way to the Lord;
Trust in Him also and He will
do it.
6 He will make your
righteousness [your pursuit
of right standing with God]
like the light,
And your judgment like [the
shining of] the noonday [sun].

speak the Word

I declare, God, that with You is the fountain of life.
In Your light, I see light.
−ADAPTED FROM PSALM 36:9

⁷Be still before the LORD;
wait patiently for Him *and*
entrust yourself to Him;
Do not fret (whine, agonize)
because of him who
prospers in his way,
Because of the man who
carries out wicked
schemes.
⁸Cease from anger and
abandon wrath;
Do not fret; *it leads* only to
evil.
⁹For those who do evil will be
cut off,

But those who wait for the
LORD, they will inherit the
land. [Is 57:13c]
¹⁰For yet a little while and the
wicked one will be gone
[forever];
Though you look carefully
where he used to be, he will
not be [found]. [Heb 10:36,
37; Rev 21:7, 8]
¹¹But the humble will [at last]
inherit the land
And will delight themselves
in abundant prosperity *and*
peace. [Ps 37:29; Matt 5:5]

delight yourself in God

Does a way exist for us to have our desires fulfilled? According to Psalm 37:4, 5, if we delight ourselves in the Lord, He will give us the desires of our hearts. I have learned that letting God give me something is so much better than trying to get it for myself. Most of us struggle greatly in our lives, trying to make things happen that only God can do. He wants us to seek Him, and He promises that He will add the things we desire if and when the time is right.

We are to commit our way unto Him and let Him bring to pass the things that we desire. Jesus said all those who labor and are heavily burdened should come to Him. He promised to renew and refresh their souls (see Matthew 11:28, 29). His ways are higher than our ways, and His thoughts are higher than ours (Isaiah 55:8, 9). In other words, God knows much better than we do what we need to do!

I spent much of my life frustrated and struggling, always trying to do something about things I could not do anything about. I worked really hard at life, but life still was not working for me.

My first Bible was a gift from my mother-in-law, and on the inside cover she wrote: "Commit your way to the LORD" from Psalm 37:5. Little did I know, when she gave me that Bible years ago, just how long it would take for me to let go of my ways and submit to God's.

I do not know why we tend to be so stubborn, but we do. I encourage you to let go of your ways and let God be God in your life. He wants to give you the desires of your heart as you commit your way to Him.

¹²The wicked plots against the righteous
And gnashes at him with his teeth.
¹³The Lord laughs at him [the wicked one—the one who oppresses the righteous],
For He sees that his day [of defeat] is coming.
¹⁴The wicked have drawn the sword and bent their bow
To cast down the afflicted and the needy,
To slaughter those who are upright in conduct [those with personal integrity and godly character].
¹⁵The sword [of the ungodly] will enter their own heart,
And their bow will be broken.

¹⁶Better is the little of the righteous [who seek the will of God]
Than the abundance (riches) of many wicked (godless). [1 Tim 6:6, 7]
¹⁷For the arms of the wicked will be broken,
But the LORD upholds *and* sustains the righteous [who seek Him].
¹⁸The LORD knows the days of the blameless,
And their inheritance will continue forever.
¹⁹They will not be ashamed in the time of evil,
And in the days of famine they will have plenty *and* be satisfied.
²⁰But the wicked (ungodly) will perish,

And the enemies of the LORD will be like the glory of the pastures *and* like the fat of lambs [that is consumed in smoke],
They vanish—like smoke they vanish away.
²¹The wicked borrows and does not pay back,
But the righteous is gracious *and* kind and gives.
²²For those blessed by God will [at last] inherit the land,
But those cursed by Him will be cut off. [Is 57:13c]

²³The steps of a [good and righteous] man are directed *and* established by the LORD,
And He delights in his way [and blesses his path].

life point

God will tell us the way to go (see Psalm 37:23), but we have to do the walking. A walk with God develops by taking one step of obedience at a time. Some people want the entire blueprint for their lives before they will make one decision. God does not usually operate that way; He leads us one step at a time.

By faith, we take the step God has shown us, and then He gives us the next one. At times we may fall down and must get back up; we may stumble, but He always helps us. We continue on by His strength and His grace, knowing that every time we face a fork in the road (a place of decision), God will guide us.

²⁴ When he falls, he will not be
  hurled down,
  Because the LORD is the One
  who holds his hand *and*
  sustains him.
²⁵ I have been young and now I
  am old,
  Yet I have not seen the
  righteous (those in right
  standing with God)
  abandoned
  Or his descendants pleading
  for bread.
²⁶ All day long he is gracious
  and lends,
  And his descendants are a
  blessing.

²⁷ Depart from evil and do
  good;
  And you will dwell [securely
  in the land] forever.
²⁸ For the LORD delights in
  justice
  And does not abandon His
  saints (faithful ones);
  They are preserved forever,
  But the descendants of the
  wicked will [in time] be cut
  off.
²⁹ The righteous will inherit the
  land
  And live in it forever.
³⁰ The mouth of the righteous
  proclaims wisdom,
  And his tongue speaks justice
  and truth.
³¹ The law of his God is in his
  heart;
  Not one of his steps will slip.
³² The wicked lies in wait for
  the righteous
  And seeks to kill him.
³³ The LORD will not leave him
  in his hand

Or let him be condemned
  when he is judged.
³⁴ Wait for *and* expect the LORD
  and keep His way,
  And He will exalt you to
  inherit the land;
  [In the end] when the
  wicked are cut off, you will
  see it.

³⁵ I have seen a wicked, violent
  man [with great power]
  Spreading *and* flaunting
  himself like a cedar in its
  native soil,
³⁶ Yet he passed away, and lo, he
  was no more;
  I sought him, but he could not
  be found.
³⁷ Mark the blameless man
  [who is spiritually complete],
  and behold the upright
  [who walks in moral
  integrity];
  There is a [good] future for
  the man of peace [because
  a life of honor blesses one's
  descendants].
³⁸ As for transgressors, they
  will be completely
  destroyed;
  The future of the wicked will
  be cut off.
³⁹ But the salvation of the
  righteous is from
  the LORD;
  He is their refuge *and*
  stronghold in the time of
  trouble.
⁴⁰ The LORD helps them and
  rescues them;
  He rescues them from the
  wicked and saves them,
  Because they take refuge in
  Him.

PSALM 38

Prayer in Time of Discipline.

A Psalm of David; to bring
to remembrance.

¹O LORD, do not rebuke me in
Your wrath,
Nor discipline me in Your
burning anger.
²For Your arrows have sunk
into me *and* penetrate
deeply,
And Your hand has pressed
down on me *and* greatly
disciplined me.
³There is no soundness in
my flesh because of Your
indignation;
There is no health in my
bones because of my sin.
⁴For my iniquities have gone
over my head [like the
waves of a flood];
As a heavy burden they weigh
too much for me.
⁵My wounds are loathsome
and foul
Because of my foolishness.
⁶I am bent over and greatly
bowed down;
I go about mourning all day
long.
⁷For my sides are filled with
burning,
And there is no health in my
flesh.
⁸I am numb and greatly
bruised [deadly cold and
completely worn out];
I groan because of the
disquiet *and* moaning of my
heart.

⁹Lord, all my desire is before
You;
And my sighing is not hidden
from You.
¹⁰My heart throbs violently, my
strength fails me;
And as for the light of my
eyes, even that has also
gone from me.
¹¹My loved ones and my friends
stand aloof from my plague;
And my neighbors stand far
away. [Luke 23:49]
¹²Those who seek my life lay
snares *for me,*
And those who seek to injure
me threaten mischievous
things *and* destruction;
They devise treachery all the
day long.

¹³But I, like a deaf man, do not
hear;
I am like a mute man who
does not open his mouth.
¹⁴Yes, I am like a man who does
not hear,
In whose mouth are no
arguments.
¹⁵For in You, O LORD, I hope;
You will answer, O Lord my
God.
¹⁶For I pray, "May they not
rejoice over me,
Who, when my foot slips,
would boast against me."
¹⁷For I am ready to fall;
My sorrow is continually
before me.
¹⁸For I do confess my guilt *and*
iniquity;
I am filled with anxiety
because of my sin. [2 Cor
7:9, 10]
¹⁹But my [numerous] enemies
are vigorous and strong,
And those who hate me
without cause are many.

20 They repay evil for good, they
　　attack *and* try to kill me,
　Because I follow what is
　　good.
21 Do not abandon me, O Lᴏʀᴅ;
　O my God, do not be far
　　from me.
22 Make haste to help me,
　O Lord, my Salvation.

PSALM 39

The Vanity of Life.

To the Chief Musician;
for Jeduthun. A Psalm
of David.

1 I SAID, "I will guard my ways
　That I may not sin with my
　　tongue;
　I will muzzle my mouth
　While the wicked are in my
　　presence."
2 I was mute and silent [before
　　my enemies],
　I refrained *even* from good,
　And my distress grew worse.
3 My heart was hot within me.
　While I was musing the fire
　　burned;
　Then I spoke with my tongue:
4 "Lᴏʀᴅ, let me know my [life's]
　　end
　And [to appreciate] the extent
　　of my days;
　Let me know how frail I am
　　[how transient is my stay
　　here].
5 "Behold, You have made my
　days as [short as] hand
　widths,

And my lifetime is as nothing
　in Your sight.
Surely every man at his best
　is a mere breath [a wisp
　of smoke, a vapor that
　vanishes]! [Eccl 1:2]　*Selah.*
6 "Surely every man walks
　around like a shadow [in a
　charade];
Surely they make an uproar
　for nothing;
Each one builds up *riches,* not
　knowing who will receive
　them. [Eccl 2:18, 19; 1 Cor
　7:31; James 4:14]

7 "And now, Lord, for what do
　I expectantly wait?
My hope [my confident
　expectation] is in You.
8 "Save me from all my
　transgressions;
Do not make me the scorn
　and reproach of the [self-
　righteous, arrogant] fool.
9 "I am mute, I do not open my
　mouth,
Because it is You who has
　done it.
10 "Remove Your plague from me;
　I am wasting away because of
　the conflict *and* opposition
　of Your hand.
11 "With rebukes You discipline
　man for sin;
You consume like a moth
　what is precious to him;
Surely every man is a mere
　breath [a wisp of smoke, a
　vapor that vanishes].　*Selah.*

speak the Word

God, all of my hope—my confident expectation—is in You.
–ADAPTED FROM Psᴀʟᴍ 39:7

¹² "Hear my prayer, O Lᴏʀᴅ, and
    listen to my cry;
Do not be silent at my tears;
For I am Your temporary
    guest,
A sojourner like all my fathers.
¹³ "O look away from me, that I
    may smile *and* again know
    joy
Before I depart and am no
    more."

PSALM 40

God Sustains His Servant.

To the Chief Musician.
A Psalm of David.

¹ I WAITED patiently *and*
    expectantly for the Lᴏʀᴅ;
And He inclined to me and
    heard my cry.
² He brought me up out of a
    horrible pit [of tumult and
    of destruction], out of the
    miry clay,
And He set my feet upon a
    rock, steadying my footsteps
    and establishing my path.
³ He put a new song in my
    mouth, a song of praise to
    our God;
Many will see and fear [with
    great reverence]
And will trust confidently in
    the Lᴏʀᴅ. [Ps 5:11]

⁴ Blessed [fortunate,
    prosperous, and favored by
    God] is the man who makes
    the Lᴏʀᴅ his trust,
And does not regard the
    proud nor those who lapse
    into lies.
⁵ Many, O Lᴏʀᴅ my God, are the
    wonderful works which You
    have done,

And Your thoughts toward
    us;
There is none to compare
    with You.
If I would declare and speak
    of *your wonders,*

life point

When the Bible speaks of "a horrible pit," as it does in Psalm 40:2, I always think of the depths of depression. The psalmist David often spoke of feeling as though he was going down into a pit and calling out to the Lord to rescue him and set his feet on solid, level ground.

Like David, nobody wants to be in the pit of depression. It is a terrible place. I cannot think of a worse place to be. When we are deeply depressed, we feel bad enough as it is. Then the devil comes along to add to our misery by bringing thoughts of every negative thing imaginable. He reminds us of every disappointing thing that has happened to us and tries to make us believe that nothing good will ever take place in our lives. His goal is to keep us so miserable and hopeless that we will never rise up to cause him any problems or to fulfill the call of God on our lives.

We must learn to resist descending into the pit of depression where we are at the mercy of the tormentor of our souls, who is determined to totally destroy us and to damage our witness for Christ. Be like David; cry out to God and allow Him to set your feet upon a rock and bring stability to your life.

pray and obey

God really wants us to hear and obey Him, and according to Psalm 40:6, He has given us the capacity to do so. In fact, God delights in the atmosphere of our obedience. Naturally, it does not do God any good to talk to us if we are not going to listen and obey!

For many years, I wanted God to talk to me, but I wanted to pick and choose what to obey. Like many others, I had "selective hearing." I wanted to do what God said to do *if* I thought it was a good idea. If I did not want to submit to what I was hearing, I could easily choose to think it was not from God.

God has given us the capacity both to hear Him and to obey Him, and obedience is the greatest sacrifice we can make to Him. Some of what God says to you will be exciting; other things may not be so thrilling to hear. But you can be assured that what God tells you will work out for good if you will just do it His way.

If God convicts you that you were rude to someone and instructs you to apologize, it is pointless to answer back, "Well, that person was rude to me too!" If you talk back with excuses, you may have prayed, and even heard, but you have not obeyed. Instead, go apologize. Say to that person, "I was rude to you, and I'm sorry." *Now* you have obeyed. Now God's anointing can flow through your life because you are obedient.

I was moved by a story about a message given at a pastors' conference by a pastor of a very large church. Hundreds of pastors had gathered from all over the nation to hear this man tell what he did to build his church. He told them simply, "I pray, and I obey. I pray, and I obey." One of the ministers who attended this meeting expressed to me his disappointment in the pastor's message. He said, "I spent all this money and came all this distance to hear this world-renowned leader tell me how his ministry grew to the point it has. For three hours, in various ways, he said the same thing, 'I pray. I obey. I pray. I obey. I pray. I obey. I pray. I obey.' I kept thinking, *Surely there is something else*."

Looking back over nearly three decades of walking with God, I would have to agree that if I put into words the simplest explanation for all the success we have enjoyed at Joyce Meyer Ministries, we too have learned to pray, hear from God, and then do what God tells us to do. Over the years, I have been seeking God about the call on my life and pressing forward in what I feel He has told me to do. The essence of it all is that I have prayed, and I have obeyed. My obedience has not always been popular with everyone else, but to the best of my ability I have prayed, I have obeyed—and it has worked. God's plan is not hard; *we* make it hard. Like everyone else I have made mistakes, but I have learned from them and have pressed on. Failing does not make you a failure. A person is a failure only if he gives up and refuses to try any longer.

If you want God's will for your life, I can give you the directions in their simplest form: *Pray and obey*. God has given you the capacity to do both.

They would be too many to count.

6 Sacrifice and meal offering You do not desire, *nor* do You delight in them;
You have opened my ears *and* given me the capacity to hear [and obey Your word];
Burnt offerings and sin offerings You do not require. [Mic 6:6–8]

7 Then I said, "Behold, I come [to the throne];
In the scroll of the book it is written of me.

8 "I delight to do Your will, O my God;
Your law is within my heart." [Jer 31:33; Heb 10:5–9]

9 I have proclaimed good news of righteousness [and the joy that comes from obedience to You] in the great assembly;

Behold, I will not restrain my lips [from proclaiming Your righteousness],
As You know, O LORD.

10 I have not concealed Your righteousness within my heart;
I have proclaimed Your faithfulness and Your salvation.
I have not concealed Your lovingkindness and Your truth from the great assembly. [Acts 20:20, 27]

11 Do not withhold Your compassion *and* tender mercy from me, O LORD;
Your lovingkindness and Your truth will continually preserve me.

12 For innumerable evils have encompassed me;
My sins have overtaken me, so that I am not able to see.
They are more numerous than the hairs of my head,
And my heart has failed me.

speak the Word

God, I delight to do Your will.
—ADAPTED FROM PSALM 40:8

¹³ Be pleased, O LORD, to save me;
　O LORD, make haste to help me.
¹⁴ Let those be ashamed and
　humiliated together
　Who seek my life to destroy it;
　Let those be turned back [in
　defeat] and dishonored
　Who delight in my hurt.
¹⁵ Let those be appalled *and*
　desolate because of their
　shame
　Who say to me, "Aha, aha
　[rejoicing in my misfortune]!"
¹⁶ Let all who seek You rejoice
　and be glad in You;
　Let those who love Your
　salvation say continually,
　"The LORD be magnified!"
¹⁷ Even though I am afflicted
　and needy,
　Still the Lord takes thought
　and is mindful of me.
　You are my help and my
　rescuer.
　O my God, do not delay.
　　[Ps 70:1–5; 1 Pet 5:7]

PSALM 41

The Psalmist in Sickness Complains of Enemies and False Friends.

To the Chief Musician.
A Psalm of David.

¹ BLESSED [by God's grace
　and compassion] is he who
　considers the helpless;
　The LORD will save him in the
　day of trouble.
² The LORD will protect him and
　keep him alive;
　And he will be called blessed
　in the land;
　You do not hand him over to
　the desire of his enemies.

³ The LORD will sustain *and*
　strengthen him on his
　sickbed;
　In his illness, You will restore
　him to health.

⁴ As for me, I said, "O LORD, be
　gracious to me;
　Heal my soul, for I have
　sinned against You."
⁵ My enemies speak evil of me,
　saying,
　"When will he die and his
　name perish?"
⁶ And when one comes to see
　me, he speaks empty words,
　While his heart gathers
　malicious gossip [against me];
　When he goes away, he tells it
　[everywhere].
⁷ All who hate me whisper
　together about me;
　Against me they devise my
　hurt [imagining the worst
　for me], *saying,*
⁸ "A wicked thing is poured out
　upon him *and* holds him;
　And when he lies down, he
　will not rise up again."
⁹ Even my own close friend in
　whom I trusted,
　Who ate my bread,
　Has lifted up his heel against
　me [betraying me]. [John
　13:18]

¹⁰ But You, O LORD, be gracious
　to me and restore me [to
　health],
　So that I may repay them.
¹¹ By this I know that You favor
　and delight in me,
　Because my enemy does not
　shout in triumph over me.
¹² As for me, You uphold me in
　my integrity,

And You set me in Your
presence forever.

13 Blessed be the LORD, the God
of Israel,
From everlasting to everlasting
[from this age to the next,
and forever].
Amen and Amen (so be it).

BOOK TWO

PSALM 42

Thirsting for God
in Trouble and Exile.

To the Chief Musician.
A skillful song, *or* a
didactic *or* reflective poem,
of the sons of Korah.

1 AS THE deer pants [longingly]
for the water brooks,
So my soul pants [longingly]
for You, O God.
2 My soul (my life, my inner
self) thirsts for God, for the
living God.

When will I come and see the
face of God? [Ps 63:1, 2; John
7:37; 1 Thess 1:9, 10]
3 My tears have been my food
day and night,
While they say to me all day
long, "Where is your God?"
4 These things I [vividly]
remember as I pour out my
soul;
How I used to go along before
the great crowd of people
and lead them in procession
to the house of God [like
a choirmaster before his
singers, timing the steps to
the music and the chant of
the song],

life point

In Psalm 42:5, we see David struggling with depression. I would like for us to examine how he handled his situation, because it shows us what to do when we are feeling depressed.

As we dissect this verse, we see three distinct responses David gives to his depressed feelings. First, he puts a question to his own soul and asks himself: "Why are you in despair, O my soul?" Then he gives an instruction to his soul: "Hope in God." Finally, he declares what he is going to do: "I shall again praise Him." We might say David has a talk with himself.

We must follow this same basic pattern of action as we confront our feelings of depression and come out of them and into victory.

putting the Word to work

Psalm 42:1 tells of a deer that longs for a refreshing stream of water. On a hot day, *knowing about* water does nothing to quench your thirst; only *drinking* water does. The same is true of our desire for God. Have you ever longed for more than just information about God? God wants you to experience Who He is. Seek Him, and He will satisfy your desire to know Him intimately.

With the voice of joy
   and thanksgiving,
   a great crowd keeping a
   festival.
⁵ Why are you in despair, O my
   soul?

And why have you become
   restless *and* disturbed
   within me?
Hope in God *and* wait
   expectantly for Him, for
   I shall again praise Him

how to deal with discouragement

In Psalm 42:5, the psalmist is discouraged. Discouragement destroys hope, so naturally the devil always tries to discourage us. Without hope we give up, which is exactly what the devil wants us to do.

The Bible repeatedly tells us not to be discouraged or dismayed. God knows that we will not be victorious if we get discouraged, so He always encourages us as we start out on a project by saying to us, "Do not get discouraged." God wants us to be *en*couraged, not *dis*couraged.

When discouragement or condemnation tries to overtake you, the first thing to do is to examine your thought life. What kind of thoughts have you been thinking? Have they sounded something like this? *I am not going to make it; this is too hard. I always fail; it has always been the same. Nothing ever changes. I am sure other people do not have this much trouble getting their minds renewed. I may as well give up. I'm tired of trying. I pray, but it seems as if God doesn't hear. He probably doesn't answer my prayers because He is so disappointed in the way I act.*

If these examples represent your thoughts, then no wonder you get discouraged or feel condemned! Remember, you become what you think. Think discouraging thoughts, and you will get discouraged. Think condemning thoughts, and you will come under condemnation. Change your thinking and be set free!

Instead of thinking negatively, think more like this: *Well, things are going a little slowly, but, thank God, I am making some progress. I am sure glad I'm on the right path that will lead me to freedom. I had a rough day yesterday. I chose wrong thinking all day long. Father, forgive me, and help me to keep on keeping on. I made a mistake, but at least that is one mistake I won't have to make again. This is a new day. You love me, Lord. Your mercy is new every morning. I refuse to be discouraged. I refuse to be condemned. Father, the Bible says that You do not condemn me. You sent Jesus to die for me. I'll be fine—today will be a great day. I ask You to help me choose right thoughts today.*

I am sure you can already feel the victory in this type of cheerful, positive, godly thinking. Practice this type of thinking today!

For the help of His
presence.
⁶O my God, my soul is in despair
within me [the burden more
than I can bear];
Therefore I will [fervently]
remember You from the
land of the Jordan
And the peaks of [Mount]
Hermon, from Mount Mizar.
⁷Deep calls to deep at the
[thundering] sound of Your
waterfalls;
All Your breakers and Your
waves have rolled over me.
⁸Yet the Lᴏʀᴅ will command
His lovingkindness in the
daytime,
And in the night His song will
be with me,
A prayer to the God of my life.

⁹I will say to God my rock,
"Why have You forgotten me?
Why do I go mourning
because of the oppression of
the enemy?"
¹⁰As a crushing of my bones
[with a sword], my
adversaries taunt me,
While they say continually to
me, "Where is your God?"
¹¹Why are you in despair, O my
soul?
Why have you become restless
and disquieted within me?
Hope in God *and* wait
expectantly for Him, for I
shall yet praise Him,

The help of my countenance
and my God.

PSALM 43
Prayer for Rescue.

¹JUDGE *AND* vindicate me,
O God; plead my case
against an ungodly nation.
O rescue me from the
deceitful and unjust man!
²For You are the God of my
strength [my stronghold—in
whom I take refuge]; why
have You rejected me?
Why do I go mourning
because of the oppression of
the enemy?

³O send out Your light and Your
truth, let them lead me;
Let them bring me to Your
holy hill
And to Your dwelling places.
⁴Then I will go to the altar of
God,
To God, my exceeding joy;
With the lyre I will praise
You, O God, my God!

⁵Why are you in despair, O my
soul?
And why are you restless *and*
disturbed within me?
Hope in God *and* wait
expectantly for Him, for I
shall again praise Him,
The help of my [sad]
countenance and my God.

speak the Word

God, send Your light and Your truth, and let them lead me.
Let them bring me into Your presence.
–ADAPTED FROM Pꜱᴀʟᴍ 43:3

PSALM 44

Former Times of Help and Present Troubles.

To the Chief Musician.
A Psalm of the sons of Korah.
A skillful song, *or* a didactic *or*
reflective poem.

¹ WE HAVE heard with our
ears, O God,
Our fathers have told us
The work You did in their days,
In the days of old.
² You drove out the [pagan]
nations with Your own hand;
Then you planted *and*
established them (Israel);
[It was by Your power that]
You uprooted the [pagan]
peoples,
Then You spread them abroad.
³ For our fathers did not possess
the land [of Canaan] by their
own sword,

be free from shame

In Psalm 44:15 the psalmist writes of "dishonor" and "humiliation."
Another way to express these is to use the word *shame.* Many people are
"rooted" in shame. This means that their shame is so deep it functions as
the root of a tree and actually produces "fruit" in the form of unhealthy
thoughts and behaviors.

If you are rooted in shame, then it's important to be aware that shame is
different from guilt. I believe shame is a deeper problem than guilt. We
may feel guilty over something we have done wrong, but shame makes
us feel bad about who we are. There is also a difference between "normal" shame and "rooted" shame.

For example, if I knock over my water glass in a fancy restaurant, I feel
ashamed or embarrassed because I have made a mess in front of everybody. That's normal. But I soon adjust to the mishap and go on. That
incident does not mar my life.

In the Garden of Eden after the Fall, Adam and Eve were ashamed when
they realized they were naked, and so they made aprons of fig leaves to
cover themselves. But that too was a normal reaction.

When you and I make mistakes or commit sin, we feel bad about them
for a while until we repent and are forgiven. Then we are able to put
them behind us and go on without any lasting harm.

But when people are rooted in shame, it affects everything about their
lives. Their bad attitudes toward themselves poison everything they try
to accomplish. They are doomed to failure because they have no confidence. Jesus bore our shame for us on the cross (see Hebrews 12:2). Ask
Jesus today to give you understanding of His work on the cross for you.
Ask Him to heal you so that you can live free from shame.

Nor did their own arm save
   them,
But Your right hand and Your
   arm and the light of Your
   presence,
Because You favored *and*
   delighted in them.

⁴You are my King, O God;
Command victories *and*
   deliverance for Jacob
   (Israel).
⁵Through You we will gore our
   enemies [like a bull];
Through Your name we will
   trample down those who
   rise up against us.
⁶For I will not trust in my bow,
Nor will my sword save me.
⁷But You have saved us from
   our enemies,
And You have put them to
   shame *and* humiliated those
   who hate us.
⁸In God we have boasted all
   the day long,
And we will praise *and*
   give thanks to Your name
   forever.   *Selah.*

⁹But now You have rejected us
   and brought us to dishonor,
And You do not go out with
   our armies [to lead us to
   victory].
¹⁰You make us turn back from
   the enemy,
And those who hate us have
   taken spoil for themselves.
¹¹You have made us like sheep
   to be eaten [as mutton]
And have scattered us [in
   exile] among the nations.
¹²You sell Your people cheaply,
And have not increased Your
   wealth by their sale.

¹³You have made us the
   reproach *and* taunt of our
   neighbors,
A scoffing and a derision to
   those around us.
¹⁴You make us a byword among
   the nations,
A laughingstock among the
   people.
¹⁵My dishonor is before me all
   day long,
And humiliation has covered
   my face,
¹⁶Because of the voice of the
   taunter and reviler,
Because of the presence of the
   enemy and the avenger.

¹⁷All this has come upon us, yet
   we have not forgotten You,
Nor have we been false to
   Your covenant [which You
   made with our fathers].
¹⁸Our heart has not turned
   back,
Nor have our steps wandered
   from Your path,
¹⁹Yet You have [distressingly]
   crushed us in the place of
   jackals
And covered us with [the
   deep darkness of] the
   shadow of death.

²⁰If we had forgotten the name
   of our God
Or stretched out our hands to
   a strange god,
²¹Would not God discover this?
For He knows the secrets of
   the heart.
²²But for Your sake we are
   killed all the day long;
We are considered as sheep
   to be slaughtered. [Rom
   8:35–39]

²³ Awake! Why do You sleep,
O Lord?
Awaken, do not reject us
forever.
²⁴ Why do You hide Your face
And forget our affliction and
our oppression?
²⁵ For our life has melted away
into the dust;
Our body clings to the ground.
²⁶ Rise up! Come be our help,
And ransom us for the sake of
Your steadfast love.

PSALM 45

A Song Celebrating the King's Marriage.

To the Chief Musician; set
to the [tune of] "Lilies." A
Psalm of the sons of Korah.
A skillful song, *or* a didactic
or reflective poem. A Song
of Love.

¹ MY HEART overflows with a
good theme;
I address my psalm to the King.
My tongue is like the pen of a
skillful writer.
² You are fairer than the sons of
men;
Graciousness is poured upon
Your lips;
Therefore God has blessed
You forever.

³ Strap Your sword on *Your*
thigh, O mighty One,
In Your splendor and Your
majesty!
⁴ And in Your majesty ride on
triumphantly
For the cause of truth and
humility and righteousness;
Let Your right hand guide You
to awesome things.

⁵ Your arrows are sharp;
The peoples (nations) fall
under You;
Your arrows pierce the hearts
of the King's enemies.

⁶ Your throne, O God, is forever
and ever;
The scepter of uprightness
is the scepter of Your
kingdom.
⁷ You have loved righteousness
(virtue, morality, justice) and
hated wickedness;
Therefore God, your God, has
anointed You
Above Your companions with
the oil of jubilation.
[Heb 1:8, 9]
⁸ All Your garments are
fragrant with myrrh, aloes
and cassia;
From ivory palaces stringed
instruments have made You
glad.
⁹ Kings' daughters are among
Your noble ladies;
At Your right hand stands the
queen in gold from Ophir.

¹⁰ Hear, O daughter, consider
and incline your ear [to my
instruction]:
Forget your people and your
father's house;
¹¹ Then the King will desire
your beauty;
Because He is your Lord, bow
down *and* honor Him.
¹² The daughter of Tyre will
come with a gift;
The rich among the people
will seek your favor.

¹³ Glorious is the King's
daughter within [the
palace];

Her robe is interwoven with
gold. [Rev 19:7, 8]
14 She will be brought to the
King in embroidered
garments;
The virgins, her companions
who follow her,
Will be brought to You.
15 With gladness and rejoicing
will they be led;
They will enter into the
King's palace.

16 In place of your fathers will
be your sons;
You shall make princes in all
the land.
17 I will make Your name to
be remembered in all
generations;
Therefore the peoples will
praise *and* give You thanks
forever and ever.

PSALM 46

God the Refuge of His People.

To the Chief Musician.
A Psalm of the sons of Korah,
set to soprano voices. A Song.

1 GOD IS our refuge and
strength [mighty and
impenetrable],

life point

What Psalm 45:13 means to me is
that God puts the Holy Spirit inside
us to work on our inner lives; our
attitudes, our reactions, and our
goals. Through His work in us, our
inner lives can be tested and refined
into an environment in which the
Lord is comfortable to reside.

A very present *and*
well-proved help in
trouble.
2 Therefore we will not fear,
though the earth should
change
And though the mountains
be shaken *and* slip into the
heart of the seas,
3 Though its waters roar and
foam,
Though the mountains
tremble at its roaring. *Selah.*

4 There is a river whose
streams make glad the city
of God,
The holy dwelling places of
the Most High.
5 God is in the midst of her
[His city], she will not be
moved;
God will help her when the
morning dawns.
6 The nations made an uproar,
the kingdoms tottered *and*
were moved;
He raised His voice, the earth
melted.
7 The Lord of hosts is
with us;
The God of Jacob is
our stronghold [our
refuge, our high tower].
Selah.

8 Come, behold the works of the
Lord,
Who has brought
desolations *and* wonders on
the earth.
9 He makes wars to cease to the
end of the earth;
He breaks the bow into
pieces and snaps the spear
in two;

He burns the chariots with fire.

10 "Be still and know (recognize, understand) that I am God.

I will be exalted among the nations! I will be exalted in the earth."

11 The LORD of hosts is with us; The God of Jacob is our stronghold [our refuge, our high tower].   *Selah.*

PSALM 47

God the King of the Earth.

To the Chief Musician. A Psalm of the sons of Korah.

1 O CLAP your hands, all you people;

Shout to God with the voice of triumph *and* songs of joy.

2 For the LORD Most High is to be feared [and worshiped with awe-inspired reverence and obedience];

He is a great King over all the earth.

life point

The Lord encourages us in Psalm 46:10 to be still and to know that He is God. Often it is difficult for us to be still or quiet because our flesh is full of energy and usually wants to be active doing something. Let me encourage you not to talk to God only when you want or need something; also spend quiet time with Him just listening for His voice. He will give you great revelation and direction if you will be still before Him and simply listen.

3 He subdues peoples under us And nations under our feet.

4 He chooses our inheritance for us,

The glory *and* excellence of Jacob whom He loves. [1 Pet 1:4, 5]   *Selah.*

5 God has ascended amid shouting,

The LORD with the sound of a trumpet.

6 Sing praises to God, sing praises;

Sing praises to our King, sing praises.

7 For God is the King of all the earth;

Sing praises in a skillful psalm *and* with understanding.

8 God reigns over the nations; God sits on His holy throne.

9 The princes of the people have gathered together as the people of the God of Abraham,

For the shields of the earth belong to God;

He is highly exalted.

PSALM 48

The Beauty and Glory of Zion.

A Song; a Psalm of the sons of Korah.

1 GREAT IS the LORD, and greatly to be praised,

In the city of our God, His holy mountain.

2 Fair *and* beautiful in elevation, the joy of all the earth,

Is Mount Zion [the City of David] in the far north,

express yourself!

The Bible instructs us to dance, to play musical instruments, and to do all kinds of outward things to express worship to the Lord (see Psalms 47:1; 150:3, 4). We need to do this; it brings a release in our lives, it honors God, and it aids in defeating the devil.

It is not enough just to say, "Well, God knows how I feel about Him. I do not have to make a big display." That would be no different from saying, "Well, God knows I believe in Him; therefore, there is no real need for me to be baptized." Or to say, "God knows I am sorry for my sins; therefore, there is no need for me to admit my sins and repent of them." We readily see how foolish this would be, and people from all denominations would agree that we need to be baptized and confess our sins. Yet not all denominations teach people to have outward expression of their praise and worship. Some teach that quiet reverence is the only proper way to worship. We definitely need to be quiet and reverent before the Lord at times, but we also need to express our emotions in worship. I am convinced that God gave us emotions for more purposes than just being enthusiastic at a ball game or about a new car. Surely God wants us to employ our emotions in expressing our love and gratitude to Him.

I am not encouraging unbridled emotion. People who just get "emotional" all the time in worship can be distracting. What we need is balance. I personally believe that if we had a proper emotional release during praise and worship, we might not release emotions at other times in improper ways. Our emotions are just as much a part of us as our body, mind, will, or spirit. God gave us emotions, and they must be cared for, just as the rest of us. We are not to be controlled by emotions because they are known to be fickle or untrustworthy, but neither can we stifle them and not be adversely affected.

I think it is tragic not to allow people the freedom to express their hearts and their love for God in a balanced way. It is wrong to be so afraid of something getting out of balance that we cut it off altogether. It also is a bad idea to do things the same way every time because "that is the way we have always done them." We all must be open to growth, which always involves change. Jesus said that He could not pour new wine into old wineskins, meaning some of the people's old ways had to go (see Matthew 9:17). They had to "let go" of old things and take hold of the new, fresh things. Knowledge and revelation are progressive; if a thing (such as your worship) is not moving forward in your life, it is at the point of dying.

I encourage you to be expressive in your praise and worship. Do this at home if you attend a church where it would be unacceptable to do so in the public services. I also encourage you to pray that everyone will be taught to worship God as He truly deserves to be worshiped.

The city of the great King.
[Matt 5:35]
³ God, in her palaces,
Has made Himself known as
a stronghold.

⁴ For, lo, the kings assembled
themselves,
They [came and] passed by
together.
⁵ They saw it, then they were
amazed;
They were stricken with
terror, they fled in alarm.
⁶ Panic seized them there,
And pain, as that of a woman
in childbirth.
⁷ With the east wind
You shattered the ships of
Tarshish.
⁸ As we have heard, so have we
seen
In the city of the LORD of
hosts, in the city of our God:
God will establish her forever.
Selah.

⁹ We have thought of Your
lovingkindness, O God,
In the midst of Your temple.
¹⁰ As is Your name, O God,

life point

David frequently wrote of meditating on all the wonderful works of the Lord—the mighty acts of God. He said that he thought about the name of the Lord, the lovingkindness of God (see Psalm 48:9), and many other such things. If you and I will do the same, we will stay encouraged, full of faith, and victorious in our everyday lives.

So is Your praise to the ends
of the earth;
Your right hand is full of
righteousness (rightness,
justice).
¹¹ Let Mount Zion be glad,
Let the daughters of Judah
rejoice
Because of Your [righteous]
judgments.
¹² Walk about Zion, go all
around her;
Count her towers,
¹³ Consider her ramparts,
Go through her palaces,
That you may tell the next
generation [about her
glory].
¹⁴ For this is God,
Our God forever and ever;
He will be our guide even
until death.

PSALM 49

The Folly of Trusting
in Riches.

To the Chief Musician.
A Psalm of the sons of Korah.

¹ HEAR THIS, all peoples;
Listen carefully, all
inhabitants of the world,
² Both low and high,
Rich and poor together:
³ My mouth will speak
wisdom,
And the meditation
of my heart will be
understanding.
⁴ I will incline my ear *and*
consent to a proverb;
On the lyre I will unfold my
riddle.
⁵ Why should I fear in the days
of evil,

When the wickedness of
those who would betray me
surrounds me [on every
side],
⁶Even those who trust in *and*
rely on their wealth
And boast of the abundance
of their riches?
⁷None of them can by any
means redeem [either
himself or] his brother,
Nor give to God a ransom for
him—
⁸For the ransom of his soul is
too costly,
And he should cease *trying*
forever—
⁹So that he should live on
eternally,
That he should never see
the pit (grave) *and* undergo
decay.
¹⁰For he sees *that even* wise
men die;
The fool and the stupid alike
perish
And leave their wealth to
others. [Eccl 2:12–16]
¹¹Their inward thought is that
their houses will continue
forever,
And their dwelling places to
all generations;
They have named their lands
after their own names
[ignoring God].
¹²But man, with all his [self]
honor *and* pomp, will not
endure;
He is like the beasts that
perish.
¹³This is the fate of those who
are foolishly confident,

And of those after them
who approve [and are
influenced by] their words.
Selah.
¹⁴Like sheep they are
appointed for Sheol (the
nether world, the place of
the dead);
Death will be their
shepherd;
And the upright shall rule
over them in the morning,
And their form *and* beauty
shall be for Sheol to
consume,
So that they have no dwelling
[on earth].
¹⁵But God will redeem my life
from the power of Sheol,
For He will receive me. *Selah.*

¹⁶Be not afraid when [an
ungodly] man becomes
rich,
When the wealth *and* glory of
his house are increased;
¹⁷For when he dies he will
carry nothing away;
His glory will not descend
after him.
¹⁸Though while he lives he
counts himself happy *and*
prosperous—
And though people praise
you when you do well for
yourself—
¹⁹He shall go to the generation
of his fathers;
They shall never again see
the light.
²⁰A man [who is held] in honor,
Yet who lacks [spiritual]
understanding *and* a
teachable heart, is like the
beasts that perish.

PSALM 50

God the Judge
of the Righteous and
the Wicked.

A Psalm of Asaph

¹ THE MIGHTY One, God, the
Lord, has spoken,
And summoned the earth from
the rising of the sun to its
setting [from east to west].
² Out of Zion, the perfection of
beauty,
God has shone forth.
³ May our God come and not
keep silent;
Fire devours before Him,
And around Him a mighty
tempest rages.
⁴ He summons the heavens
above,
And the earth, to judge His
people:
⁵ "Gather My godly ones to Me,
Those who have made a
covenant with Me by
sacrifice."
⁶ And the heavens declare His
righteousness,
For God Himself is judge.
Selah.

⁷ "Hear, O My people, and I will
speak;
O Israel, I will testify against
you:
I am God, your God.
⁸ "I do not reprove you for your
sacrifices;
Your burnt offerings are
continually before Me.

⁹ "I will accept no young bull
from your house
Nor male goat from your folds.
¹⁰ "For every beast of the forest
is Mine,
And the cattle on a thousand
hills.
¹¹ "I know every bird of the
mountains,
And everything that moves in
the field is Mine.
¹² "If I were hungry, I would not
tell you,
For the world and all it contains
are Mine. [1 Cor 10:26]
¹³ "Shall I eat the flesh of bulls
Or drink the blood of male
goats?
¹⁴ "Offer to God the sacrifice of
thanksgiving
And pay your vows to the Most
High;
¹⁵ Call on Me in the day of
trouble;
I will rescue you, and you
shall honor *and* glorify Me."

¹⁶ But to the wicked God says:
"What right have you to recite
My statutes
Or to take My covenant on your
lips?
¹⁷ "For you hate instruction *and*
discipline
And cast My words behind
you [discarding them].
¹⁸ "When you see a thief, you
are pleased with him *and*
condone his behavior,
And you associate with
adulterers.

speak the Word

Lord, You are not only God, but You are my God.
—ADAPTED FROM PSALM 50:7

19 "You give your mouth to evil
And your tongue frames
deceit.
20 "You sit and speak against
your brother;
You slander your own
mother's son.
21 "These things you have done
and I kept silent;
You thought that I was just
like you.
Now I will reprimand *and*
denounce you and state *the
case* in order before your
eyes.
22 "Now consider this, you who
forget God,
Or I will tear you in pieces, and
there will be no one to rescue
[you].
23 "He who offers a sacrifice of
praise *and* thanksgiving
honors Me;
And to him who orders his
way rightly [who follows the
way that I show him],
I shall show the salvation of
God."

PSALM 51

A Contrite Sinner's Prayer
for Pardon.

To the Chief Musician.
A Psalm of David; when
Nathan the prophet came
to him after he had sinned
with Bathsheba.

1 HAVE MERCY on me,
O God, according to Your
lovingkindness;
According to the greatness of
Your compassion blot out
my transgressions.

2 Wash me thoroughly from my
wickedness *and* guilt
And cleanse me from my sin.
3 For I am conscious of my
transgressions *and* I
acknowledge them;
My sin is always before me.
4 Against You, You only, have I
sinned
And done that which is evil in
Your sight,
So that You are justified when
You speak [Your sentence]

life point

In Psalm 51, King David cries out
to God for mercy and forgiveness
because the Lord had been dealing
with him about his sin with
Bathsheba and the murder of her
husband. Many people do not realize
that David had done these things
one full year before he wrote this
psalm. Apparently, he never really
acknowledged this sin until long
after it happened. He had not faced
the truth, and as long as he refused
to face the truth, he could not truly
repent. And as long as he could not
truly repent, he could not receive
forgiveness from God.

Psalm 51:6 conveys a powerful
message. It says that God desires
truth "in the innermost being." That
means if we want to receive God's
blessings, we must be honest with
Him about our sins and ourselves.
Let me encourage you not to let sin
linger in your life. We all sin, and
when we do, we need to be quick to
repent.

And faultless in Your
judgment. [Rom 3:4]

⁵I was brought forth in [a state
of] wickedness;
In sin my mother conceived
me [and from my beginning
I, too, was sinful]. [John 3:6;
Rom 5:12; Eph 2:3]
⁶Behold, You desire truth in
the innermost being,
And in the hidden part [of my
heart] You will make me
know wisdom.
⁷Purify me with hyssop, and I
will be clean;
Wash me, and I will be whiter
than snow.
⁸Make me hear joy and
gladness *and* be satisfied;
Let the bones which You have
broken rejoice.
⁹Hide Your face from my sins
And blot out all my iniquities.

¹⁰Create in me a clean heart,
O God,
And renew a right *and*
steadfast spirit within me.
¹¹Do not cast me away from
Your presence
And do not take Your Holy
Spirit from me.
¹²Restore to me the joy of Your
salvation
And sustain me with a willing
spirit.
¹³Then I will teach
transgressors Your ways,
And sinners shall be
converted *and* return to
You.
¹⁴Rescue me from
bloodguiltiness,
O God, the God of my
salvation;

Then my tongue will
sing joyfully of Your
righteousness *and* Your
justice.
¹⁵O Lord, open my lips,
That my mouth may declare
Your praise.
¹⁶For You do not delight in
sacrifice, or else I would
give it;
You are not pleased with
burnt offering. [1 Sam
15:22]
¹⁷My [only] sacrifice
[acceptable] to God is a
broken spirit;
A broken and contrite heart
[broken with sorrow for sin,
thoroughly penitent], such,
O God, You will not despise.

¹⁸By Your favor do good to Zion;
May You rebuild the walls of
Jerusalem.
¹⁹Then will You delight in the
sacrifices of righteousness,
In burnt offering and whole
burnt offering;
Then young bulls will be
offered on Your altar.

PSALM 52

Futility of Boastful Wickedness.

To the Chief Musician.
A skillful song, *or* a didactic
or reflective poem.
A Psalm of David, when
Doeg the Edomite came and
told Saul, "David has come
to the house of Ahimelech."

¹WHY DO you boast of evil,
O mighty man?
The lovingkindness of God
endures all day long.

2 Your tongue devises
  destruction,
 Like a sharp razor, working
  deceitfully.
3 You love evil more than good,
 And falsehood more than
  speaking what is right.
                              Selah.
4 You love all words that devour,
 O deceitful tongue.

5 But God will break you down
  forever;
 He will take you away and
  tear you away from your
  tent,
 And uproot you from the land
  of the living.   *Selah.*
6 The righteous will see it and
  fear,
 And will [scoffingly] laugh,
  saying,
7 "Look, [this is] the man who
  would not make God his
  strength [his stronghold
  and fortress],
 But trusted in the abundance
  of his riches,
 Taking refuge in his wealth."

8 But as for me, I am like a
  green olive tree in the
  house of God;
 I trust [confidently] in the
  lovingkindness of God
  forever and ever.
9 I will thank You forever,
  because You have done it,
  [You have rescued me and
  kept me safe].

I will wait on Your name, for
 it is good, in the presence of
 Your godly ones.

PSALM 53

Folly and Wickedness of Men.

To the Chief Musician; in a
mournful strain. A skillful
song, *or* didactic *or* reflective
poem of David.

1 THE [empty-headed] fool has
  said in his heart, "There is
  no God."
 They are corrupt *and* evil, and
  have committed repulsive
  injustice;
 There is no one who does good.
2 God has looked down from
  heaven upon the children of
  men
 To see if there is anyone who
  understands,
 Who seeks after God [who
  requires Him, who longs for
  Him as essential to life].
3 Every one of them has turned
  aside *and* fallen away;
 Together they have become
  filthy *and* corrupt;
 There is no one who does
  good, no, not even one.
  [Rom 3:10–12]

4 Have workers of wickedness
  no knowledge *or* no
  understanding?
 They eat up My people *as
  though* they ate bread

speak the Word

*Lord, I will thank You forever because You have rescued me and
kept me safe. I will wait on Your name, for it is good.*
–ADAPTED FROM PSALM 52:9

And have not called upon
God.
5 There they were, in great
terror *and* dread, where
there had been no terror *or*
dread;
For God scattered the bones
of him who besieged you;
You have put them to shame,
because God has rejected
them.
6 Oh, that the salvation of
Israel would come out of
Zion!
When God restores [the
fortunes of] His people,
Let Jacob rejoice, let Israel be
glad.

PSALM 54

Prayer for Defense against Enemies.

To the Chief Musician;
with stringed instruments.
A skillful song, *or* a didactic
or reflective poem, of David,
when the Ziphites went and
told Saul, "David is hiding
among us."

1 SAVE ME, O God, by Your
name;
And vindicate me by Your
[wondrous] power.
2 Hear my prayer, O God;
Listen to the words of my
mouth.
3 For strangers have risen
against me

And violent men have sought
my life;
They have not set God before
them.   *Selah.*

4 Behold, God is my helper *and*
ally;
The Lord is the sustainer of
my soul [my upholder].
5 He will pay back the evil to
my enemies;
In Your faithfulness destroy
them.

6 With a freewill offering I will
sacrifice to You;
I will give thanks *and* praise
Your name, O Lord, for it is
good.
7 For He has rescued me from
every trouble,
And my eye has looked *with
satisfaction* (triumph) on my
enemies.

PSALM 55

Prayer for the Destruction of the Treacherous.

To the Chief Musician;
with stringed instruments.
A skillful song, *or* a didactic
or reflective poem, of David.

1 LISTEN TO my prayer,
O God,
And do not hide Yourself
from my plea.
2 Listen to me and answer me;
I am restless *and* distraught
in my complaint and
distracted

speak the Word

Thank You, God, for being my helper and my ally.
−ADAPTED FROM PSALM 54:4

3 Because of the voice of the
  enemy,
  Because of the pressure of the
  wicked;
  For they bring down trouble
  on me,
  And in anger they
  persecute me.

4 My heart is in anguish within
  me,
  And the terrors of death have
  fallen upon me.
5 Fear and trembling have
  come upon me;
  Horror has
  overwhelmed me.
6 And I say, "Oh, that I had
  wings like a dove!
  I would fly away and be at
  rest.
7 "I would wander far away,
  I would lodge in the [peace of
  the] wilderness.   *Selah*.
8 "I would hurry to my refuge
  [my tranquil shelter far
  away]
  From the stormy wind *and*
  from the tempest."

9 Confuse [my enemies],
  O Lord, divide their
  tongues [destroying their
  schemes],
  For I have seen violence and
  strife in the city.
10 Day and night they go around
  her walls;
  Wickedness and mischief are
  in her midst.

11 Destruction is within her;
  Oppression and deceit do not
  depart from her streets *and*
  market places.

12 For it is not an enemy who
  taunts me—
  Then I could bear it;
  Nor is it one who has hated
  me who insolently exalts
  himself against me—
  Then I could hide from him.
13 But it is you, a man my equal
  and my counsel,
  My companion and my
  familiar friend;
14 We who had sweet fellowship
  together,
  Who walked to the house of
  God in company.
15 Let death come deceitfully
  upon them;
  Let them go down alive to
  Sheol (the nether world, the
  place of the dead),
  For evil [of every kind] is in
  their dwelling *and* in their
  hearts, in their midst.

16 As for me, I shall call upon
  God,
  And the LORD will save me.
17 Evening and morning and at
  noon I will complain and
  murmur,
  And He will hear my voice.
18 He has redeemed my life in
  peace from the battle that
  was against me,

speak the Word

*God, I thank You that You have redeemed my life in peace
from the battle that was against me.*
–ADAPTED FROM PSALM 55:18

For there were many
against me.
19 God will hear and humble
them,
Even He who sits enthroned
from old—   *Selah.*
Because in them there
has been no change
[of heart],
And they do not fear God [at
all].
20 He [my companion] has
put out his hands against
those who were at peace
with him;
He has broken his covenant
[of friendship and loyalty].
21 The words of his mouth were
smoother than butter,
But his heart was hostile;
His words were softer than
oil,
Yet they were drawn swords.

22 Cast your burden on the LORD
[release it] and He will
sustain *and* uphold you;
He will never allow the
righteous to be shaken (slip,
fall, fail). [1 Pet 5:7]
23 But You, O God, will bring
down the wicked to the pit
of destruction;
Men of blood and treachery
will not live out half their
days.
But I will [boldly and
unwaveringly] trust
in You.

PSALM 56

Supplication for Rescue and Grateful Trust in God.

To the Chief Musician; set
to [the tune of] "Silent Dove
Among Those Far Away." A
Mikhtam of David. [A record
of memorable thoughts]
when the Philistines seized
him in Gath.

1 BE GRACIOUS to me, O God,
for man has trampled on
me;
All day long the adversary
oppresses *and* torments me.
2 My enemies have trampled
upon me all day long,
For they are many who fight
proudly against me.
3 When I am afraid,
I will put my trust *and* faith in
You.
4 In God, whose word I praise;
In God I have put my trust;
I shall not fear.
What can mere man do to
me?
5 All day long they twist my
words *and* say hurtful
things;
All their thoughts are against
me for evil.
6 They attack, they hide *and*
lurk,
They watch my steps,
As they have [expectantly]
waited *to take* my life.

speak the Word

*God, I will cast my burdens on You and release them, knowing
that You will sustain and uphold me. I declare, God, that You will
never allow the righteous to be shaken!*
—ADAPTED FROM PSALM 55:22

7 Cast them out because of their
  wickedness.
In anger bring down the
  peoples, O God!

8 You have taken account of my
  wanderings;
Put my tears in Your bottle.
Are they not recorded in Your
  book?
9 Then my enemies will turn
  back in the day when I call;
This I know, that God is for me.
  [Rom 8:31]
10 In God, *whose* word I praise,
In the LORD, *whose* word I
  praise,
11 In God have I put my trust
  and confident reliance; I
  will not be afraid.
What can man do to me?
12 Your vows are *binding* upon
  me, O God;
I will give thank offerings to
  You.
13 For You have rescued my soul
  from death,
Yes, and my feet from
  stumbling,
So that I may walk before God
In the light of life.

PSALM 57

Prayer for Rescue
from Persecutors.

To the Chief Musician;
set to [the tune of] "Do
Not Destroy." A Mikhtam
of David. [A record
of memorable thoughts
of David] when he fled from
Saul in the cave.

1 BE GRACIOUS to me, O God,
  be gracious *and* merciful to
  me,
For my soul finds shelter *and*
  safety in You,
And in the shadow of
  Your wings I will take
  refuge *and* be confidently
  secure
Until destruction
  passes by.
2 I will cry to God Most
  High,
Who accomplishes *all things*
  on my behalf [for He
  completes my purpose in
  His plan].
3 He will send from heaven and
  save me;
He calls to account him who
  tramples me down.   *Selah.*
God will send out His
  lovingkindness and His
  truth.

4 My life is among lions;
I must lie among those who
  breathe out fire—
The sons of men whose teeth
  are spears and arrows,
And their tongue a sharp
  sword.
5 Be exalted above the heavens,
  O God;
Let Your glory *and* majesty be
  over all the earth.
6 They set a net for my steps;
My very life was bowed
  down.
They dug a pit before me;
Into the midst of it they
  themselves have fallen.
                    Selah.

⁷My heart is steadfast, O God,
  my heart is steadfast *and*
  confident!

I will sing, yes, I will sing
  praises [to You]!
  ⁸Awake, my glory!

steadfast and confident

In Psalm 57:7, we read about a heart that is not only steadfast, but also confident.

I have discovered that staying confident at all times is vital to successful ministry and to an overcoming life. Even while I am in front of an audience teaching and ministering, the devil will try to introduce thoughts into my head to make me lose confidence. For example, there have been times when if I noticed two or three people glance at their watches, the devil whispered to me, "They are so bored they can't wait to get out of here." If a couple of people got up and left to go to the restroom, the devil would say, "They are leaving because they don't like your preaching."

I know that when people are singing or leading worship, it is not uncommon for the devil to tell them, "Nobody likes this. You picked the wrong music. You should have chosen a different song. Your voice sounds lousy. You are singing off-key," and so on and so on.

The mind is a battlefield, and the devil lies to us by putting wrong thoughts in our minds. He is constantly trying to steal our confidence. He does not want us to believe we can hear from God or to believe in the power of prayer. He does not want us to have any confidence concerning God's call on our lives or to be confident that we look nice, that we have any wisdom, or that we know anything at all. He wants us to go around feeling that we are failures. That is why we need to keep our hearts confident within us all the time. I have learned that we do not have to *feel* confident to *be* confident. We can be confident by faith because our confidence should be in Christ, not in ourselves. No matter how I feel, I still believe that I can do whatever I need to do through Christ, Who strengthens me (see Philippians 4:13). If we do not feel confident, then we feel afraid, and I have learned at those times to "do it afraid."

We do not have to drag ourselves out of bed each day in fear or discouragement. Instead, we should get up every morning prepared to keep Satan under our feet. How do we do that? We do it by confidently declaring what the Word says about us, confessing scriptures such as, "I am more than a conqueror through Jesus. I can do all things through Christ Who strengthens me. I am triumphant in every situation because God always causes me to triumph" (see Romans 8:37; Philippians 4:13; 2 Corinthians 2:14). Speaking God's Word not only causes the devil to leave us alone, but it also strengthens our confidence—and confidence is essential if we are going to keep growing and keep going in God.

Awake, harp and lyre!
I will awaken the dawn.
⁹I will praise *and* give thanks
   to You, O Lord, among the
   people;
I will sing praises to You
   among the nations.
¹⁰For Your faithfulness
   and lovingkindness are
   great, reaching to the
   heavens,
And Your truth to the
   clouds.
¹¹Be exalted above the
   heavens, O God;
Let Your glory *and*
   majesty be over all
   the earth.

PSALM 58

Prayer for the Punishment of the Wicked.

To the Chief Musician;
set to [the tune of] "Do
Not Destroy." A Mikhtam
of David. [A record
of memorable thoughts
of David.]

¹DO YOU indeed speak
   righteousness, O gods
   (heavenly beings)?
Do you judge fairly,
   O sons of men?
   [Ps 82:1, 2]
²No, in your heart you devise
   wrongdoing;
On earth you deal out
   the violence of your hands.
³The wicked are estranged
   from the womb;
These go astray from birth,
   speaking lies [even twisted
   partial truths].

⁴Their poison is like the venom
   of a serpent;
They are like the deaf
   horned viper that stops up
   its ear,
⁵So that it does not listen to
   the voice of charmers,
Or of the skillful enchanter
   casting [cunning] spells.

⁶O God, break their teeth in
   their mouth;
Break out the fangs of the
   young lions, O LORD.
⁷Let them flow away like
   water that runs off;
When he aims his arrows,
   let them be as headless
   shafts.
⁸*Let them be* as a snail which
   melts away (secretes slime)
   as it goes along,
Like the miscarriage of a
   woman which never sees
   the sun.
⁹Before your cooking pots
   can feel the *fire of* thorns
   [burning under them as
   fuel],
He will sweep them away
   with a whirlwind, the
   green and the burning
   ones alike.

¹⁰The [unyieldingly]
   righteous will rejoice
   when he sees the
   vengeance [of God];
He will wash his feet in the
   blood of the wicked.
¹¹Men will say, "Surely there
   is a reward for the
   righteous;
Surely there is a God
   who judges on
   the earth."

PSALM 59

Prayer for Rescue from Enemies.

To the Chief Musician;
set to [the tune of] "Do
Not Destroy." A Mikhtam
of David, [a record
of memorable thoughts]
when Saul sent men to watch
his house in order to kill him.

¹DELIVER ME from my
enemies, O my God;
Set me *securely* on an
inaccessibly high place
away from those who rise
up against me.
²Deliver me from those who
practice wrongdoing,
And save me from
bloodthirsty men.
³Look! They lie in wait for my
life;
Fierce *and* powerful men [are
uniting together to] launch
an attack against me,
Not for my wrongdoing nor
for any sin of mine, O LORD.
⁴They run and set themselves
against me though there is
no guilt in me;
Stir Yourself to meet *and* help
me, and see [what they are
doing]!
⁵You, O LORD God of hosts, the
God of Israel,
Arise to punish all the
nations;

Spare no one *and* do not
be merciful to any who
treacherously plot evil.
Selah.
⁶They return at evening, they
howl *and* snarl like dogs,
And go [prowling] around the
city.
⁷Look how they belch out
[insults] with their mouths;
Swords [of sarcasm, ridicule,
slander, and lies] are in
their lips,
For *they say,* "Who hears us?"
⁸But You, O LORD, will laugh at
them [in scorn];
You scoff at *and* deride all the
nations.

⁹O [God] my strength, I will
watch for You;
For God is my stronghold [my
refuge, my protector, my
high tower].
¹⁰My God in His [steadfast]
lovingkindness will meet me;
God will let me look
triumphantly on my enemies
[who lie in wait for me].
¹¹Do not kill them, or my people
will forget;
Scatter them *and* make them
wander [endlessly] back
and forth by Your power,
and bring them down,
O Lord our shield!
¹²For the sin of their mouths
and the words of their lips,

speak the Word

*Thank You, God, for always meeting me with
steadfast loving-kindness.*
—ADAPTED FROM PSALM 59:10

Let them even be trapped in
their pride,
And on account of the curses
and lies which they tell.
13 Destroy *them* in wrath,
destroy *them* so that they
may be no more;
Let them know that God rules
over Jacob (Israel)
To the ends of the earth. *Selah.*
14 They return at evening, they
howl *and* snarl like dogs,
And go [prowling] around the
city.
15 They wander around for food
[to devour]
And growl all night if they are
not satisfied.

16 But as for me, I will sing of
Your mighty strength *and*
power;
Yes, I will sing joyfully of
Your lovingkindness in the
morning;
For You have been my
stronghold
And a refuge in the day of my
distress.
17 To You, O [God] my strength,
I will sing praises;
For God is my stronghold
[my refuge, my protector,
my high tower], the God
who shows me [steadfast]
lovingkindness.

PSALM 60

Lament over Defeat in Battle, and Prayer for Help.

To the Chief Musician; set
to [the tune of] "The Lily
of the Testimony." A Mikhtam
of David [intended to record

memorable thoughts and]
to teach; when he struggled
with the Arameans
of Mesopotamia and
the Arameans of Zobah,
and when Joab returned
and struck twelve thousand
Edomites in the Valley
of Salt.

1 O GOD, You have rejected us
and cast us off. You have
broken [down our defenses
and scattered] us;
You have been angry;
O restore us *and* turn again
to us.
2 You have made the land
quake, You have split it
open;
Heal its rifts, for it shakes *and*
totters.
3 You have made Your people
experience hardship;
You have given us wine to
drink that makes us stagger
and fall.
4 You have set up a banner for
those who fear You [with
awe-inspired reverence
and submissive wonder—a
banner to shield them from
attack],
A banner that may be
displayed because of the
truth.   *Selah.*
5 That Your beloved ones may
be rescued,
Save with Your right hand
and answer us.

6 God has spoken in His
holiness [in His promises]:
"I will rejoice, I will divide
[the land of] Shechem and
measure out the Valley of
Succoth [west to east].

7 "Gilead is Mine, and
     Manasseh is Mine;
     Ephraim is My helmet;
     Judah is My scepter.
8 "Moab is My washbowl;
     Over Edom I shall throw My
     shoe [in triumph];
     Over Philistia I raise the
     shout [of victory]."

9 Who will bring me into the
     besieged city [of Petra]?
     Who will lead me to Edom?
10 Have You not rejected us,
     O God?
     And will You not go out with
     our armies?
11 Give us help against the enemy,
     For the help of man is
     worthless (ineffectual,
     without purpose).
12 Through God we will have
     victory,
     For He will trample down our
     enemies.

putting the Word to work

Has life ever seemed so overwhelming that you wanted to run and hide? You can be sure of God's eternal protection and ability to be your refuge (see Psalm 61:3, 4). Whether you need the strength of a strong tower or the comfort of His arms around you, cry out to God; He will answer in your time of need.

PSALM 61

Confidence in God's Protection.

To the Chief Musician; on
stringed instruments.
A Psalm of David.

1 HEAR MY cry, O God;
     Listen to my prayer.
2 From the end of the earth I
     call to You, when my heart
     is overwhelmed *and* weak;
     Lead me to the rock that is
     higher than I [a rock that
     is too high to reach without
     Your help].
3 For You have been a shelter
     and a refuge for me,
     A strong tower against the
     enemy.
4 Let me dwell in Your tent
     forever;
     Let me take refuge in the
     shelter of Your wings. *Selah.*

5 For You have heard my vows,
     O God;
     You have given me the
     inheritance of those who fear
     Your name [with reverence].
6 You will prolong the king's
     life [adding days upon days];
     His years will be like many
     generations.
7 He will sit enthroned forever
     before [the face of] God;
     Appoint lovingkindness and
     truth to watch over *and*
     preserve him.

speak the Word

God, through You, I will have victory.
—ADAPTED PSALM 60:12

stability releases ability

Psalm 62:8 teaches us that we are not to have faith in God just once in a while, but at all times. We need to learn to live from faith to faith (see Romans 1:17), trusting the Lord when things are good and when things are bad.

It is easy to trust God when things are going well. But when things are not going well, we develop character by trusting God in our difficult situations. And the more character we develop, the more our ability can be released. That is why I say that *stability releases ability*. The more stable we become, the more our ability will be released because God will know that He can trust us.

Many people have gifts that can take them to places where their character cannot keep them. Gifts are *given*, but character is *developed*. I have learned this in my own life.

Throughout my childhood, one thing I could do well was talk. In school, I could talk enough to make the teacher think I understood everything she was teaching, when I really knew nothing about it. I have always been a communicator and a convincer. But in order for God to allow me in the pulpit to preach to millions every day, not only did I have to have a gift, I also had to have character so that He could trust me to use my mouth to teach His Word and communicate His heart. Otherwise, He could not allow me to teach that many people, because I might say one thing one day and something else the next day. Or, even worse, I might preach to others what I was unable to do in my own private life.

By disciplining our emotions, our moods, and our mouths, we become stable enough to remain peaceful whatever our situation or circumstances, so that we can walk in the fruit of the Spirit—whether we feel like it or not. The more stable we become, the more ability can be released through us. Desire and pursue stability in every area of your life so that all the ability in you can be released!

---

[8] So I will sing praise to Your name forever,
Paying my vows day by day.

PSALM 62

God Alone a Refuge from Treachery and Oppression.

To the Chief Musician; to Jeduthun [Ethan, the noted musician, founder of an official musical family].
A Psalm of David.

[1] FOR GOD alone my soul *waits* in silence;
From Him comes my salvation.
[2] He alone is my rock and my salvation,
My defense *and* my strong tower; I will not be shaken *or* disheartened.

³ How long will you attack a man
So that you may murder him,
all of you,
Like a leaning wall, like a
tottering fence?
⁴ They consult only to throw
him down from his high
position [to dishonor him];
They delight in lies.
They bless with [the words
of] their mouths,
But inwardly they curse.
Selah.

⁵ For God alone my soul waits
in silence *and* quietly
submits to Him,
For my hope is from Him.
⁶ He only is my rock and my
salvation;
My fortress *and* my defense,
I will not be shaken *or*
discouraged.
⁷ On God my salvation and my
glory rest;
He is my rock of [unyielding]
strength, my refuge is in God.
⁸ Trust [confidently] in Him at
all times, O people;
Pour out your heart before Him.
God is a refuge for us.   *Selah.*

⁹ Men of low degree are only
a breath (emptiness), and
men of [high] rank are a lie
(delusion).
In the balances they go up
[because they have no
measurable weight or value];

They are together lighter than
a breath.
¹⁰ Do not trust in oppression,
And do not vainly hope in
robbery;
If riches increase, do not set
your heart on them.

¹¹ God has spoken once,
Twice I have heard this:
That power belongs to God.
¹² Also to You, O Lord, belong
lovingkindness *and*
compassion,
For You compensate every man
according to [the value of] his
work. [Jer 17:10; Rev 22:12]

PSALM 63

The Thirsting Soul Satisfied
in God.

A Psalm of David; when he was
in the wilderness of Judah.

¹ O GOD, You are my God; with
deepest longing I will seek
You;
My soul [my life, my very self]
thirsts for You, my flesh
longs *and* sighs for You,
In a dry and weary land
where there is no water.
² So I have gazed upon You in
the sanctuary,
To see Your power and Your
glory. [Ps 42:1, 2]
³ Because Your lovingkindness
is better than life,

speak the Word

God, I am trusting confidently in You at all times.
You are a refuge for me!
–ADAPTED FROM PSALM 62:8

My lips shall praise You.
⁴ So will I bless You as long as I
  live;
  I will lift up my hands in Your
  name.
⁵ My soul [my life, my very
  self] is satisfied as with
  marrow and fatness,
  And my mouth offers praises
  [to You] with joyful lips.

⁶ When I remember You on my
  bed,
  I meditate *and* thoughtfully
  focus on You in the night
  watches,

⁷ For You have been my help,
  And in the shadow of Your
  wings [where I am always
  protected] I sing for joy.
⁸ My soul [my life, my very self]
  clings to You;
  Your right hand upholds me.

⁹ But those who seek my life to
  destroy it
  Will [be destroyed and] go
  into the depths of the earth
  [into the underworld].
¹⁰ They will be given over to the
  power of the sword;
  They will be a prey for foxes.
¹¹ But the king will rejoice in God;

life point

Sacrifice and Christianity have always been connected. In the Old Testament, the Law required sacrifices of various kinds. David speaks of lifting up the hands "as the evening offering" in Psalm 141:2.

Other scriptures talk about the lifting up of hands in worship (see Psalm 28:2; 119:48; 134:2; 1 Timothy 2:8). Lifting our hands to God seems a natural thing to do when we are in His presence. To me, it is an expression of adoration, reverence, and surrender. We should continually surrender ourselves to God and His plan for us.

You can lift up your hands and speak a word of praise all throughout the day. Even at work, you can go to the restroom and take a moment to praise God. When we willingly surrender and worship God as a sacrifice, He responds.

life point

David spoke frequently about meditating on God, His goodness, His works, and His ways. It is tremendously uplifting to think on the goodness of God and all the marvelous works of His hands.

I enjoy watching television shows about nature, animals, ocean life, and other things in the physical world because they depict the greatness and the awesomeness of God, His infinite creativity and the fact that He is upholding all things by His power (see Hebrews 1:3). Always remember that—and know that He is not only upholding and maintaining the moon, the stars, the planets including the earth, the animals, and all of creation, but that He is also upholding and maintaining everything about you and your life in the palm of His hand.

Everyone who swears by Him
[honoring the true God,
acknowledging His authority
and majesty] will glory,
For the mouths of those who
speak lies will be stopped.

life point

In Psalm 63:1, David cries out: "O
God, You are my God; with deepest
longing I will seek You" Throughout
the Psalms, David prayed similar prayers, which I call "seeking
prayers." Many times per day, I find
myself whispering in my heart or
even aloud, "Oh, God, I need You."
This is a very simple but very powerful way to pray. I encourage you to
join me in seeking God in this quick
and effective way.

PSALM 64

Prayer for Protection from
Secret Enemies.

To the Chief Musician.
A Psalm of David.

¹HEAR MY voice, O God, in
my complaint;
Guard my life from the terror of
the enemy.
²Hide me from the secret
counsel *and* conspiracy of
the ungodly,
From the scheming of those
who do wrong,
³Who have sharpened their
tongues like a sword.
They aim venomous words as
arrows,
⁴To shoot from ambush at the
blameless [one];

Suddenly they shoot at him,
without fear.
⁵They encourage themselves
in [their pursuit of] an evil
agenda;
They talk of laying snares
secretly;
They say, "Who will discover
us?"
⁶They devise acts of injustice,
saying,
"We are ready with a well-
conceived plan."
For the inward thought and
the heart of a man are deep
(mysterious, unsearchable).
⁷But God will shoot them with
an [unexpected] arrow;
Suddenly they will be
wounded.
⁸So they will be caused to
stumble;
Their own tongue is against
them;
All who gaze at them will
shake the head [in scorn].
⁹Then all men will fear [God's
judgment];
They will declare the work of
God,
And they will consider *and*
wisely acknowledge what
He has done.
¹⁰The righteous will rejoice in
the LORD and take refuge in
Him;
All the upright in heart will
glory *and* offer praise.

PSALM 65

God's Abundant Favor
to Earth and Man.

To the Chief Musician.
A Psalm of David. A Song.

1 TO YOU belongs silence
   [the submissive wonder of
   reverence], and [it bursts
   into] praise in Zion, O God;
  And to You the vow shall be
   performed.
2 O You who hear prayer,
  To You all mankind comes.
3 Wickedness *and* guilt prevail
   against me;
  Yet as for our transgressions,
  You forgive them [removing
   them from Your sight].
4 Blessed is the one whom You
   choose and bring near
  To dwell in Your courts.
  We will be filled with the
   goodness of Your house,
  Your holy temple.

5 By awesome *and* wondrous
   things You answer us in
   righteousness, O God of our
   salvation,
  You who are the trust *and*
   hope of all the ends of the
   earth and of the farthest sea;
6 Who creates the mountains
   by His strength,
  Being clothed with power,
7 Who stills the roaring of the
   seas,
  The roaring of their waves,
  And the tumult of the peoples,
8 So they who dwell at the
   ends *of the earth* stand
   in awe of Your signs [the
   evidence of Your presence].
   [Mark 4:36–41]
  You make the dawn and the
   sunset shout for joy.

9 You visit the earth and make
   it overflow [with water];
  You greatly enrich it;

The stream of God is full of
   water;
  You provide their grain, when
   You have prepared the earth.
10 You water its furrows
   abundantly,
  You smooth its ridges;
  You soften it with showers,
  You bless its growth.
11 You crown the year with Your
   bounty,
  And Your paths overflow.
12 The pastures of the
   wilderness drip [with dew],
  And the hills are encircled
   with joy.

life point

In his writings the psalmist often uses the word *selah*, which means "pause, and calmly think of that." This phrase lets the reader know that this is a good place to stop and to slowly digest the meaning of what has just been said. The reader is given the opportunity to do this at the end of Psalm 66:4.

Jeremiah talked about stopping to feed on and digest the words of God. He said, "Your words were found and I ate them, and Your words became a joy to me and the delight of my heart" (Jeremiah 15:16). We must, so to speak, "chew" on the Word of God. Often we read the Bible for *quantity* when we should read for *quality*. Whatever passage you are reading, read in a manner that allows the Word to go down into your innermost being and feed your spirit.

¹³ The meadows are clothed
with flocks
And the valleys are covered
with grain;
They shout for joy and they
sing.

PSALM 66

Praise for God's Mighty
Deeds and for His Answer
to Prayer.

To the Chief Musician.
A Song. A Psalm.

¹ SHOUT JOYFULLY to God,
all the earth;
² Sing of the honor *and* glory
and magnificence of His
name;
Make His praise glorious.
³ Say to God, "How awesome
and fearfully glorious are
Your works!
Because of the greatness of
Your power Your enemies
will pretend to be obedient
to You.
⁴ "All the earth will [bow
down to] worship You [in
submissive wonder],
And will sing praises to You;
They will praise Your name
in song."   *Selah.*

⁵ Come and see the works of
God,
He is awesome in His deeds
toward the children of men.

⁶ He turned the sea into dry land;
They crossed through the
river on foot;
There we rejoiced in Him.
[Ex 14–15]
⁷ Who rules by His might
forever,
His eyes keep watch on the
nations;
Do not let the rebellious exalt
themselves.   *Selah.*

⁸ Bless our God, O peoples,
And make the sound of His
praise *be heard* abroad,
⁹ Who keeps us among the living,
And does not allow our feet to
slip *or* stumble.
¹⁰ For You have tested us, O God;
You have refined us as silver
is refined.
¹¹ You brought us into the net;
You laid a heavy burden [of
servitude] on us.
¹² You made men (charioteers)
ride over our heads [in
defeat];
We went through fire and
through water,
Yet You brought us out into a
[broad] *place of* abundance
[to be refreshed].
¹³ I shall come into Your house
with burnt offerings;
I shall pay You my vows,
¹⁴ Which my lips uttered
And my mouth spoke as a
promise when I was in
distress.

speak the Word

*I bless You, Lord, because You have not turned away my prayer
nor Your loving-kindness from me.*
–ADAPTED FROM PSALM 66:20

15 I shall offer to You burnt
   offerings of fat lambs,
With the [sweet] smoke of
   rams;
I will offer bulls with male
   goats.   *Selah.*

16 Come and hear, all who fear
   God [and worship Him with
   awe-inspired reverence and
   obedience],
And I will tell what He has
   done for me.
17 I cried aloud to Him;
He was highly praised with
   my tongue.
18 If I regard sin *and* baseness in
   my heart [that is, if I know
   it is there and do nothing
   about it],
The Lord will not hear [me];
   [Prov 15:29; 28:9; Is 1:15;
   John 9:31; James 4:3]
19 But certainly God has heard
   [me];
He has given heed to the voice
   of my prayer.
20 Blessed be God,
Who has not turned away my
   prayer
Nor His lovingkindness
   from me.

PSALM 67

The Nations Exhorted
to Praise God.

To the Chief Musician; on
   stringed instruments.
   A Psalm. A Song.

1 GOD BE gracious *and* kind-
   hearted to us and bless us,
And make His face shine
   [with favor] on us—   *Selah.*
2 That Your way may be known
   on earth,

Your salvation *and*
   deliverance among all
   nations.
3 Let the peoples praise You,
   O God;
Let all the peoples praise You.
4 Let the nations be glad and
   sing for joy,
For You will judge the people
   fairly
And guide the nations on
   earth.   *Selah.*
5 Let the peoples praise You,
   O God;
Let all the peoples praise You.
6 The earth has yielded its
   harvest [as evidence of His
   approval];
God, our God, blesses us.
7 God blesses us,
And all the ends of the earth
   shall fear Him [with awe-
   inspired reverence and
   submissive wonder].

putting the Word to work

God wants all nations and people to
know Him, worship Him, and enjoy
Him. How can you be involved in
God's work in the world?

PSALM 68

The God of Sinai and
of the Sanctuary.

To the Chief Musician.
   A Psalm of David. A Song.

1 LET GOD arise, and His
   enemies be scattered;
Let those who hate Him flee
   before Him.

²As smoke is driven away, so
  drive *them* away;
As wax melts before
  the fire,
So let the wicked *and* guilty
  perish before [the presence
  of] God.
³But let the righteous be glad;
  let them be in good spirits
  before God,
Yes, let them rejoice with
  delight.
⁴Sing to God, sing praises to
  His name;
Lift up *a song* for Him
  who rides through the
  desert—
His name is the Lᴏʀᴅ—be in
  good spirits before Him.

⁵A father of the fatherless and
  a judge *and* protector of the
  widows,
Is God in His holy habitation.
⁶God makes a home for the
  lonely;
He leads the prisoners into
  prosperity,
Only the stubborn *and*
  rebellious dwell in a
  parched land.

⁷O God, when You went out
  before Your people,
When You marched through
  the wilderness,   *Selah.*
⁸The earth trembled;
The heavens also poured
  down *rain* at the presence
  of God;

Sinai itself trembled at the
  presence of God, the God of
  Israel.
⁹You, O God, sent abroad
  plentiful rain;
You confirmed Your
  inheritance when it was
  parched *and* weary.
¹⁰Your flock found a dwelling
  place in it;
O God, in Your goodness You
  provided for the poor.

¹¹The Lord gives the command
  [to take Canaan];
The women who proclaim the
  good news are a great host
  (army);

¹²"The kings of the [enemies']
  armies flee, they flee,
And the beautiful woman
  who remains at home
  divides the spoil [left
  behind]."
¹³When you lie down [to rest]
  among the sheepfolds,
You [Israel] are like the
  wings of a dove [of victory]
  overlaid with silver,
Its feathers glistening with
  gold [trophies taken from
  the enemy].
¹⁴When the Almighty scattered
  [the Canaanite] kings in the
  land of Canaan,
It was snowing on Zalmon.

¹⁵A mountain of God is the
  mountain of Bashan;

speak the Word

Thank You, God, for bearing my burdens day by day.
You are the God of my salvation, Who sets me free.
–ADAPTED FROM PSALM 68:19, 20

A [high] mountain of many summits is Mount Bashan [rising east of the Jordan].
¹⁶ Why do you look with envy, mountains with many peaks,
At the mountain [of the city of Zion] which God has desired for His dwelling place?
Yes, the Lord will dwell *there* forever.
¹⁷ The chariots of God are myriads, thousands upon thousands;
The Lord is among them as He was at Sinai, in holiness.
¹⁸ You have ascended on high, You have led away captive *Your* captives;
You have received gifts among men,
Even from the rebellious also, that the Lord God may dwell there. [Eph 4:8]

¹⁹ Blessed be the Lord, who bears our burden day by day,
The God who is our salvation! *Selah.*
²⁰ God is to us a God of acts of salvation;
And to God the Lord belong escapes from death [setting us free].
²¹ Surely God will shatter the head of His enemies,
The hairy scalp of one who goes on in his guilty ways.
²² The Lord said, "I will bring your enemies back from Bashan;
I will bring them back from the depths of the [Red] Sea,

²³ That your foot may crush them in blood,
That the tongue of your dogs *may have* its share from your enemies."

²⁴ They have seen Your [solemn] procession, O God,
The procession of my God, my King, into the sanctuary [in holiness].
²⁵ The singers go in front, the players of instruments last;
Between them the maidens playing on tambourines.
²⁶ Bless God in the congregations, [give thanks, gratefully praise Him],
The Lord, *you who are* from [Jacob] the fountain of Israel.
²⁷ The youngest is there, Benjamin, ruling them,
The princes of Judah and their company [the southern tribes],
The princes of Zebulun and the princes of Naphtali [the northern tribes].

²⁸ Your God has commanded your strength [your power in His service and your resistance to temptation];
Show Yourself strong, O God, who acted on our behalf.
²⁹ Because of Your temple at Jerusalem
[Pagan] kings will bring gifts to You [out of respect].
³⁰ Rebuke the beasts [living] among the reeds [in Egypt],
The herd of bulls (the leaders) with the calves of the peoples;

Trampling underfoot the
pieces of silver;
He has scattered the peoples
who delight in war.
31 Princes *and* envoys shall
come from Egypt;
Ethiopia will quickly stretch
out her hands [with the
offerings of submission] to
God.

32 Sing to God, O kingdoms of
the earth,
Sing praises to the Lord! *Selah.*
33 To Him who rides in the
highest heavens, the
ancient heavens,
Behold, He sends out His
voice, a mighty *and* majestic
voice.
34 Ascribe strength to God;
His majesty is over Israel
And His strength is in the
skies.
35 O God, *You are* awesome *and*
profoundly majestic from
Your sanctuary;
The God of Israel gives
strength and power to His
people.
Blessed be God!

PSALM 69

A Cry of Distress and
Imprecation on Adversaries.

To the Chief Musician; set
to [the tune of] "Lilies."
A Psalm of David.

1 SAVE ME, O God,
For the waters have
threatened my life [they
have come up to my neck].
2 I have sunk in deep mire,
where there is no foothold;

I have come into deep
waters, where a flood
overwhelms me.
3 I am weary with my crying;
my throat is parched;
My eyes fail while I wait [with
confident expectation] for
my God.
4 Those who hate me without
cause are more than the
hairs of my head;
Those who would destroy
me are powerful, being my
enemies wrongfully;
I am forced to restore what I
did not steal. [John 15:25]

5 O God, You know my folly;
My wrongs are not hidden
from You.
6 Do not let those who wait
[confidently] for You be
ashamed through me,
O Lord God of hosts;
Do not let those who seek You
[as necessary for life itself]
be dishonored through me,
O God of Israel,
7 Because for Your sake I have
borne reproach;
Confusion *and* dishonor have
covered my face.
8 I have become estranged from
my brothers
And an alien to my mother's
sons. [John 7:3–5]
9 For zeal for Your house has
consumed me,
And the [mocking] insults of
those who insult You have
fallen on me. [John 2:17;
Rom 15:3]
10 When I wept *and* humbled
myself with fasting,
It became my reproach.

¹¹When I made sackcloth
  my clothing [as one in
  mourning],
  I became a byword [a mere
  object of scorn] to them.
¹²They who sit in the [city's]
  gate talk about me *and* mock
  me,
  And I am the song of the
  drunkards.

¹³But as for me, my prayer
  is to You, O Lᴏʀᴅ, at an
  acceptable *and* opportune
  time;
  O God, in the greatness
  of Your favor *and* in
  the abundance of Your
  lovingkindness,
  Answer me with truth [that
  is, the faithfulness of Your
  salvation].
¹⁴Rescue me from the mire and
  do not let me sink;
  Let me be rescued from those
  who hate me and from the
  deep waters.
¹⁵Do not let the floodwater
  overwhelm me,
  Nor the deep waters swallow
  me up,
  Nor the pit [of Sheol] shut its
  mouth over me.

¹⁶Answer me, O Lᴏʀᴅ, for Your
  lovingkindness is sweet *and*
  good *and* comforting;
  According to the greatness
  of Your compassion, turn
  to me.
¹⁷Do not hide Your face from
  Your servant,
  For I am in distress; answer
  me quickly.
¹⁸Draw near to my soul and
  redeem it;

Ransom me because of my
  enemies [so that they do not
  delight in my distress].
¹⁹You know my reproach and
  my shame and my dishonor
  [how I am insulted];
  My adversaries are all before
  You [each one fully known].

²⁰Reproach *and* insults have
  broken my heart and I am
  so sick.
  I looked for sympathy, but
  there was none,
  And for comforters, but I
  found none.
²¹They (self-righteous
  hypocrites) also gave me
  gall [poisonous and bitter]
  for my food,
  And for my thirst they gave
  me vinegar to drink. [Matt
  27:34, 48]

²²May their table [with all its
  abundance and luxury]
  become a snare [to them];
  And when they are in peace
  [secure at their sacrificial
  feasts], *may it become* a trap.
²³May their eyes be dimmed so
  that they cannot see,
  And make their loins shake
  continually [in terror and
  weakness].
²⁴Pour out Your indignation on
  them,
  And let [the fierceness
  of] Your burning anger
  overtake them.
²⁵May their encampment be
  desolate;
  May no one dwell in their
  tents. [Matt 23:38; Acts 1:20]
²⁶For they have persecuted him
  whom You have struck,

And they tell of the pain
  of those whom You have
  pierced *and* wounded.
²⁷ Add [unforgiven] iniquity
  to their iniquity [in Your
  book],
  And may they not come into
  Your righteousness.
²⁸ May they be blotted out of the
  book of life [and their lives
  come to an end]
  And may they not be recorded
  with the righteous (those in
  right standing with God).
  [Rev 3:4, 5; 20:12, 15; 21:27]

²⁹ But I am sorrowful and in pain;
  May Your salvation, O God,
  set me [securely] on high.
³⁰ I will praise the name of God
  with song
  And magnify Him with
  thanksgiving.
³¹ And it will please the Lᴏʀᴅ
  better than an ox
  Or a young bull with horns
  and hoofs.
³² The humble have seen it and
  are glad;
  You who seek God [requiring
  Him as your greatest need],
  let your heart revive *and*
  live. [Ps 22:26; 42:1]
³³ For the Lᴏʀᴅ hears the needy
  And does not despise His *who
  are* prisoners.

³⁴ Let heaven and earth praise
  Him,
  The seas and everything that
  moves in them.
³⁵ For God will save Zion and
  rebuild the cities of Judah,
  That His servants may
  remain there and
  possess it.
³⁶ The descendants of His
  servants will inherit it,
  And those who love His name
  will dwell in it.

PSALM 70

Prayer for Help
against Persecutors.

To the Chief Musician.
A Psalm of David, to bring
  to remembrance.

¹ O GOD, *come quickly* to save
  me;
  O Lᴏʀᴅ, come quickly to help
  me!
² Let those be ashamed and
  humiliated
  Who seek my life;
  Let them be turned back and
  humiliated
  Who delight in my hurt.
³ Let them be turned back
  because of their shame *and*
  disgrace
  Who say, "Aha, aha!"

⁴ May all those who seek You
  [as life's first priority]
  rejoice and be glad in You;

speak the Word

*God, I am seeking You as life's first priority and I am rejoicing
in You. I love Your salvation and I will say continually,
"Let God be magnified!"*
–ᴀᴅᴀᴘᴛᴇᴅ ꜰʀᴏᴍ Pꜱᴀʟᴍ 70:4

May those who love
Your salvation say
continually,
"Let God be magnified!"
⁵But I am afflicted and
needy;
Come quickly to me, O God!
You are my help and my
rescuer;
O Lord, do not delay.

PSALM 71

Prayer of an Old Man
for Rescue.

¹IN YOU, O Lord, I have put
my trust *and* confidently
taken refuge;
Let me never be put to
shame.
²In Your righteousness deliver
me and rescue me;
Incline Your ear to me and
save me.
³Be to me a rock of refuge *and*
a sheltering stronghold to
which I may continually
come;
You have given the
commandment to save me,
For You are my rock and my
fortress.
⁴Rescue me, O my God, from
the hand of the wicked
(godless),
From the grasp of the
unrighteous and ruthless
man.
⁵For You are my hope;
O Lord God, *You are* my
trust *and* the source of my
confidence from my youth.
⁶Upon You have I relied *and*
been sustained from my
birth;

You are He who took me from
my mother's womb *and* You
have been my benefactor
from that day.
My praise is continually of
You.

⁷I am as a wonder to many,
For You are my strong refuge.
⁸My mouth is filled with Your
praise
And with Your glory all day
long.
⁹Do not cast me off *nor* send
me away in the time of old
age;
Do not abandon me when
my strength fails *and* I am
weak.
¹⁰For my enemies have spoken
against me;
Those who watch for my life
have consulted together,
¹¹Saying, "God has abandoned
him;
Pursue and seize him, for
there is no one to rescue
him."

¹²O God, do not be far from me;
O my God, come quickly to
help me!
¹³Let those who attack my life
be ashamed and consumed;
Let them be covered with
reproach and dishonor, who
seek to injure me.
¹⁴But as for me, I will wait *and*
hope continually,
And will praise You yet more
and more.
¹⁵My mouth shall tell of Your
righteousness
And of Your [deeds of]
salvation all day long,

For their number is more than
I know.

¹⁶I will come with the mighty
acts of the Lord GOD [and in
His strength];
I will make mention of Your
righteousness, Yours alone.

¹⁷O God, You have taught me
from my youth,
And I still declare Your
wondrous works *and*
miraculous deeds.

¹⁸And even when I am old and
gray-headed, O God, do not
abandon me,
Until I declare Your
[mighty] strength to
this generation,
Your power to all who are to
come.

¹⁹Your righteousness, O God,
reaches to the [height of
the] heavens,
You who have done great
things;
O God, who is like You, [who
is Your equal]?

²⁰You who have shown
me many troubles and
distresses
Will revive *and* renew me
again,
And will bring me up again
from the depths of the
earth.

²¹May You increase my
greatness (honor)
And turn to comfort me.

²²I will also praise You with the
harp,
Your truth *and* faithfulness,
O my God;
To You I will sing praises with
the lyre,
O Holy One of Israel.

²³My lips will shout for joy
when I sing praises to You,
And my soul, which You have
redeemed.

²⁴My tongue also will speak of
Your righteousness all day
long;
For they are ashamed, for
they are humiliated who
seek my injury.

PSALM 72

The Reign of the Righteous King.

A Psalm of Solomon.

¹GIVE THE king [knowledge
of] Your judgments, O God,
And [the spirit of] Your
righteousness to the king's
son [to guide all his ways].

²May he judge Your people
with righteousness,
And Your afflicted with
justice. [1 Kin 3:1–5]

³The mountains will bring
peace *and* prosperity to the
people,
And the hills, in [the
establishment of]
righteousness.

speak the Word

God, I will wait and hope continually.
I will praise You more and more.
—ADAPTED FROM PSALM 71:14

⁴May he bring justice to the poor among the people,
Save the children of the needy
And crush the oppressor,

⁵Let them fear You [with awe-inspired reverence and worship You with obedience] while the sun endures,
And as long as the moon [reflects light], throughout all generations.
⁶May he come down like rain on the mown grass,
Like showers that water the earth.
⁷In his days may the righteous flourish,
And peace abound until the moon is no more. [Is 11:1–9]

⁸May he also rule from sea to sea
And from the River [Euphrates] to the ends of the earth. [Zech 14:9]
⁹The nomads of the desert will bow before him,
And his enemies will lick the dust.
¹⁰The kings of Tarshish and of the islands will bring offerings;
The kings of Sheba and Seba will offer gifts.
¹¹Yes, all kings will bow down before him,
All nations will serve him. [Ps 138:4]

¹²For he will rescue the needy when he cries for help,
The afflicted *and* abused also, and him who has no helper.

¹³He will have compassion on the poor and needy,
And he will save the lives of the needy.
¹⁴He will redeem their life from oppression *and* fraud and violence,
And their blood will be precious in His sight.
¹⁵So may he live, and may the gold of Sheba be given to him;
And let them pray for him continually;
Let them bless *and* praise him all day long.

¹⁶There will be an abundance of grain in the soil on the top of the mountains;
Its fruit will wave like [the cedars of] Lebanon,
And those of the city will flourish like grass of the earth.
¹⁷May his name endure forever;
May his name continue as long as the sun;
And let men bless themselves by him;
Let all nations call him blessed.

¹⁸Blessed be the Lᴏʀᴅ God, the God of Israel,
Who alone does wonderful things.
¹⁹Blessed be His glorious name ⁻ forever;
And may the whole earth be filled with His glory.
Amen and Amen.
²⁰The prayers of David son of Jesse are ended.

BOOK THREE

PSALM 73

The End of the Wicked Contrasted with That of the Righteous.

A Psalm of Asaph.

¹ TRULY GOD is good to Israel,
To those who are pure in heart.
² But as for me, my feet came close to stumbling,
My steps had almost slipped.
³ For I was envious of the arrogant
As I saw the prosperity of the wicked.
⁴ For there are no pains in their death,
Their body is fat *and* pampered.
⁵ They are not in trouble *as other* men,
Nor are they plagued like mankind.
⁶ Therefore pride is their necklace;
Violence covers them like a garment [like a long, luxurious robe].
⁷ Their eye bulges from fatness [they have more than the heart desires];
The imaginations of their mind run riot [with foolishness].
⁸ They mock and wickedly speak of oppression;
They speak loftily [with malice].
⁹ They set their mouth against the heavens,
And their tongue swaggers through the earth.
[Rev 13:6]
¹⁰ Therefore his people return to this place,
And waters of abundance [offered by the irreverent] are [blindly] drunk by them.
¹¹ They say, "How does God know?
Is there knowledge [of us] with the Most High?"
¹² Behold, these are the ungodly,
Who always prosper *and* are at ease [in the world]; they have increased in wealth.
¹³ Surely then in vain I have cleansed my heart
And washed my hands in innocence. [Mal 3:14]
¹⁴ For all the day long have I been stricken,
And punished every morning.
¹⁵ If I had said, "I will say this," [and expressed my feelings],
I would have betrayed the generation of Your children.
¹⁶ When I considered how to understand this,
It was too great an effort for me *and* too painful
¹⁷ Until I came into the sanctuary of God;
Then I understood [for I considered] their end.
¹⁸ Surely You set the wicked-minded *and* immoral on slippery places;
You cast them down to destruction.
¹⁹ How they are destroyed in a moment!
They are completely swept away by sudden terrors!

²⁰ Like a dream [which seems real] until one awakens,
O Lord, when stirred, [You observe the wicked], You will despise their image.

²¹ When my heart was embittered
And I was pierced within [as with the fang of an adder],
²² Then I was senseless and ignorant;
I was like a beast before You.
²³ Nevertheless I am continually with You;
You have taken hold of my right hand.
²⁴ You will guide me with Your counsel,
And afterward receive me to honor *and* glory.

²⁵ Whom have I in heaven [but You]?
And besides You, I desire nothing on earth.
²⁶ My flesh and my heart may fail,
But God is the rock *and* strength of my heart and my portion forever.

putting the Word to work

Have you ever wondered who will be there for you when times are really tough? Even when you feel as though you cannot go on, God promises to be your strength (see Psalm 73:25–28). Ask God to draw you nearer to Himself, so you can experience His goodness and strength even more fully.

²⁷ For behold, those who are far from You will perish;
You have destroyed all those who are unfaithful *and* have abandoned You.
²⁸ But as for me, it is good for me to draw near to God;
I have made the Lord G_{OD} my refuge *and* placed my trust in Him,
That I may tell of all Your works.

PSALM 74

An Appeal against the Devastation of the Land by the Enemy.

A skillful song, *or* a didactic *or* reflective poem, of Asaph.

¹ O GOD, why have You rejected us forever?
Why does Your anger smoke against the sheep of Your pasture?
² Remember Your congregation, which You have purchased of old,
Which You have redeemed to be the tribe of Your inheritance;
Remember Mount Zion, where You have dwelt.
³ Turn your footsteps [quickly] toward the perpetual ruins;
The enemy has damaged everything within the sanctuary.
⁴ In the midst of Your meeting place Your enemies have roared [with their battle cry];
They have set up their own emblems for signs [of victory].

⁵It seems as if one had lifted up
An axe in a forest of trees [to
set a record of destruction].
⁶And now all the carved work
[of the meeting place]
They smash with hatchets and
hammers.
⁷They have burned Your
sanctuary to the ground;
They have profaned the
dwelling place of Your name.
⁸They said in their heart, "Let
us completely subdue them."
They have burned all the
meeting places of God in
the land.
⁹We do not see our symbols;
There is no longer any
prophet [to guide us],
Nor does any among us know
for how long.
¹⁰O God, how long will the
adversary scoff?
Is the enemy to revile Your
name forever?
¹¹Why do You withdraw Your
hand, even Your right hand
[from judging the enemy]?
Remove Your hand from Your
chest, destroy *them!*

¹²Yet God is my King of old,
Working salvation in the
midst of the earth.
¹³You divided the [Red] Sea by
Your strength;
You broke the heads of the sea
monsters in the waters. [Ex
14:21]
¹⁴You crushed the heads of
Leviathan (Egypt);
You gave him as food for the
creatures of the wilderness.
[Job 41:1]
¹⁵You broke open fountains and
streams;

You dried up ever-flowing
rivers. [Ex 17:6; Num 20:11;
Josh 3:13]
¹⁶The day is Yours, the night
also is Yours;
You have established *and*
prepared the [heavenly]
light and the sun.
¹⁷You have defined *and*
established all the borders
of the earth [the divisions
of land and sea and of the
nations];
You have made summer and
winter. [Acts 17:26]

¹⁸Remember this, O Lᴏʀᴅ, the
enemy has scoffed,
And a foolish *and* impious
people has spurned Your
name.
¹⁹Oh, do not hand over the soul
of your turtledove to the
wild beast;
Do not forget the life of Your
afflicted forever.
²⁰Consider the covenant [You
made with Abraham],
For the dark places of the land
are full of the habitations of
violence.
²¹Let not the oppressed return
dishonored;
Let the afflicted and needy
praise Your name.

²²Arise, O God, plead Your own
cause;
Remember how the foolish
man scoffs at You all day
long.
²³Do not forget the [clamoring]
voices of Your adversaries,
The uproar of those who rise
against You, which ascends
continually [to Your ears].

PSALM 75

God Abases the Proud, but Exalts the Righteous.

To the Chief Musician; set to [the tune of] "Do Not Destroy." A Psalm of Asaph. A Song.

[1] WE GIVE thanks *and* praise to You, O God, we give thanks,
For Your [wonderful works declare that Your] name is near;
People declare Your wonders.
[2] "When I select an appointed time,
I will judge with equity," [says the LORD].
[3] "The earth and all the inhabitants of it melt [in tumultuous times].
It is I who will steady its pillars. *Selah.*
[4] "I said to the arrogant, 'Do not boast;'
And to the wicked, 'Do not lift up the horn [of self-glorification].
[5] 'Do not lift up your [defiant and aggressive] horn on high,
Do not speak with a stiff neck.'"

[6] For not from the east, nor from the west,
Nor from the desert comes exaltation. [Is 14:13]
[7] But God is the Judge;
He puts down one and lifts up another.
[8] For a cup [of His wrath] is in the hand of the LORD, and the wine foams;
It is well mixed *and* fully spiced, and He pours out from it;

And all the wicked of the earth must drain it and drink down to its dregs. [Ps 60:3; Jer 25:15; Rev 14:9, 10; 16:19]

[9] But as for me, I will declare it *and* rejoice forever;
I will sing praises to the God of Jacob.
[10] All the horns of the wicked He will cut off,
But the horns of the righteous will be lifted up.

PSALM 76

The Victorious Power of the God of Jacob.

To the Chief Musician; on stringed instruments. A Psalm of Asaph. A Song.

[1] GOD IS known in Judah;
His name is great in Israel.
[2] His tabernacle is in Salem (Jerusalem);
His dwelling place is in Zion.
[3] There He broke the flaming arrows,
The shield, the sword, and the weapons of war. *Selah.*

[4] You are glorious *and* resplendent,
More majestic than the mountains of prey.
[5] The stouthearted have been stripped of their spoil,
They have slept the sleep [of death];
And none of the warriors could use his hands.
[6] At Your rebuke, O God of Jacob,

Both rider and horse were cast into a dead sleep [of death]. [Ex 15:1, 21; Nah 2:13; Zech 12:4]

7 You, even You, are to be feared [with the submissive wonder of reverence];
Who may stand in Your presence when once You are angry?

8 You caused judgment to be heard from heaven;
The earth feared and was quiet

9 When God arose to [establish] judgment,
To save all the humble of the earth.   *Selah.*

10 For the wrath of man shall praise You;
With a remnant of wrath You will clothe *and* arm Yourself.

11 Make vows to the L ORD your God and fulfill them;
Let all who are around Him bring gifts to Him who is to be feared [with awe-inspired reverence].

12 He will cut off the spirit of princes;
He is awesome *and* feared by the kings of the earth.

PSALM 77

Comfort in Trouble from Recalling God's Mighty Deeds.

To the Chief Musician; according to Jeduthun [one of David's three chief musicians, founder of an official musical family]. A Psalm of Asaph.

1 MY VOICE rises to God, and I will cry aloud;
My voice rises to God, and He will hear me.

2 In the day of my trouble I [desperately] sought the Lord;
In the night my hand was stretched out [in prayer] without weariness;
My soul refused to be comforted.

3 I remember God; then I am disquieted *and* I groan;
I sigh [in prayer], and my spirit grows faint.   *Selah.*

4 You have held my eyelids open;
I am so troubled that I cannot speak.

5 I have considered the ancient days,
The years [of prosperity] of long, long ago.

6 I will remember my song in the night;
I will meditate with my heart,
And my spirit searches:

7 Will the Lord reject forever?
And will He never be favorable again?

8 Has His lovingkindness ceased forever?

life point

In Psalm 77:6, David shows us how he sought God's leading. The next time you have a decision to make, do not try to figure it out with your mind. Go somewhere to get still and let your spirit search diligently for God's voice.

Have His promises ended for
  all time?
⁹ Has God forgotten to be
  gracious?
Or has He in anger
  withdrawn His compassion?
                              Selah.
¹⁰ And I said, "This is my grief,
That the right hand of the
  Most High has changed
  [and His lovingkindness is
  withheld]."

¹¹ I will [solemnly] remember
  the deeds of the LORD;
Yes, I will [wholeheartedly]
  remember Your wonders of
  old.
¹² I will meditate on all Your
  works
And thoughtfully consider all
  Your [great and wondrous]
  deeds.
¹³ Your way, O God, is holy [far
  from sin and guilt].
What god is great like our
  God?
¹⁴ You are the [awesome] God
  who works [powerful]
  wonders;
You have demonstrated Your
  power among the people.
¹⁵ You have with Your [great]
  arm redeemed Your people,
The sons of Jacob and Joseph.
                              Selah.

¹⁶ The waters [of the Red Sea]
  saw You, O God;
The waters saw You, they
  were in anguish;
The deeps also trembled.
¹⁷ The clouds poured down
  water;
The skies sent out a sound [of
  rumbling thunder];

Your arrows (lightning)
  flashed here and there.
¹⁸ The voice of Your thunder
  was in the whirlwind;
The lightnings illumined the
  world;
The earth trembled and
  shook.
¹⁹ Your way [of escape for Your
  people] was through the
  sea,
And Your paths through the
  great waters,
And Your footprints were not
  traceable.
²⁰ You led Your people like a
  flock
By the hand of Moses and
  Aaron [to the promised
  goal].

PSALM 78

God's Guidance of His People in Spite of Their Unfaithfulness.

*A skillful song, or a didactic
or reflective poem, of Asaph.*

¹ LISTEN, O my people, to my
  teaching;
Incline your ears to the words
  of my mouth [and be willing
  to learn].
² I will open my mouth in a
  parable [to instruct using
  examples];
I will utter dark *and* puzzling
  sayings of old [that contain
  important truth] — [Matt
  13:34, 35]
³ Which we have heard and
  known,
And our fathers have told us.

leave your stubbornness behind

Psalm 78 describes some of the things that happened to the Israelites as they journeyed from Egypt to the Promised Land. Despite God's gracious and miraculous provision for them time and time again, verse 8 tells us that they were very stubborn and rebellious during their years in the wilderness. That is precisely what caused them to die there. They simply would not do what God told them to do! They would cry out to God to get them out of trouble when they got into a mess. They would even respond to His instructions with obedience—until circumstances improved. Then, repeatedly, they would go right back into rebellion.

This same cycle is repeated and recorded so many times in the Old Testament that it is almost unbelievable. And yet, if we are not walking in wisdom, we will spend our lives doing the same thing. As we read about the Israelites and their time in the wilderness, let us learn from their mistakes and not repeat them in our own lives.

I suppose some of us are just by nature a little more strong-willed than others. And then, of course, we must consider our roots and how we got started in life, because that affects us too.

I was born with a strong personality. The years I spent being abused and controlled, plus my already-strong personality, combined to develop in me the mind-set that nobody was going to tell me what to do. Obviously, God had to deal with this bad attitude before He could use me.

The Lord demands that we learn to give up our own way and be pliable and moldable in His hands. As long as we are stubborn and rebellious, He cannot use us.

I describe "stubborn" as obstinate, or difficult to handle or work with; and "rebellious" as resisting control, resisting correction, unruly, or refusing to follow ordinary guidelines. Both these definitions describe me as I used to be! The abuse I had suffered in my early life caused a lot of my out-of-balance attitudes toward authority. But in order to grow as a person and be successful in life, I could not allow my past to become an excuse to stay trapped in stubbornness, rebellion, or anything else.

Victorious living requires prompt and precise obedience to God. We grow in our ability and willingness to lay aside our will and do His. It is vital that we continue to make progress in this area. It is not enough to reach a certain plateau and think, *I have gone as far as I am going to go.* We must be obedient in all things—not holding back anything or keeping any doors in our lives closed to the Lord.

Let Him do a thorough work in you so that you can leave your "wilderness" behind and enter your Promised Land.

⁴We will not hide them from
their children,
But [we will] tell to the
generation to come the
praiseworthy deeds of the
LORD,
And [tell of] His great
might *and* power and the
wonderful works that He
has done.

⁵For He established a
testimony (a specific
precept) in Jacob
And appointed a law in
Israel,
Which He commanded our
fathers
That they should teach to
their children [the great
facts of God's transactions
with Israel],
⁶That the generation to come
might know them, that the
children still to be born
May arise and recount them
to their children,
⁷That they should place their
confidence in God
And not forget the works of
God,
But keep His commandments,
⁸And not be like their fathers—
A stubborn and rebellious
generation,
A generation that did not
prepare its heart to know
and follow God,
And whose spirit was not
faithful to God.

⁹The sons of Ephraim were
armed as archers and
carrying bows,
Yet they turned back in the
day of battle.

¹⁰They did not keep the
covenant of God
And refused to walk
according to His law;
¹¹And they forgot His
[incredible] works
And His miraculous
wonders that He had shown
them.
¹²He did marvelous things in
the sight of their fathers
In the land of Egypt, in
the field of Zoan [where
Pharaoh resided].
¹³He divided the [Red] Sea
and allowed them to pass
through it,
And He made the waters
stand up like [water behind]
a dam. [Ex 14:22]
¹⁴In the daytime He led them
with a cloud
And all the night with a light
of fire. [Ex 13:21; 14:24]
¹⁵He split rocks in the
wilderness
And gave *them* abundant
[water to] drink like the
ocean depths.
¹⁶He brought streams also from
the rock [at Rephidim and
Kadesh]
And caused waters to run
down like rivers. [Ex 17:6;
Num 20:11]

¹⁷Yet they still continued to sin
against Him
By rebelling against the Most
High in the desert.
¹⁸And in their hearts they put
God to the test
By asking for food according
to their [selfish] appetite.
¹⁹Then they spoke against
God;

They said, "Can God prepare [food for] a table in the wilderness?

20 "Behold, He struck the rock so that waters gushed out
And the streams overflowed;
Can He give bread also?
Or will He provide meat for His people?"

21 Therefore, when the Lord heard, He was full of wrath;
A fire was kindled against Jacob,
And His anger mounted up against Israel,
22 Because they did not believe in God [they did not rely on Him, they did not adhere to Him],
And they did not trust in His salvation (His power to save).
23 Yet He commanded the clouds from above
And opened the doors of heaven;
24 And He rained down manna upon them to eat
And gave them the grain of heaven. [Ex 16:14; John 6:31]
25 Man ate the bread of angels;
God sent them provision in abundance.
26 He caused the east wind to blow in the heavens
And by His [unlimited] power He guided the south wind.
27 He rained meat upon them like the dust,
And winged birds (quail) like the sand of the seas. [Num 11:31]
28 And He let them fall in the midst of their camp,
Around their tents.

29 So they ate and were well filled,
He gave them what they craved.
30 Before they had satisfied their desire,
And while their food was in their mouths,
[Num 11:33]
31 The wrath of God rose against them
And killed some of the strongest of them,
And subdued the choice young men of Israel.
32 In spite of all this they still sinned,
For they did not believe in His wonderful *and* extraordinary works.
33 Therefore He consumed their days like a breath [in emptiness and futility]
And their years in sudden terror.

34 When He killed [some of] them, then those remaining sought Him,
And they returned [to Him] and searched diligently for God [for a time].
35 And they remembered that God was their rock,
And the Most High God their Redeemer.
36 Nevertheless they flattered Him with their mouths
And lied to Him with their tongues.
37 For their heart was not steadfast toward Him,
Nor were they faithful to His covenant. [Acts 8:21]

38 But He, the source
of compassion *and*
lovingkindness, forgave
their wickedness and did
not destroy them;
Many times He restrained His
anger
And did not stir up all His
wrath.
39 For He [graciously]
remembered that they were
mere [human] flesh,
A wind that goes and does not
return.

40 How often they rebelled
against Him in the
wilderness
And grieved Him in the
desert!
41 Again and again they tempted
God,
And distressed the Holy One
of Israel.
42 They did not remember [the
miracles worked by] His
[powerful] hand,
Nor the day when He
redeemed them from the
enemy,
43 How He worked His miracles
in Egypt
And His wonders in the field
of Zoan [where Pharaoh
resided],
44 And turned their rivers into
blood,
And their streams, so that
they could not drink.
45 He sent among them swarms
of flies which devoured
them,
And frogs which destroyed
them.
46 He also gave their crops to the
grasshopper,

And the fruit of their labor to
the locust.
47 He destroyed their vines with
[great] hailstones
And their sycamore trees
with frost.
48 He gave over their cattle also
to the hailstones,
And their flocks *and* herds to
thunderbolts. [Ex 9:18–21]
49 He sent upon them His
burning anger, [Ex 12:23]
His fury and indignation and
distress,
A band of angels of
destruction [among them].
50 He leveled a path for His
anger [to give it free run];
He did not spare their souls
from death,
But turned over their lives to
the plague.
51 He killed all the firstborn in
Egypt,
The first and best of
their strength in the tents
[of the land of the sons] of
Ham.
52 But God led His own people
forward like sheep
And guided them in the
wilderness like [a good
shepherd with] a flock.
53 He led them safely, so that
they did not fear;
But the sea engulfed their
enemies. [Ex 14:27, 28]

54 So He brought them to His
holy land,
To this mountain [Zion]
which His right hand had
acquired.
55 He also drove out the
nations before the
sons of Israel

And allotted *their land* as an inheritance, measured out *and* partitioned;
And He had the tribes of Israel dwell in their tents [the tents of those who had been dispossessed].

⁵⁶ Yet they tempted and rebelled against the Most High God
And did not keep His testimonies (laws).

⁵⁷ They turned back and acted unfaithfully like their fathers;
They were twisted like a warped bow [that will not respond to the archer's aim].

⁵⁸ For they provoked Him to [righteous] anger with their high places [devoted to idol worship]
And moved Him to jealousy with their carved images [by denying Him the love, worship, and obedience that is rightfully and uniquely His].

⁵⁹ When God heard this, He was filled with [righteous] wrath;
And utterly rejected Israel, [greatly hating her ways],

⁶⁰ So that He abandoned the tabernacle at Shiloh,
The tent in which He had dwelled among men,

⁶¹ And gave up His strength *and* power (the ark of the covenant) into captivity,
And His glory into the hand of the enemy (the Philistines). [1 Sam 4:21]

⁶² He also handed His people over to the sword,

And was infuriated with His inheritance (Israel). [1 Sam 4:10]

⁶³ The fire [of war] devoured His young men,
And His [bereaved] virgins had no wedding songs.

⁶⁴ His priests [Hophni and Phinehas] fell by the sword,
And His widows could not weep. [1 Sam 4:11, 19, 20]

⁶⁵ Then the Lord awakened as from sleep,
Like a [mighty] warrior who awakens from the sleep of wine [fully conscious of his power].

⁶⁶ He drove His enemies backward;
He subjected them to lasting shame *and* dishonor.

⁶⁷ Moreover, He rejected the tent of Joseph,
And did not choose the tribe of Ephraim [in which the tabernacle stood].

⁶⁸ But He chose the tribe of Judah [as Israel's leader],
Mount Zion, which He loved [to replace Shiloh as His capital].

⁶⁹ And He built His sanctuary [exalted] like the heights [of the heavens],
Like the earth which He has established forever.

⁷⁰ He also chose David His servant
And took him from the sheepfolds; [1 Sam 16:11, 12]

⁷¹ From tending the ewes with nursing young He brought him
To shepherd Jacob His people,

And Israel His inheritance.
[2 Sam 7:7, 8]
⁷²So David shepherded them
according to the integrity of
his heart;
And guided them with his
skillful hands.

PSALM 79

A Lament over
the Destruction of Jerusalem,
and Prayer for Help.

A Psalm of Asaph.

¹O GOD, the nations have
invaded [the land of Your
people] Your inheritance;
They have defiled Your
sacred temple;
They have laid Jerusalem in
ruins.
²They have given the dead
bodies of Your servants
as food to the birds of the
heavens,
The flesh of Your godly
ones to the beasts of the
earth.
³They have poured out their
blood like water all around
Jerusalem,
And there was no one to bury
them.
⁴We have become an
object of taunting to our
neighbors [because of our
humiliation],
A derision and mockery to
those who encircle us.
⁵How long, O Lord? Will You
be angry forever?
Will Your jealousy [which
cannot endure a divided
allegiance] burn like fire?

⁶Pour out Your wrath on the
[Gentile] nations that do not
know You,
And on the kingdoms that
do not call on Your name.
[2 Thess 1:8]
⁷For they have devoured Jacob
And made his pasture
desolate.

⁸O do not remember against
us the sins *and* guilt of our
forefathers.
Let Your compassion *and*
mercy come quickly to meet
us,
For we have been brought
very low.
⁹Help us, O God of our
salvation, for the glory of
Your name;
Rescue us, forgive us our sins
for Your name's sake.
¹⁰Why should the [Gentile]
nations say, "Where is their
God?"
Let there be known [without
delay] among the nations
in our sight [and to this
generation],
Your vengeance for the blood
of Your servants which has
been poured out.
¹¹Let the groaning *and* sighing
of the prisoner come before
You;
According to the greatness of
Your power keep safe those
who are doomed to die.
¹²And return into the lap of our
neighbors sevenfold
The taunts with which they
have taunted You, O Lord.
¹³So we Your people, the sheep
of Your pasture,
Will give You thanks forever;

We will declare *and* publish
Your praise from generation
to generation.

PSALM 80

God Implored to Rescue His People from Their Calamities.

To the Chief Musician;
set to [the tune of] "Lilies,
a Testimony." A Psalm
of Asaph.

¹HEAR US O Shepherd of
Israel,
You who lead Joseph like a
flock;
You who sit enthroned
above the cherubim
[of the ark of the covenant],
shine forth!
²Before Ephraim and
Benjamin and Manasseh,
stir up Your power
And come to save us!
³Restore us, O God;
Cause Your face to shine on us
[with favor and approval],
and we will be saved.

⁴O Lᴏʀᴅ God of hosts,
How long will You be angry
with the prayers of Your
people?
⁵You have fed them the bread
of tears,
And You have made them
drink [bitter] tears in
abundance.
⁶You make us an object of
contention to our neighbors,
And our enemies laugh
[at our suffering] among
themselves.
⁷Restore us, O God of hosts;

And cause Your face to shine
on us [with favor and
approval], and we will be
saved.

⁸You uprooted a vine (Israel)
from Egypt;
You drove out the [Canaanite]
nations and planted the
vine [in Canaan].
⁹You cleared away *the ground*
before it,
And it took deep root and
filled the land.
¹⁰The mountains were covered
with its shadow,
And its branches were like
the cedars of God.
¹¹Israel sent out its branches to
the [Mediterranean] Sea,
And its branches to the
[Euphrates] River. [1 Kin
4:21]
¹²Why have You broken down
its walls *and* hedges,
So that all who pass by pick
its fruit?
¹³A boar from the woods eats it
away,
And the insects of the field
feed on it.

¹⁴Turn again [in favor to us],
O God of hosts;
Look down from heaven and
see, and take care of this
vine,
¹⁵Even the stock which Your
right hand has planted,
And [look down on] the son
that You have reared *and*
strengthened for Yourself.
¹⁶It is burned with fire, it is cut
down;
They perish at the rebuke of
Your [angry] appearance.

17 Let Your hand be upon the
   man of Your right hand,
Upon the son of man whom
   You have made strong for
   Yourself.
18 Then we shall not turn back
   from You;
Revive us and we will call on
   Your name.
19 Restore us, O Lord God of
   hosts;
Cause Your face to shine on
   us [in favor and approval],
   and we shall be saved.

PSALM 81

God's Goodness and Israel's Waywardness.

To the Chief Musician; set
to the Philistine lute. *A Psalm*
of Asaph.

1 SING ALOUD to God our
   strength;
Shout for joy to the God of
   Jacob (Israel).
2 Raise a song, sound the
   timbrel,
The sweet sounding lyre with
   the harp.
3 Blow the trumpet at the New
   Moon,
At the full moon, on our feast
   day.
4 For this is a statute for Israel,
An ordinance of the God of
   Jacob.
5 He established it for a
   testimony in Joseph
When He went throughout
   the land of Egypt.
I heard the language [of One
   whom] I did not know,
   saying,

6 "I removed the burden from
   his shoulder;
His hands were freed from
   the basket.
7 "You called in [the time of]
   trouble and I rescued you;
I answered you in the secret
   place of thunder;
I tested you at the waters of
   Meribah. [Num 20:3, 13, 24]
                        Selah.
8 "Hear, O My people, and I will
   admonish you—
O Israel, if you would listen
   to Me!
9 "Let there be no strange god
   among you,
Nor shall you worship any
   foreign god.
10 "I am the Lord your God,
Who brought you up from the
   land of Egypt.
Open your mouth wide and I
   will fill it.

11 "But My people would not
   listen to My voice,
And Israel did not [consent
   to] obey Me.
12 "So I gave them up to the
   stubbornness of their heart,
To walk in [the path of] their
   own counsel. [Acts 7:42, 43;
   14:16; Rom 1:24, 26]
13 "Oh, that My people would
   listen to Me,
That Israel would walk in My
   ways!
14 "Then I would quickly subdue
   and humble their enemies
And turn My hand against
   their adversaries;
15 Those who hate the Lord
   would pretend obedience
   to Him *and* cringe before
   Him,

And their time *of punishment*
would be forever.
16 "But I would feed Israel
with the finest of the wheat;
And with honey from the rock
I would satisfy you."

PSALM 82

Unjust Judgments Rebuked.

A Psalm of Asaph.

1 GOD STANDS in the divine
assembly;
He judges among the gods
(divine beings).
2 How long will you judge
unjustly
And show partiality to the
wicked?   *Selah.*
3 Vindicate the weak and
fatherless;
Do justice *and* maintain the
rights of the afflicted and
destitute.
4 Rescue the weak and needy;
Rescue them from the hand of
the wicked.

5 The rulers do not know nor do
they understand;
They walk on in the
darkness [of complacent
satisfaction];
All the foundations of the
earth [the fundamental
principles of the
administration of justice]
are shaken.
6 I said, "You are gods;
Indeed, all of you are sons of
the Most High. [Gen 6:1–4;
John 10:34–36; Rom 13:1, 2]
7 "Nevertheless you will die
like men

And fall like any one of the
princes."
8 Arise, O God, judge the earth!
For to You belong all the
nations. [Matt 28:18–20; Rev
11:15]

PSALM 83

God Implored to Confound
His Enemies.

A Song. A Psalm of Asaph.

1 DO NOT keep silent, O God;
Do not hold Your peace or be
still, O God.
2 For behold, Your enemies are
in tumult,
And those who hate You have
raised their heads [in hatred
of You]. [Acts 4:25, 26]
3 They concoct crafty schemes
against Your people,
And conspire together against
Your hidden *and* precious
ones.
4 They have said, "Come, and
let us wipe them out as a
nation;
Let the name of Israel be
remembered no more."
5 For they have conspired
together with one mind;
Against You they make a
covenant—
6 The tents of Edom and the
Ishmaelites,
Of Moab and the Hagrites,
7 Gebal and Ammon and
Amalek,
Philistia with the inhabitants
of Tyre.
8 Assyria also has joined with
them;

They have helped the
children of Lot [the
Ammonites and the
Moabites] *and* have been an
arm [of strength] to them.
                        Selah.

⁹Deal with them as [You did]
with Midian,
As with Sisera and Jabin at
the brook of Kishon, [Judg
4:12–24]
¹⁰Who were destroyed at En-dor,
Who became like dung for the
earth.
¹¹Make their nobles like Oreb
and Zeeb
And all their princes like
Zebah and Zalmunna, [Judg
7:23–25; 8:10–21]
¹²Who said, "Let us possess for
ourselves
The pastures of God."

¹³O my God, make them like
whirling dust,
Like chaff before the wind
[worthless and without
substance].
¹⁴Like fire consumes the forest,
And like the flame sets the
mountains on fire,
¹⁵So pursue them with Your
tempest
And terrify them with [the
violence of] Your storm.
¹⁶Fill their faces with shame
and disgrace,
That they may [persistently]
seek Your name, O Lord.
¹⁷Let them be ashamed and
dismayed forever;
Yes, let them be humiliated
and perish,
¹⁸That they may know that You
alone, whose name is the
Lord,

Are the Most High over all
the earth.

PSALM 84

Longing for the Temple Worship.

To the Chief Musician;
set to a Philistine lute.
A Psalm of the sons of Korah.

¹HOW LOVELY are Your
dwelling places,
O Lord of hosts!
²My soul (my life, my inner self)
longs for and greatly desires
the courts of the Lord;
My heart and my flesh sing
for joy to the living God.
³The bird has found a house,
And the swallow a nest for
herself, where she may lay
her young—
Even Your altars, O Lord of
hosts,
My King and my God.
⁴Blessed *and* greatly favored
are those who dwell in Your
house *and* Your presence;

life point

When our strength is in God,
the difficult places in life can be
turned into blessings; the valleys of
weeping can be turned into springs
(see Psalm 84:5, 6). Whenever
you face a tough situation or a
place of sadness and despair, draw
your strength from God. As you
do, you will find yourself going
"from strength to strength" and
"increasing in victorious power,"
as Psalm 84:7 promises.

They will be singing Your
praises all the day long.
Selah.

⁵Blessed *and* greatly favored is
the man whose strength is
in You,
In whose heart are the
highways *to Zion.*
⁶Passing through the Valley of
Weeping (Baca), they make
it a place of springs;
The early rain also covers it
with blessings.
⁷They go from strength to
strength [increasing in
victorious power];
Each of them appears before
God in Zion.

⁸O Lᴏʀᴅ God of hosts, hear my
prayer;
Listen, O God of Jacob! *Selah.*
⁹See our shield, O God,
And look at the face of Your
anointed [the king as Your
representative].

putting the Word to work

The Bible teaches us that God is our home. We view our homes as places of rest and comfort, shelters from all the other parts of life. Psalm 84:10 reminds us that dwelling in the presence of God is where the greatest blessing is to be found. Spend time every day with God through prayer, worship, and time in His Word, and you will find there is no place you would rather be than in His presence. When you are with Him, you will feel as though you are at home!

¹⁰For a day in Your courts is
better than a thousand
[anywhere else];
I would rather stand [as
a doorkeeper] at the
threshold of the house of
my God
Than to live [at ease] in the
tents of wickedness.
¹¹For the Lᴏʀᴅ God is a sun and
shield;
The Lᴏʀᴅ bestows grace *and*
favor and honor;
No good thing will He
withhold from those who
walk uprightly.
¹²O Lᴏʀᴅ of hosts,
How blessed *and* greatly
favored is the man who
trusts in You [believing in
You, relying on You, and
committing himself to You
with confident hope and
expectation].

PSALM 85

Prayer for God's Mercy upon the Nation.

To the Chief Musician.
A Psalm of the sons of Korah.

¹O LORD, You have [at last]
shown favor to Your land [of
Canaan];
You have restored [from
Babylon] the captives of
Jacob (Israel).
²You have forgiven the
wickedness of Your people;
You have covered all their sin.
Selah.
³You have withdrawn all Your
wrath,
You have turned away from
Your burning anger.

4 Restore us, O God of our
   salvation,
 And cause Your indignation
   toward us to cease.
5 Will You be angry with us
   forever?
 Will You prolong Your anger
   to all generations?
6 Will You not revive us *and*
   bring us to life again,
 That Your people may rejoice
   in You?
7 Show us Your lovingkindness,
   O Lord,
 And grant us Your salvation.

8 I will hear [with expectant
   hope] what God the Lord
   will say,
 For He will speak peace to His
   people, to His godly ones—
 But let them not turn again to
   folly.
9 Surely His salvation is near to
   those who [reverently] fear
   Him [and obey Him with
   submissive wonder],
 That glory [the manifest
   presence of God] may dwell
   in our land.
10 Steadfast love and truth *and*
    faithfulness meet together;
 Righteousness and peace kiss
   each other.
11 Truth springs from the earth,
 And righteousness looks
   down from heaven.
12 Indeed, the Lord will give
    what is good,

And our land will yield its
  produce.
13 Righteousness will go before
   Him
 And will make His footsteps
   into a way [in which to
   walk].

PSALM 86

A Psalm of Supplication and Trust.

A Prayer of David.

1 INCLINE YOUR ear, O Lord,
   and answer me,
 For I am distressed and needy
   [I long for Your help].
2 Protect my life (soul), for I am
   godly *and* faithful;
 O You my God, save Your
   servant, who trusts in
   You [believing in You and
   relying on You, confidently
   committing everything to
   You].
3 Be gracious *and* merciful to
   me, O Lord,
 For to You I cry out all the day
   long.
4 Make Your servant rejoice,
 For to You, O Lord, I lift up
   my soul [all that I am—in
   prayer].
5 For You, O Lord, are good,
   and ready to forgive [our
   sins, sending them away,
   completely letting them go
   forever and ever];

speak the Word

God, I know that You will give what is good.
Righteousness goes before You and will make Your footsteps
into a way in which I can walk.
—ADAPTED FROM PSALM 85:12, 13

And abundant in
lovingkindness *and*
overflowing in mercy to all
those who call upon You.
⁶Hear, O Lᴏʀᴅ, my prayer;
And listen attentively to the
voice of my supplications
(specific requests)!
⁷In the day of my trouble I will
call upon You,
For You will answer me.
⁸There is no one like You
among the gods, O Lord,
Nor are there any works [of
wonder and majesty] like
Yours.
⁹All nations whom You have
made shall come and kneel
down in worship before
You, O Lord,
And they shall glorify Your
name.
¹⁰For You are great and do
wondrous works!
You alone are God.

¹¹Teach me Your way, O Lᴏʀᴅ,
I will walk *and* live in Your
truth;
Direct my heart to fear Your
name [with awe-inspired
reverence and submissive
wonder]. [Ps 5:11; 69:36]
¹²I will give thanks *and* praise
You, O Lord my God, with all
my heart;
And will glorify Your name
forevermore.

putting the Word to work

Have you ever bent over to let a
child whisper something in your ear?
God does this for us—He inclines His
ear to hear our every cry (see Psalm
86:1–7). If you have ever felt that no
one is listening to you, take heart;
God hears every one of your prayers,
and He will be faithful
to answer.

¹³For great is Your
lovingkindness *and*
graciousness toward me;
And You have rescued my life
from the depths of Sheol
[from death].

¹⁴O God, arrogant *and* insolent
men have risen up against
me;
A band of violent men have
sought my life,
And they have not set You
before them.
¹⁵But You, O Lord, are a God
[who protects and is]
merciful and gracious,
Slow to anger and abounding
in lovingkindness and
truth.
¹⁶Turn to me, and be gracious
to me;
Grant Your strength [Your
might and the power to
resist temptation] to Your
servant,

speak the Word

Teach me Your way, Lord, that I may walk and live in Your truth.
Direct my heart to fear Your name with awe-inspired
reverence and submissive wonder.
—ᴀᴅᴀᴘᴛᴇᴅ ꜰʀᴏᴍ Pꜱᴀʟᴍ 86:11

And save the son of Your
  handmaid.
[17] Show me a sign of [Your]
  goodwill,
That those who hate me may
  see it and be ashamed,
Because You, O LORD, helped
  and comforted me.

PSALM 87

The Privileges of Citizenship
in Zion.

A Psalm of the sons of Korah.
A Song.

[1] HIS FOUNDATION is on the
  holy mountain.
[2] The LORD loves the gates of
  Zion
More than all the dwellings of
  Jacob (Israel).
[3] Glorious things are spoken of
  you,
O city of God [Jerusalem].
                              Selah.
[4] "I will mention Rahab
  (Egypt) and Babylon
  among those who know
  Me—
Behold, Philistia and
  Tyre with Ethiopia
  (Cush)—
'This one was born there.'"
[5] But of Zion it will be said,
  "This one and that one were
  born in her,"
And the Most High Himself
  will establish her.
[6] The LORD will count, when He
  registers the peoples,
"This one was born there."
                              Selah.
[7] The singers as well as the
  players of flutes *will say,*

"All my springs *and* sources of
  joy are in you [Jerusalem,
  city of God]."

PSALM 88

A Petition to Be Saved
from Death.

A Song. A Psalm of the sons
  of Korah. To the Chief
  Musician; set to chant
  mournfully. A didactic *or*
  reflective poem of Heman
  the Ezrahite.

[1] O LORD, the God of my
  salvation,
I have cried out [for help] by
  day and in the night before
  You. [Luke 18:7]
[2] Let my prayer come before
  You *and* enter into Your
  presence;
Incline Your ear to my cry!
[3] For my soul is full of troubles,
And my life draws near the
  grave (Sheol, the place of
  the dead).
[4] I am counted among those
  who go down to the pit
  (grave);
I am like a man who has
  no strength [a mere
  shadow],
[5] Cast away [from the living]
  and abandoned among the
  dead,
Like the slain who lie in a
  [nameless] grave,
Whom You no longer
  remember,
And they are cut off from
  Your hand.
[6] You have laid me in the lowest
  pit,
In dark places, in the depths.

7 Your wrath has rested heavily
upon me,
And You have afflicted me
with all Your waves. [Ps
42:7]   *Selah.*
8 You have put my friends far
from me;
You have made me an object
of loathing to them.
I am shut up and I cannot go
out.
9 My eye grows dim with
sorrow.
O Lord, I have called on You
every day;
I have spread out my hands to
You [in prayer].

10 Will You perform wonders for
the dead?
Shall the departed spirits
arise and praise You? *Selah.*
11 Will Your lovingkindness be
declared in the grave
Or Your faithfulness in
Abaddon (the underworld)?
12 Will Your wonders be known
in the darkness?
And Your righteousness in
the land of forgetfulness
[where the dead forget and
are forgotten]?

13 But I have cried out to You,
O Lord, for help;
And in the morning my
prayer will come to You.
14 O Lord, why do You reject me?
Why do You hide Your face
from me? [Matt 27:46]

15 I was afflicted and close
to death from my youth
on;
I suffer Your terrors; I am
overcome.
16 Your fierce wrath has swept
over me;
Your terrors have
destroyed me.
17 They have surrounded me
like flood waters all day
long;
They have completely
encompassed me.
18 Lover and friend You have
placed far from me;
My familiar friends are in
darkness.

PSALM 89

The Lord's Covenant
with David, and Israel's
Afflictions.

A skillful song, *or* a didactic
or reflective poem, of Ethan
the Ezrahite.

1 I WILL sing of the goodness
and lovingkindness of the
Lord forever;
With my mouth I will make
known Your faithfulness
from generation to
generation.
2 For I have said, "Goodness
and lovingkindness will be
built up forever;

speak the Word

Lord, I will sing of Your goodness and loving-kindness forever.
I will tell others of Your faithfulness from generation to generation.
—ADAPTED FROM PSALM 89:1

In the heavens [unchangeable and majestic] You will establish Your faithfulness."

3 [God has said] "I have made a covenant with My chosen one;

I have sworn to David My servant,

4 I will establish your seed forever

And I will build up your throne for all generations." [Is 9:7; Jer 33:14–26; Luke 1:32, 33; Gal 3:16]   *Selah.*

5 The heavens (angels) praise Your wonders, O Lord,

Your faithfulness also in the assembly of the holy ones.

6 For who in the heavens can be compared to the Lord?

Who among the divine beings is like the Lord,

7 A God greatly feared *and* reverently worshiped in the council of the holy [angelic] ones,

And awesome above all those who are around Him?

8 O Lord God of hosts, who is like You, O mighty Lord?

Your faithfulness surrounds You [as an intrinsic, unchangeable part of Your very being].

9 You rule the swelling of the sea;

When its waves rise, You still them. [Ps 65:7; 107:29; Mark 4:39]

10 You have crushed Rahab (Egypt) like one who is slain;

You have scattered Your enemies with Your mighty arm.

11 The heavens are Yours, the earth also is Yours;

The world and all that is in it, You have founded *and* established them. [Gen 1:3]

12 The north and the south, You have created them;

Mount Tabor and Mount Hermon shout for joy at Your name.

13 You have a strong arm;

Mighty is Your hand, Your right hand is exalted.

14 Righteousness and justice are the foundation of Your throne;

Lovingkindness and truth go before You.

15 Blessed *and* happy are the people who know the joyful sound [of the trumpet's blast]!

They walk, O Lord, in the light *and* favor of Your countenance!

16 In Your name they rejoice all the day,

And in Your righteousness they are exalted.

17 For You are the glory of their strength [their proud adornment],

And by Your favor our horn is exalted.

18 For our shield belongs to the Lord,

And our king to the Holy One of Israel.

19 Once You spoke in a vision to Your godly ones,

And said, "I have given help to one who is mighty [giving him the power to be a champion for Israel];

I have exalted one chosen
from the people.

20 "I have found David My
servant;
With My holy oil I have
anointed him, [Acts 13:22]

21 With whom My hand
shall be established *and*
steadfast;
My arm also shall strengthen
him.

22 "The enemy will not outwit
him,
Nor will the wicked man
afflict *or* humiliate him.

23 "I will crush his adversaries
before him,
And strike those who hate
him.

24 "My faithfulness and My
steadfast lovingkindness
shall be with him,
And in My name shall his
horn be exalted [great
power and prosperity shall
be conferred upon him].

25 "I will also set his hand on the
[Mediterranean] sea,
And his right hand on the
rivers [the tributaries of the
Euphrates].

26 "He will cry to Me, 'You are
my Father,
My God, and the rock of my
salvation.'

27 "I will also make him My
firstborn (preeminent),
The highest of the kings of
the earth. [Rev 1:5]

28 "My lovingkindness I will
keep for him forevermore,
And My covenant will be
confirmed to him.

29 "His descendants I will
establish forever,

And his throne [will endure]
as the days of heaven. [Is
9:7; Jer 33:14–26; Gal 3:16]

30 "If his children turn away
from My law
And do not walk in My
ordinances,

31 If they break My statutes
And do not keep My
commandments,

32 Then I will punish their
transgression with the rod
[of discipline],
And [correct] their
wickedness with stripes.
[2 Sam 7:14]

33 "Nevertheless, I will not break
off My lovingkindness from
him,
Nor allow My faithfulness to
fail.

34 "My covenant I will not
violate,
Nor will I alter the utterance
of My lips.

35 "Once [for all] I have sworn
by My holiness, [My vow
which cannot be violated];
I will not lie to David.

36 "His descendants shall
endure forever
And his throne [will continue]
as the sun before Me. [Is 9:7;
Jer 33:14–26; Gal 3:16]

37 "It shall be established
forever like the moon,
And the witness in the
heavens is ever faithful."
[Rev 1:5; 3:14]   *Selah.*

38 But [in apparent
contradiction of all this]
You [the faithful LORD]
have cast off and
rejected;

You have been full of wrath
   against Your anointed.
[39] You have spurned *and*
   repudiated the covenant
   with Your servant;
   You have profaned his crown
   [by casting it] in the dust.
[40] You have broken down all his
   [city] walls;
   You have brought his
   strongholds to ruin.
[41] All who pass along the road
   rob him;
   He has become the scorn of
   his neighbors.
[42] You have exalted the right
   hand of his foes;
   You have made all his
   enemies rejoice.
[43] Also, You have turned back
   the edge of his sword
   And have not made him
   [strong enough] to stand in
   battle.
[44] You have put an end to his
   splendor
   And have hurled his throne to
   the ground.
[45] You have shortened the days
   of his youth;
   You have covered him with
   shame.   *Selah.*

[46] How long, O LORD?
   Will You hide Yourself forever?
   Will Your wrath burn like
   fire?
[47] Remember how fleeting my
   lifetime is;
   For what vanity, [for what
   emptiness, for what futility,
   for what wisp of smoke] You
   have created all the sons of
   men!
[48] What man can live and not
   see death?

Can he rescue his soul from
   the [powerful] hand of
   Sheol (the nether world, the
   place of the dead)?   *Selah.*

[49] O Lord, where are Your
   former lovingkindnesses
   [so abundant in the days of
   David and Solomon],
   Which You swore to David in
   Your faithfulness?
[50] Remember, O Lord, the
   reproach of Your servants
   [scorned, insulted, and
   disgraced];
   How I bear in my heart the
   reproach of all the many
   peoples,
[51] With which Your enemies
   have taunted, O LORD,
   With which they have mocked
   the footsteps of Your
   anointed.

[52] Blessed be the LORD
   forevermore!
   Amen and Amen.

BOOK FOUR

PSALM 90

God's Eternity and Man's Transitoriness.

A Prayer of Moses the man
of God.

[1] LORD, YOU have been our
   dwelling place [our refuge,
   our sanctuary, our stability]
   in all generations.
[2] Before the mountains were
   born
   Or before You had given birth
   to the earth and the world,

Even from everlasting to
everlasting, You are [the
eternal] God.

³ You turn man back to dust,
And say, "Return [to the earth],
O children of [mortal] men!"
⁴ For a thousand years in Your
sight
Are like yesterday when it is
past,
Or as a watch in the night.
[2 Pet 3:8]
⁵ You have swept them away
like a flood, they fall asleep
[forgotten as soon as they
are gone];
In the morning they are like
grass which grows anew—
⁶ In the morning it flourishes
and springs up;
In the evening it wilts and
withers away.

⁷ For we have been consumed
by Your anger
And by Your wrath we have
been terrified.
⁸ You have placed our
wickedness before you,
Our secret *sins* [which we
tried to conceal, You have
placed] in the [revealing]
light of Your presence.
⁹ For all our days pass away in
Your wrath;

We have finished our years
like a whispered sigh.
[Num 14:26–35]
¹⁰ The days of our life are
seventy years—
Or even, if because of
strength, eighty years;
Yet their pride [in additional
years] is only labor and
sorrow,
For it is soon gone and we fly
away.
¹¹ Who understands the power of
Your anger? [Who connects
this brevity of life among us
with Your judgment of sin?]

life point

When you and I feel a tide of
emotions beginning to swell within
us, we need to return to the secret
place of the Most High (see Psalm
91:1), crying out to Him: "Father,
help me resist this surge of emotions
that threatens to overwhelm me!"
If we will do that, the Lord has
promised to intervene on our behalf.
We need to learn to take refuge
under His shadow, where we will
be safe and secure, knowing that
no power in heaven or on earth can
withstand Him.

speak the Word

*Lord, teach me to number my days, that I may cultivate
and bring to You a heart of wisdom.*
–ADAPTED FROM PSALM 90:12

*God, let Your gracious favor be upon me.
Confirm for me the work of my hands.*
–ADAPTED FROM PSALM 90:17

And Your wrath, [who connects
it] with the [reverent] fear
that is due You?
¹²So teach us to number our days,
That we may cultivate *and*
bring to You a heart of
wisdom.

¹³Turn, O LORD [from Your fierce
anger]; how long will it be?
Be compassionate toward
Your servants—revoke Your
sentence.
¹⁴O satisfy us with Your
lovingkindness in the
morning [now, before we
grow older],

That we may rejoice and be
glad all our days.
¹⁵Make us glad in proportion to
the days You have afflicted
us,
And the years we have
suffered evil.
¹⁶Let Your work [the signs of
Your power] be revealed to
Your servants
And Your [glorious] majesty
to their children.
¹⁷And let the [gracious] favor of
the Lord our God be on us;
Confirm for us the work of
our hands—

what do you say?

David frequently spoke about the goodness and character of God. In Psalm 91:2, David says God is his refuge, his fortress—a God he can really trust. It is interesting to note that David also wrote in this verse, "I will *say* of the LORD . . ." (italics mine). Perhaps we should also regularly ask ourselves, "What am I saying of the Lord?"

We need to *say* right things, not just *think* them. We may think, *I believe all those good things about the Lord*, but are we also *saying* anything that is helping us? Often we claim to believe something, yet the opposite comes out of our mouths.

We need to speak aloud the goodness of God. We need to do it at proper times and in proper places, but we need to be sure we do it. I cannot encourage you strongly enough to make verbal confessions part of your fellowship time with God.

I often take walks in the morning. While I walk, I pray, I sing, and I confess the Word out loud. I say something like, "God is on my side. I can do whatever He assigns me to do." Or "God is good, and He has a good plan for my life. Blessings are chasing me and overflowing in my life." When I speak words like these, I am nullifying the evil plan Satan has for me.

Verbalize your thanksgiving, your praise, and your worship. Say aloud the things that are in your heart about God; sing songs that are filled with praise and worship. Take aggressive action against the enemy by speaking of the goodness of God!

Yes, confirm the work of our
hands.

PSALM 91

Security of the One Who Trusts in the LORD.

¹HE WHO dwells in the shelter
of the Most High
Will remain secure *and* rest in
the shadow of the Almighty
[whose power no enemy can
withstand].
²I will say of the LORD, "He is
my refuge and my fortress,
My God, in whom I trust [with
great confidence, and on
whom I rely]!"
³For He will save you from the
trap of the fowler,
And from the deadly
pestilence.
⁴He will cover you *and*
completely protect you with
His pinions,
And under His wings you will
find refuge;
His faithfulness is a shield
and a wall.

⁵You will not be afraid of the
terror of night,
Nor of the arrow that flies by
day,
⁶Nor of the pestilence that
stalks in darkness,
Nor of the destruction
(sudden death) that lays
waste at noon.
⁷A thousand may fall at your
side
And ten thousand at your
right hand,
But danger will not come near
you.

⁸You will only [be a spectator
as you] look on with your
eyes
And witness the [divine]
repayment of the wicked
[as you watch safely from
the shelter of the Most
High].
⁹Because you have made the
LORD, [who is] my refuge,
Even the Most High, your
dwelling place, [Ps 91:1, 14]
¹⁰No evil will befall you,
Nor will any plague come near
your tent.

¹¹For He will command His
angels in regard to you,
To protect *and* defend *and*
guard you in all your ways
[of obedience and service].
¹²They will lift you up in their
hands,
So that you do not [even] strike
your foot against a stone.
[Luke 4:10, 11; Heb 1:14]
¹³You will tread upon the lion
and cobra;
The young lion and the
serpent you will trample
underfoot. [Luke 10:19]

¹⁴"Because he set his love on
Me, therefore I will save
him;
I will set him [securely] on
high, because he knows My
name [he confidently trusts
and relies on Me, knowing I
will never abandon him, no,
never].
¹⁵"He will call upon Me, and I
will answer him;
I will be with him in trouble;
I will rescue him and honor
him.

16 "With a long life I will satisfy
    him
  And I will let him see My
    salvation."

PSALM 92

Praise for the Lord's Goodness.

A Psalm. A Song
for the Sabbath day.

1 IT IS a good *and* delightful
    thing to give thanks to the
    Lord,
  To sing praises to Your name,
    O Most High,
2 To declare Your
    lovingkindness in the
    morning
  And Your faithfulness by
    night,
3 With an instrument of ten
    strings and with the harp,
  With a solemn sound on the
    lyre.
4 For You, O Lord, have made
    me glad by Your works;
  At the works of Your hands I
    joyfully sing.

5 How great are Your works,
    O Lord!
  Your thoughts are very
    deep [beyond man's
    understanding].
6 A senseless man [in his crude
    and uncultivated state]
    knows nothing,
  Nor does a [self-righteous]
    fool understand this:
7 That though the wicked
    sprout up like grass
  And all evildoers flourish,
  They will be destroyed
    forever.

8 But You, Lord, are on high
    forever.
9 For behold, Your enemies,
    O Lord,
  For behold, Your enemies will
    perish;
  All who do evil will be
    scattered.

10 But my horn [my emblem of
    strength and power] You
    have exalted like that of a
    wild ox;
  I am anointed with fresh oil
    [for Your service].
11 My eye has looked on my foes;
  My ears hear of the evildoers
    who rise up against me.
12 The righteous will flourish
    like the date palm [long-
    lived, upright and useful];
  They will grow like a cedar
    in Lebanon [majestic and
    stable].
13 Planted in the house of the
    Lord,
  They will flourish in the
    courts of our God.
14 [Growing in grace] they will
    still thrive *and* bear fruit
    and prosper in old age;
  They will flourish *and* be vital
    and fresh [rich in trust and
    love and contentment];
15 [They are living memorials]
    to declare that the Lord is
    upright *and* faithful [to His
    promises];
  He is my rock, and there is no
    unrighteousness in Him.
    [Rom 9:14]

PSALM 93

The Majesty of the Lord.

¹THE LORD reigns, He is
clothed with majesty *and*
splendor;
The LORD has clothed and
encircled Himself with
strength;
the world is firmly
established, it cannot be
moved.
²Your throne is established
from of old;
You are from everlasting.

³The floods have lifted up,
O LORD,
The floods have lifted up their
voice;
The floods lift up their
pounding waves.
⁴More than the sounds of
many waters,
More than the mighty
breakers of the sea,
The LORD on high is mighty.
⁵Your precepts are fully
confirmed *and* completely
reliable;
Holiness adorns Your house,
O LORD, forever.

PSALM 94

The LORD Implored to Avenge
His People.

¹O LORD God, You to whom
vengeance belongs,
O God, You to whom
vengeance belongs, shine
forth [in judgment]!
²Rise up, O Judge of the earth;
Give to the proud a fitting
compensation.

³O LORD, how long will the
wicked,
How long will the wicked
rejoice in triumph?
⁴They pour out *words,*
speaking arrogant things;
All who do evil boast proudly.
[Jude 14, 15]
⁵They crush Your people,
O LORD,
And afflict *and* abuse Your
heritage.
⁶They kill the widow and the
alien
And murder the fatherless.
⁷Yet they say, "The LORD does
not see,
Nor does the God of Jacob
(Israel) notice it."

⁸Consider thoughtfully, you
senseless (stupid ones)
among the people;
And you [dull-minded] fools,
when will you become wise
and understand?
⁹He who made the ear, does He
not hear?
He who formed the eye, does
He not see?
¹⁰He who instructs the nations,
Does He not rebuke *and* punish,
He who teaches man
knowledge?
¹¹The LORD knows the thoughts
of man,
That they are a mere breath
(vain, empty, futile). [1 Cor
3:20]

¹²Blessed [with wisdom and
prosperity] is the man
whom You discipline *and*
instruct, O LORD,
And whom You teach from
Your law,

¹³ That You may grant
   him [power to calm
   himself and find]
   peace in the days of
   adversity,
Until the pit is dug for the
   wicked *and* ungodly.
¹⁴ For the LORD will not abandon
   His people,
Nor will He abandon His
   inheritance.

life point

In Psalm 94:12–15, God is saying that He deals with us and disciplines us for a reason. He wants us to come to the point where we can keep ourselves calm in the day of adversity.

In verses 14 and 15, notice the emphasis on God's faithfulness and justice toward His children. We can be sure that if we are being obedient to His Word and His will, and we are being led by His Holy Spirit, we have nothing to fear from our enemies, because the Lord Himself will fight our battles for us (see 2 Chronicles 20:15). Do you want God's help? If the answer is yes, then ask for His help and receive it by faith. God cannot help someone who does not want to be helped. Decide that you sincerely want God's help, and He will run to your aid and move mightily on your behalf.

¹⁵ For judgment will again be
   righteous,
And all the upright in heart
   will follow it.
¹⁶ Who will stand up for me
   against the evildoers?
Who will take a stand for
   me against those who do
   wickedness?

¹⁷ If the LORD had not been my
   help,
I would soon have dwelt in
   [the land of] silence.
¹⁸ If I say, "My foot has slipped,"
Your compassion *and*
   lovingkindness, O LORD, will
   hold me up.
¹⁹ When my anxious thoughts
   multiply within me,
Your comforts delight me.
²⁰ Can a throne of destruction
   be allied with You,
One which frames *and*
   devises mischief by decree
   [under the sacred name of
   law]?
²¹ They band themselves
   together against the life of
   the righteous
And condemn the innocent to
   death.
²² But the LORD has become my
   high tower *and* defense,
And my God the rock of my
   refuge.
²³ He has turned back their own
   wickedness upon them
And will destroy them by
   means of their own evil;

speak the Word

God, when my anxious thoughts multiply within me,
Your comforts delight me.
—ADAPTED FROM PSALM 94:19

The LORD our God will wipe
them out.

PSALM 95

Praise to the LORD,
and Warning against
Unbelief.

¹O COME, let us sing joyfully to
the LORD;
Let us shout joyfully to the
rock of our salvation.
²Let us come before
His presence with a
song of thanksgiving;
Let us shout joyfully to Him
with songs.
³For the LORD is a great God
And a great King above all
gods,
⁴In whose hand are the depths
of the earth;
The peaks of the mountains
are His also.
⁵The sea is His, for He made it
[by His command];
And His hands formed the
dry land. [Gen 1:9]

⁶O come, let us worship and
bow down,
Let us kneel before
the LORD our Maker
[in reverent praise and
prayer].
⁷For He is our God
And we are the people of His
pasture and the sheep of
His hand.
Today, if you will hear His
voice, [Heb 3:7–11]
⁸Do not harden your hearts
and become spiritually dull
as at Meribah [the place of
strife],

And as at Massah [the
place of testing] in the
wilderness, [Ex 17:1–7; Num
20:1–13; Deut 6:16]
⁹"When your fathers tested
Me,
They tried Me, even though
they had seen My work [of
miracles].
¹⁰"For forty years I was grieved
and disgusted with that
generation,
And I said, 'They are a people
who err in their heart,
And they do not acknowledge
or regard My ways.'
¹¹"Therefore I swore [an oath]
in My wrath,
'They absolutely shall not
enter My rest [the land of
promise].' " [Heb 4:3–11]

PSALM 96

A Call to Worship the LORD
the Righteous Judge.

¹O SING to the LORD a new
song;
Sing to the LORD, all the
earth!
²Sing to the LORD, bless His
name;
Proclaim good news of His
salvation from day to day.
³Declare His glory among the
nations,
His marvelous works *and*
wonderful deeds among all
the peoples.
⁴For great is the LORD and
greatly to be praised;
He is to be feared above all
gods. [Deut 6:5; Rev 14:7]

⁵For all the gods of the peoples
  are [worthless, lifeless]
  idols,
But the Lord made the
  heavens.
⁶Splendor and majesty are
  before Him;
Strength and beauty are in
  His sanctuary.

⁷Ascribe to the Lord,
  O families of the peoples,
Ascribe to the Lord glory and
  strength.
⁸Ascribe to the Lord the glory
  of His name;
Bring an offering and come
  into His courts.
⁹Worship the Lord in the
  splendor of holiness;
Tremble [in submissive
  wonder] before Him, all the
  earth.
¹⁰Say among the nations, "The
  Lord reigns;
Indeed, the world is firmly
  and securely established, it
  shall not be moved;
He will judge *and* rule the
  people with fairness."
  [Rev 11:15; 19:6]

¹¹Let the heavens be glad, and
  let the earth rejoice;
Let the sea roar, and all the
  things it contains;
¹²Let the field be exultant, and
  all that is in it.
Then all the trees of the forest
  will sing for joy
¹³Before the Lord, for He is
  coming,
For He is coming to judge the
  earth.
He will judge the world with
  righteousness

And the peoples in
  His faithfulness.
  [1 Chr 16:23–33; Rev 19:11]

PSALM 97

The Lord's Power and
Dominion.

¹THE LORD reigns, let the
  earth rejoice;
Let the many islands *and*
  coastlands be glad.
²Clouds and thick darkness
  surround Him [as at Sinai];
Righteousness and justice are
  the foundation of His throne.
  [Ex 19:9]
³Fire goes before Him
And burns up His adversaries
  on all sides.
⁴His lightnings have
  illuminated the world;
The earth has seen and
  trembled.
⁵The mountains melted like
  wax at the presence of the
  Lord,
At the presence of the Lord of
  the whole earth.
⁶The heavens declare His
  righteousness,
And all the peoples see His
  glory *and* brilliance.

⁷Let all those be [deeply]
  ashamed who serve carved
  images,
Who boast in idols.
Worship Him, all you gods!
  [Heb 1:6]
⁸Zion heard this and was glad,
And the daughters (cities) of
  Judah rejoiced [in relief]
Because of Your judgments,
  O Lord.

9 For You are the LORD Most
   High over all the earth;
You are exalted far above all
   gods.

10 You who love the LORD, hate
   evil;
He protects the souls of His
   godly ones (believers),
He rescues them from the
   hand of the wicked. [Rom
   8:13–17]
11 Light is sown [like seed]
   for the righteous *and*
   illuminates their path,
And [irrepressible] joy [is
   spread] for the upright in
   heart [who delight in His
   favor and protection].
12 Rejoice in the LORD, you
   righteous ones [those
   whose moral and spiritual
   integrity places them in
   right standing with God],
And praise *and* give thanks
   at the remembrance of His
   holy name.

PSALM 98

A Call to Praise the LORD
for His Righteousness.

A Psalm.

1 O SING to the LORD a new
   song,
For He has done marvelous
   and wonderful things;

His right hand and His holy
   arm have gained the victory
   for Him.
2 The LORD has made known His
   salvation;
He has [openly] revealed
   His righteousness in the
   sight of the nations.
   [Luke 2:30, 31]
3 He has [graciously]
   remembered His
   lovingkindness and His
   faithfulness to the house of
   Israel;
All the ends of the earth have
   witnessed the salvation of
   our God. [Acts 13:47; 28:28]

4 Shout joyfully to the LORD, all
   the earth;
Shout [in jubilation] and sing
   for joy and sing praises.
5 Sing praises to the LORD with
   the lyre,
With the lyre and the sound
   of melody.
6 With trumpets and the sound
   of the horn
Shout with joy before the
   King, the LORD.

7 Let the sea thunder *and*
   roar, and all the things it
   contains,
The world and those who
   dwell in it.
8 Let the rivers clap their
   hands;

speak the Word

*Thank You, God, that light is sown like seed for the righteous and
it illuminates their path. Thank you for giving irrepressible joy
to those who are upright in heart, for those who delight in
Your favor and protection.*
—ADAPTED FROM PSALM 97:11

Let the mountains sing
  together for joy *and* delight
⁹Before the Lord, for He is
  coming to judge the earth;
He will judge the world with
  righteousness
And the peoples with fairness.

PSALM 99

Praise to the Lord for His Fidelity to Israel.

¹THE LORD reigns, let the
  peoples tremble [with
  submissive wonder]!
He sits enthroned above the
  cherubim, let the earth
  shake!
²The Lord is great in Zion,
And He is exalted *and*
  magnified above all the
  peoples.
³Let them [reverently] praise
  Your great and awesome
  name;
Holy is He. [Rev 15:4]
⁴The strength of the King
  loves justice *and* righteous
  judgment;
You have established fairness;
You have executed justice
  and righteousness in Jacob
  (Israel).
⁵Exalt the Lord our God
And worship at His footstool;
Holy is He.

⁶Moses and Aaron were among
  His priests,
And Samuel was among those
  who called on His name;
They called upon the Lord
  and He answered them.
⁷He spoke to them in the pillar
  of cloud;

They kept His testimonies
And the statutes that He gave
  them. [Ps 105:9, 10]
⁸You answered them, O Lord
  our God;
You were a forgiving God to
  them,
And yet an avenger of their
  evil practices.
⁹Exalt the Lord our God
And worship at His holy hill
  [Zion, the temple mount],
For the Lord our God is holy.

PSALM 100

All Men Exhorted to Praise God.

A Psalm of Thanksgiving.

¹SHOUT JOYFULLY to the
  Lord, all the earth.
²Serve the Lord with gladness
  and delight;
Come before His presence
  with joyful singing.
³Know *and* fully recognize
  with gratitude that the Lord
  Himself is God;
It is He who has made us, not
  we ourselves [and we are
  His].
We are His people and the
  sheep of His pasture. [Eph
  2:10]

⁴Enter His gates with a song of
  thanksgiving
And His courts with praise.
Be thankful to Him, bless *and*
  praise His name.
⁵For the Lord is good;
His mercy *and* lovingkindness
  are everlasting,
His faithfulness [endures] to
  all generations.

life point

When we have the mind of Christ, our thoughts will be filled with praise and thanksgiving. When we complain, we open many doors to the enemy. Complaining—either in thought or word—causes us to live weak, powerless lives and can sometimes bring on physical illness. Do you want to live a powerful life? Take the advice of Psalm 100; be thankful to God and *say* you are thankful. Realize that complaining is a death principle, but being thankful and saying so is a life principle that will bring joy to your everyday life.

PSALM 101

The Psalmist's Profession of Uprightness.

A Psalm of David.

¹I WILL sing of [steadfast] lovingkindness and justice;
To You, O Lord, I will sing praises.
²I will behave wisely *and* follow the way of integrity.
When will You come to me?
I will walk in my house in integrity *and* with a blameless heart.

³I will set no worthless *or* wicked thing before my eyes.
I hate the practice of those who fall away [from the right path];
It will not grasp hold of me.
⁴A perverse heart shall depart from me;
I will not tolerate evil.
⁵Whoever secretly slanders his neighbor, him I will silence;
The one who has a haughty look and a proud (arrogant) heart I will not tolerate.

⁶My eyes will be on the faithful (honorable) of the land, that they may dwell with me;
He who walks blamelessly is the one who will minister to *and* serve me.
⁷He who practices deceit will not dwell in my house;
He who tells lies *and* half-truths will not continue [to remain] in my presence.
⁸Morning after morning I will destroy all the wicked in the land,
That I may cut off from the city of the Lord all those who do evil.

speak the Word

Lord, I will behave wisely, and I will follow the way of integrity.
I will walk within my house in integrity and with a blameless heart.
–ADAPTED FROM PSALM 101:2

PSALM 102

Prayer of an Afflicted Man for Mercy on Himself and on Zion.

A Prayer of the afflicted;
when he is overwhelmed
and pours out his complaint
to God.

¹HEAR MY prayer, O Lᴏʀᴅ,
And let my cry for help come
to You!
²Do not hide Your face from
me in the day of my
distress!
Incline Your ear to me;
In the day when I call, answer
me quickly.
³For my days have vanished in
smoke,
And my bones have been
scorched like a hearth.
⁴My heart has been struck like
grass and withered,
Indeed, [absorbed by my
heartache] I forget to eat my
food.
⁵Because of the sound of my
groaning [in suffering and
trouble]
My bones cling to my flesh.
⁶I am like a [mournful] vulture
of the wilderness;
I am like a [desolate] owl of
the wasteland.
⁷I am sleepless *and* lie awake
[mourning],
I have become like a lonely
bird on a housetop.

⁸My enemies taunt me all day
long;
Those who ridicule me use
my *name* as a curse.
⁹For I have eaten ashes like
bread,

And have mingled my drink
with tears [Is 44:20]
¹⁰Because of Your indignation
and Your wrath,
For You have lifted me up and
thrown me away.
¹¹My days are like an evening
shadow that lengthens *and*
vanishes [with the sun];
And as for me, I wither away
like grass.

¹²But You, O Lᴏʀᴅ, are
enthroned forever [ruling
eternally as sovereign];
And [the fame and glory of]
Your name [endures] to all
generations.
¹³You will arise and have
compassion on Zion,
For it is time to be gracious
and show favor to her;
Yes, the appointed time [the
moment designated] has
come. [Ps 12:5; 119:126]
¹⁴For Your servants find
[melancholy] pleasure in
the stones [of her ruins]
And feel pity for her dust.
¹⁵So the nations will fear the
name of the Lᴏʀᴅ,
And all the kings of the earth
[will recognize] Your glory.
[Ps 96:9]
¹⁶For the Lᴏʀᴅ has built up
Zion;
He has appeared in His glory
and brilliance;
¹⁷He has regarded the prayer of
the destitute,
And has not despised their
prayer.

¹⁸Let this be recorded for the
generation to come,
That a people yet to be
created will praise the Lᴏʀᴅ.

19 For He looked down from
His holy height [of His
sanctuary],
From heaven the Lord gazed
on the earth,
20 To hear the sighing of the
prisoner,
To set free those who were
doomed to death,
21 So that people may declare the
name of the Lord in Zion
And His praise in Jerusalem,
22 When the peoples are
gathered together,
And the kingdoms, to serve the
Lord.

23 He has exhausted my
strength [humbling me with
sorrow] in the way;
He has shortened my days.
24 I said, "O my God, do not take
me away in the midst of my
days;
Your years are [eternal]
throughout all generations.
25 "At the beginning You
founded the earth;
The heavens are the work of
Your hands.
26 "Even they will perish, but
You endure;
Yes, all of them will wear out
like a garment.
Like clothing You will change
them and they shall be
changed.
27 "But You remain the same,
And Your years will never
end. [Heb 1:10–12]

28 "The children of Your
servants will continue,
And their descendants will be
established before You."

PSALM 103

Praise for the Lord's Mercies.

A Psalm of David.

1 BLESS *AND* affectionately
praise the Lord, O my soul,
And all that is [deep] within
me, *bless* His holy name.
2 Bless *and* affectionately praise
the Lord, O my soul,
And do not forget any of His
benefits;
3 Who forgives all your sins,
Who heals all your diseases;
4 Who redeems your life from
the pit,
Who crowns you [lavishly]
with lovingkindness and
tender mercy;
5 Who satisfies your years with
good things,
So that your youth is renewed
like the [soaring] eagle. [Is
40:31]

6 The Lord executes
righteousness
And justice for all the
oppressed.
7 He made known His ways [of
righteousness and justice]
to Moses,
His acts to the children of
Israel.

speak the Word

*God, I am Your servant. I declare that my descendants
will be established before You.*
–ADAPTED FROM PSALM 102:28

⁸ The Lord is merciful and
   gracious,
   Slow to anger and abounding
   in compassion *and*
   lovingkindness.
   [James 5:11]
⁹ He will not always strive *with
   us,*
   Nor will He keep *His anger*
   forever.
¹⁰ He has not dealt with us
   according to our sins [as we
   deserve],
   Nor rewarded us [with
   punishment] according to
   our wickedness.
¹¹ For as the heavens are high
   above the earth,
   So great is His lovingkindness
   toward those who fear *and*
   worship Him [with awe-
   filled respect and deepest
   reverence].
¹² As far as the east is from the
   west,
   So far has He removed our
   transgressions from us.
¹³ Just as a father loves his
   children,
   So the Lord loves those who
   fear *and* worship Him [with
   awe-filled respect and
   deepest reverence].
¹⁴ For He knows our [mortal]
   frame;
   He remembers that we are
   [merely] dust.

¹⁵ As for man, his days are like
   grass;
   Like a flower of the field, so
   he flourishes.
¹⁶ For the wind passes over it
   and it is no more,
   And its place knows it no
   longer.

¹⁷ But the lovingkindness of the
   Lord is from everlasting to
   everlasting on those who
   [reverently] fear Him,
   And His righteousness to
   children's children, [Deut
   10:12]
¹⁸ To those who honor *and* keep
   His covenant,
   And remember to do His
   commandments [imprinting
   His word on their hearts].

¹⁹ The Lord has established His
   throne in the heavens,
   And His sovereignty rules
   over all [the universe].
²⁰ Bless the Lord, you His angels,
   You mighty ones who do His
   commandments,
   Obeying the voice of His
   word!
²¹ Bless the Lord, all you His
   hosts,
   You who serve Him and do His
   will.
²² Bless the Lord, all you works
   of His, in all places of His
   dominion;
   Bless *and* affectionately praise
   the Lord, O my soul!

PSALM 104

The Lord's Care over All
His Works.

¹ BLESS *AND* affectionately
   praise the Lord, O my soul!
   O Lord my God, You are very
   great;
   You are clothed with splendor
   and majesty,
² [You are the One] who covers
   Yourself with light as with a
   garment,

Who stretches out the
heavens like a tent curtain,
³Who lays the beams of
His upper chambers in
the waters [above the
firmament],
Who makes the clouds His
chariot,
Who walks on the wings of
the wind,
⁴Who makes winds His
messengers,
Flames of fire His ministers.
[Heb 1:7]

⁵He established the earth on
its foundations,
So that it will not be moved
forever and ever. [Job
38:4, 6]
⁶You covered it with the deep
as with a garment;
The waters were standing
above the mountains. [Gen
1:2; 2 Pet 3:5]
⁷At Your rebuke they fled;
At the sound of Your thunder
they hurried away.
⁸The mountains rose, the
valleys sank down
To the place which You
established for them.
⁹You set a boundary [for the
waters] that they may not
cross over,
So that they will not return to
cover the earth.

¹⁰You send springs into the
valleys;
Their waters flow among the
mountains.
¹¹They give drink to every
beast of the field;
The wild donkeys quench
their thirst there.

¹²Beside them the birds of the
heavens have their nests;
They lift up their voices *and*
sing among the branches.
[Matt 13:32]
¹³He waters the mountains
from His upper chambers;
The earth is satisfied with the
fruit of His works.

¹⁴He causes grass to grow for
the cattle,
And all that the earth
produces for cultivation by
man,
So that he may bring food
from the earth—
¹⁵And wine which makes the
heart of man glad,
So that he may make his face
glisten with oil,
And bread to sustain *and*
strengthen man's heart.
¹⁶The trees of the Lord drink
their fill,
The cedars of Lebanon which
He has planted,
¹⁷Where the birds make their
nests;
As for the stork, the fir trees
are her house.

¹⁸The high mountains are for
the wild goats;
The rocks are a refuge for the
shephanim.
¹⁹He made the moon for the
seasons;
The sun knows the [exact]
place of its setting.
²⁰You [O Lord] make darkness
and it becomes night,
In which prowls about every
wild beast of the forest.
²¹The young lions roar after
their prey

And seek their food from God.
22 When the sun arises, they
  withdraw
And lie down in their dens.
23 Man goes out to his work
And remains at his labor until
  evening.

24 O Lord, how many *and* varied
  are Your works!
In wisdom You have made
  them all;
The earth is full of Your
  riches *and* Your creatures.
25 There is the sea, great and
  broad,
In which are swarms without
  number,
Creatures both small and great.
26 There the ships [of the sea]
  sail,
And Leviathan [the sea
  monster], which You have
  formed to play there.

27 They all wait for You
To give them their food in its
  appointed season.
28 You give it to them, they
  gather it up;
You open Your hand, they
  are filled *and* satisfied with
  good [things].
29 You hide Your face, they are
  dismayed;
You take away their breath,
  they die
And return to their dust.
30 You send out Your Spirit, they
  are created;
You renew the face of the
  ground.

31 May the glory of the Lord
  endure forever;
May the Lord rejoice *and* be
  glad in His works—

32 He looks at the earth, and it
  trembles;
He touches the mountains,
  and they smoke.
33 I will sing to the Lord as long
  as I live;
I will sing praise to my God
  while I have my being.
34 May my meditation be sweet
  and pleasing to Him;
As for me, I will rejoice *and* be
  glad in the Lord.
35 Let sinners be consumed from
  the earth,
And let the wicked be no
  more.
Bless *and* affectionately praise
  the Lord, O my soul.
Praise the Lord! (Hallelujah!)

PSALM 105

The Lord's Wonderful Works in Behalf of Israel.

1 O GIVE thanks to the Lord,
  call upon His name;
Make known His deeds
  among the people.
2 Sing to Him, sing praises to
  Him;
Speak of all His wonderful
  acts *and* devoutly praise
  them.
3 Glory in His holy name;
Let the hearts of those who
  seek *and* require the Lord
  [as their most essential
  need] rejoice.
4 Seek *and* deeply long for the
  Lord and His strength [His
  power, His might];
Seek *and* deeply long for
  His face *and* His presence
  continually.

putting the Word to work

Remembering God's faithfulness to us is an important means of building our faith. Psalm 105:5 encourages us to recall the wonderful things He has done for us. What are some of your favorite memories? Regularly take time to remember God's faithfulness in your life and what He has done for you, and thank Him. Share with others God's goodness to you so they too can hear what He has done!

5 Remember [with awe and gratitude] the wonderful things which He has done,
His amazing deeds and the judgments uttered by His mouth [on His enemies, as in Egypt], [Ps 78:43–51]
6 O you offspring of Abraham, His servant,
O you sons of Jacob, His chosen ones!
7 He is the LORD our God;
His judgments are in all the earth.

8 He has remembered His covenant forever,
The word which He commanded *and* established to a thousand generations,
9 *The covenant* which He made with Abraham,
And His sworn oath to Isaac, [Luke 1:72, 73]
10 Which He confirmed to Jacob as a statute,
To Israel as an everlasting covenant,

11 Saying, "To you I will give the land of Canaan
As the measured portion of your inheritance."
12 When there were only a few men in number,
Very few [in fact], and strangers in it;
13 And they wandered from one nation to another,
From one kingdom to another people,
14 He allowed no man to oppress them;
He rebuked kings for their sakes, *saying,* [Gen 12:17; 20:3–7]
15 "Do not touch My anointed ones,
And do My prophets no harm." [1 Chr 16:8–22]

16 And He called for a famine upon the land [of Egypt];
He cut off every source of bread. [Gen 41:54]
17 He sent a man before them, Joseph, who was sold as a slave. [Gen 45:5; 50:20, 21]
18 His feet they hurt with shackles;
He was put in chains of iron,
19 Until the time that his word [of prophecy regarding his brothers] came true,
The word of the LORD tested *and* refined him.
20 The king sent and released him,
The ruler of the peoples [of Egypt], and set him free.
21 He made Joseph lord of his house
And ruler of all his possessions, [Gen 41:40]
22 To imprison his princes at his will,

That he might teach his elders
wisdom.
²³Israel also came into Egypt;
Thus Jacob sojourned
in the land of Ham.
[Gen 46:6]
²⁴There the LORD greatly
increased [the number of]
His people,

And made them more powerful
than their enemies.

²⁵He turned the heart
[of the Egyptians]
to hate His people,
To deal craftily with His
servants.
²⁶He sent Moses His servant,

remember Joseph

Psalm 105 is another wonderful place in the Bible where the writer takes time to recall God's working throughout history. Similar accounts can be found in Nehemiah 9 and in Hebrews 11. Each time a biblical writer recounts stories from the past, our faith can be strengthened and our hearts can be encouraged.

In Psalm 105:17–19, we are reminded of Joseph and of the unjust treatment he received from his brothers. They sold him into slavery and told his father that a wild animal had killed him. Meanwhile, a wealthy man named Potiphar purchased Joseph and took him into his home as a slave. God gave Joseph favor everywhere he went, and soon he found favor with his new master.

Joseph kept getting promoted, but then something unjust happened to him. Potiphar's wife tried to entice him into having an affair, but because he was a man of integrity, he would have nothing to do with her. Lying to her husband, she said Joseph had attacked her, which caused him to be imprisoned for something he had not done!

Joseph tried to help others the entire time he was in prison. He did not complain, and because he had a proper attitude in his suffering, God eventually delivered and promoted him. He ultimately had so much authority in Egypt that no one else in the entire land was above him except Pharaoh himself.

God also vindicated Joseph concerning the situation with his brothers, in that they had to come to Joseph for food when the whole land was in a state of famine. Once again, Joseph displayed a godly attitude by not mistreating them even though they deserved it. He told them what they had meant for his harm, God had worked out for his good—that they were in God's hands, not his, and that he had no right to do anything but bless them (see Genesis 37–45 for the details of this story). We can expect similar results when we stay patient through suffering and keep a positive, forgiving attitude.

And Aaron, whom He had chosen.

27 They exhibited His wondrous signs among them,
Great miracles in the land of Ham (Egypt).

28 He sent [thick, oppressive] darkness and made *the land* dark;
And Moses and Aaron did not rebel against His words. [Ex 10:22; Ps 99:7]

29 He turned Egypt's waters into blood
And caused their fish to die. [Ex 7:20, 21]

30 Their land swarmed with frogs,
Even in the chambers of their kings. [Ex 8:6]

31 He spoke, and there came swarms of flies
And gnats in all their territory. [Ex 8:17, 24]

32 He gave them hail for rain,
With flaming fire in their land. [Ex 9:23, 25]

33 He struck their vines also and their fig trees,
And shattered the [ice-laden] trees of their territory. [Ps 78:47]

34 He spoke, and the [migratory] locusts came,
And the young locusts, even without number, [Ex 10:4, 13, 14]

35 And ate up all the vegetation in their land,
And devoured the fruit of their ground.

36 He also struck down all the firstborn in their land,
The first fruits *and* chief substance of all their strength. [Ex 12:29; Ps 78:51]

37 He brought the sons of Israel out [of Egypt] with silver and gold,
And among their tribes there was not one who stumbled. [Ex 12:35]

38 Egypt was glad when they departed,
For the dread *and* fear of them had fallen on the Egyptians. [Ex 12:33]

39 The LORD spread a cloud as a covering [by day],
And a fire to illumine the night. [Ex 13:21]

40 The Israelites asked, and He brought quail,
And satisfied them with the bread of heaven. [Ex 16:12–15]

41 He opened the rock and water flowed out;
It ran in the dry places like a river. [Ex 17:6; Num 20:11]

42 For He remembered His holy word
To Abraham His servant; [Gen 15:14]

43 He brought out His people with joy,
And His chosen ones with a joyful shout,

44 He gave them the lands of the nations [of Canaan],
So that they would possess *the fruits of* those peoples' labor, [Deut 6:10, 11]

45 So that they might observe His precepts
And keep His laws [obediently accepting and honoring and valuing them].
Praise the LORD! (Hallelujah!)

PSALM 106

Israel's Rebelliousness and the LORD's Deliverances.

¹PRAISE THE LORD!
(Hallelujah!)
Oh give thanks to the LORD,
for He is good;
For His mercy *and*
lovingkindness endure
forever! [1 Chr 16:34]
²Who can put into words the
mighty deeds of the LORD?
Or who can proclaim all
His praise [that is due
Him]?
³Blessed are those who
observe justice [by
honoring God's precepts],
Who practice righteousness at
all times.

⁴Remember me, O LORD, when
You favor Your people.
Visit me with Your salvation
[when You rescue them],
⁵That I may see the prosperity
of Your chosen ones,
That I may rejoice in the
gladness of Your nation,
That I may glory with Your
inheritance.

⁶We have sinned like our
fathers;
We have committed iniquity,
we have behaved wickedly.
[Lev 26:40–42]
⁷Our fathers in Egypt did not
understand *nor* appreciate
Your miracles;
They did not remember
the abundance of Your
mercies *nor* imprint Your
lovingkindnesses on their
hearts,

But they were rebellious at
the sea, at the Red Sea. [Ex
14:21]
⁸Nevertheless He saved them
for His name's sake,
That He might make His
[supreme] power known.
⁹He rebuked the Red Sea, and
it dried up;
And He led them through
the depths as through a
pasture.
[Ex 14:21]
¹⁰So He saved them from the
hand of the one that hated
them,
And redeemed them from
the hand of the [Egyptian]
enemy. [Ex 14:30]
¹¹And the waters covered their
adversaries;
Not one of them was left. [Ex
14:27, 28; 15:5]
¹²Then Israel believed in [the
validity of] His words;
They sang His praise.

¹³But they quickly forgot His
works;
They did not [patiently] wait
for His counsel *and* purpose
[to be revealed regarding
them],
¹⁴But lusted intensely in the
wilderness
And tempted God [with their
insistent desires] in the
desert. [Num 11:4]
¹⁵So He gave them their request,
But sent a wasting disease
among them. [Ps 78:29–31]

¹⁶They envied Moses in the
camp,
And Aaron [the high priest],
the holy one of the LORD,
[Num 16:1–32]

¹⁷ Therefore the earth opened
and swallowed Dathan,

And engulfed the company of
Abiram. [Num 16:31, 32]

be happy

Psalm 106:12–15 reminds us of the Israelites when they became greedy and demanding. It warns us of the dangers of a greedy, lustful heart because such a heart is never satisfied—and that is an unsafe spiritual condition.

Although God had led the Israelites out of bondage in Egypt and had destroyed Pharaoh and his army, who were chasing after them, the Israelites were not satisfied. They continued to gripe and complain every step of the way. No matter how much He provided for them, they always wanted more. They were on the way to the Promised Land, but they were not enjoying the journey. Many times, we have the same problem.

Early in my ministry, I taught twenty-five people every Tuesday evening in my living room. That was all I was mature enough to handle. I had a vision to do what I am doing now, so I grumbled, murmured, pleaded, prayed, fasted, but I never got out of my living room. All my efforts were a waste of time and energy. I could have been relaxing, praising God, laughing, and enjoying my family and my life. But no, I had to be miserable all the time because I was not getting my way.

I finally had an opportunity to teach another Bible study. I was happy with that for a little while, but not for long. Then I went to work for a church where I was associate pastor for five years, but after a while I was not satisfied there anymore. Then I started my own ministry, and before long, I was unhappy with that. No matter what I was doing, I always wanted something else.

If people are not careful, they can waste their entire lives by always wanting what they do not have. They fall in love and cannot wait to get married. Then once they are married, they think about everything that is wrong with their spouse and they are still not happy. They have children and cannot wait for them to grow up and start school. As soon as the children are in school, they cannot wait until they graduate.

On and on it goes. No matter what their place in life, they always want something else. They keep murmuring and grumbling to God about what they want. Then as soon as He gives it to them, they start complaining again because they want something more.

The moral of the story of the Israelites is that they got what they asked for, but they were not really ready to handle it. Ask God to give you a heart that is satisfied and content at every point along your life's journey and to be able to handle increase when it comes. Learn to enjoy where you are on the way to where you are going!

18 And a fire broke out in their
   company;
   The flame consumed the
   wicked. [Num 16:35, 46]

19 They made a calf in Horeb
   (Sinai)
   And worshiped a cast image.
   [Ex 32:4]
20 Thus they exchanged [the
   true God who was] their
   glory
   For the image of an ox that
   eats grass.
21 They forgot God their Savior,
   Who had done such great
   things in Egypt,
22 Wonders in the land of Ham,
   Awesome things at the Red
   Sea.
23 Therefore He said He would
   destroy them,
   [And He would have done so]
   had not Moses, His chosen
   one, stepped into the gap
   before Him,
   To turn away His wrath from
   destroying them. [Ex 32:10,
   11, 32]
24 Then they despised the
   pleasant land [of Canaan];
   They did not believe in His
   word *nor* rely on it,
25 But they sulked *and*
   complained in their tents;
   They did not listen to the
   voice of the LORD.
26 Therefore He lifted up His
   hand [swearing] to them,
   That He would cause them to
   fall in the wilderness,
27 And that He would cast out
   their descendants among
   the nations
   And scatter them in the lands
   [of the earth].

28 They joined themselves also
   to [the idol] Baal of Peor,
   And ate sacrifices offered to
   the dead.
29 Thus they provoked Him to
   anger with their practices,
   And a plague broke out among
   them.
30 Then Phinehas [the priest]
   stood up and interceded,
   And so the plague was halted.
   [Num 25:7, 8]
31 And that was credited to him
   for righteousness,
   To all generations forever.

32 They provoked Him to anger
   at the waters of Meribah,
   So that it went hard with
   Moses on their account;
   [Num 20:3–13]
33 Because they were rebellious
   against His Spirit,
   Moses spoke recklessly with
   his lips.

34 They did not destroy the
   [pagan] peoples [in
   Canaan],
   As the LORD commanded
   them,
35 But they mingled with the
   [idolatrous] nations
   And learned their ways,
36 And served their idols,
   Which became a [dreadful]
   snare to them.
37 They even sacrificed their
   sons and their daughters to
   demons [Deut 32:17; 2 Kin
   16:3]
38 And shed innocent blood,
   Even the blood of their sons
   and of their daughters,
   Whom they sacrificed to the
   idols of Canaan;

And the land was polluted
with their blood.

³⁹ In this way they became
unclean in their practices;
They played the prostitute
in their own deeds [by
giving their worship, which
belongs to God alone, to
other "gods"].

⁴⁰ Therefore the anger of the
Lord was kindled against
His people
And He detested His own
inheritance. [Deut 32:17]

⁴¹ He gave them into the hands
of the nations,
And those who hated them
ruled over them.

⁴² Their enemies also oppressed
them,
And they were subdued under
the [powerful] hand of their
enemies.

⁴³ Many times He rescued them;
But they were rebellious in
their counsel,
And sank down in their
wickedness.

⁴⁴ Nevertheless He looked
[sympathetically] at their
distress
When He heard their cry;

⁴⁵ And He remembered His
covenant for their sake,
And relented [rescinding
their sentence] according
to the greatness of His
lovingkindness [when they
cried out to Him],

⁴⁶ He also made them *objects* of
compassion
Among those who had carried
them away captive. [2 Kin
25:27–30]

⁴⁷ Save us, O Lord our God,
And gather us from among
the nations,
That we may give thanks to
Your holy name
And glory in praising You.

⁴⁸ Blessed be the Lord, the God
of Israel,
From everlasting even to
everlasting.
And let all the people say,
"Amen."
Praise the Lord! (Hallelujah!)
[1 Chr 16:35, 36]

BOOK FIVE

PSALM 107

The Lord Rescues People
from Many Troubles.

¹ O GIVE thanks to the Lord,
for He is good;
For His compassion *and*
lovingkindness endure
forever!

² Let the redeemed of the Lord
say so,
Whom He has redeemed
from the hand of the
adversary,

³ And gathered them from the
lands,
From the east and from the
west,
From the north and from the
south.

⁴ They wandered in the
wilderness in a [solitary]
desert region;
And did not find a way to an
inhabited city.

⁵ Hungry and thirsty,
They fainted.

⁶ Then they cried out to the
LORD in their trouble,
And He rescued them from
their distresses.
⁷ He led them by the straight
way,
To an inhabited city [where
they could establish their
homes].
⁸ Let them give thanks
to the LORD for His
lovingkindness,
And for His wonderful acts to
the children of men!
⁹ For He satisfies the parched
throat,
And fills the hungry appetite
with what is good.

¹⁰ Some dwelt in darkness
and in the deep (deathly)
darkness,
Prisoners [bound] in misery
and chains, [Luke 1:79]
¹¹ Because they had rebelled
against the precepts of God
And spurned the counsel of
the Most High.
¹² Therefore He humbled their
heart with hard labor;
They stumbled and there was
no one to help.
¹³ Then they cried out to the
LORD in their trouble,
And He saved them from
their distresses.
¹⁴ He brought them out of
darkness and the deep
(deathly) darkness
And broke their bonds apart.
[Ps 68:6; Acts 12:7; 16:26]
¹⁵ Let them give thanks
to the LORD for His
lovingkindness,
And for His wonderful acts to
the children of men!

¹⁶ For He has shattered the gates
of bronze
And cut the bars of iron apart.

¹⁷ Fools, because of their
rebellious way,
And because of their sins,
were afflicted.
¹⁸ They detested all kinds of food,
And they drew near to the
gates of death.
¹⁹ Then they cried out to the
LORD in their trouble,
And He saved them from
their distresses.
²⁰ He sent His word and healed
them,
And rescued them from their
destruction. [2 Kin 20:4, 5;
Matt 8:8]
²¹ Let them give thanks to the
LORD for His lovingkindness,
And for His wonderful acts to
the children of men! [Heb
13:15]
²² And let them offer the
sacrifices of thanksgiving,
And speak of His deeds with
shouts of joy!

²³ Those who go down to the sea
in ships,
Who do business on great
waters;
²⁴ They have seen the works of
the LORD,
And His wonders in the deep.
²⁵ For He spoke and raised up a
stormy wind,
Which lifted up the waves of
the sea.
²⁶ They went up toward the
heavens [on the crest of
the wave], they went down
again to the depths [of the
watery trough];

Their courage melted away in their misery.

27 They staggered and trembled like a drunken man,
And were at their wits' end [all their wisdom was useless].

28 Then they cried out to the LORD in their trouble,
And He brought them out of their distresses.

29 He hushed the storm to a gentle whisper,
So that the waves of the sea were still. [Ps 65:7; 89:9; Matt 8:26]

30 Then they were glad because of the calm,
And He guided them to their desired haven (harbor).

31 Let them give thanks to the LORD for His lovingkindness,
And for His wonderful acts to the children of men!

32 Let them exalt Him also in the congregation of the people,
And praise Him at the seat of the elders.

33 He turns rivers into a wilderness,
And springs of water into a thirsty ground; [1 Kin 17:1, 7]

34 A productive land into a [barren] salt waste,
Because of the wickedness of those who dwell in it. [Gen 13:10; 14:3; 19:25]

35 He turns a wilderness into a pool of water
And a dry land into springs of water; [Is 41:18]

36 And there He has the hungry dwell,

So that they may establish an inhabited city,

37 And sow fields and plant vineyards,
And produce an abundant harvest.

38 Also He blesses them so that they multiply greatly,
And He does not let [the number of] their cattle decrease.

39 When they are diminished and bowed down (humbled)
Through oppression, misery, and sorrow,

40 He pours contempt on princes
And makes them wander in a pathless wasteland.

41 Yet He sets the needy securely on high, away from affliction,
And makes their families like a flock.

42 The upright see it and rejoice;
But all unrighteousness shuts its mouth.

43 Who is wise? Let him observe *and* heed these things;
And [thoughtfully] consider the lovingkindness of the LORD.

PSALM 108

Praise and Supplication to God for Victory.

A Song. A Psalm of David.

1 O GOD, my heart is steadfast [with confident faith];
I will sing, I will sing praises, even with my soul.

2 Awake, harp and lyre;
I will awaken the dawn!

3 I will praise *and* give thanks
to You, O LORD, among the
people;
And I will sing praises to You
among the nations.
4 For Your lovingkindness is
great *and* higher than the
heavens;
Your truth *reaches* to the
skies. [Ps 57:7–11]
5 Be exalted [in majesty],
O God, above the heavens,
And Your glory above all the
earth.
6 That Your beloved [ones] may
be rescued,
Save with Your right hand,
and answer me!

7 God has spoken in His
holiness:
"I will rejoice, I will portion
out Shechem [as I divide
Canaan among My people],
And measure out the Valley of
Succoth.
8 "Gilead is Mine, Manasseh is
Mine;
Ephraim also is the helmet
of My head [My stronghold,
My defense];
Judah is My scepter. [Gen
49:10]
9 "Moab is My washbowl;
Over Edom I will throw My
shoe [to show Edom is
Mine];
Over Philistia I will shout [in
triumph]."

10 Who will bring me into the
fortified city [of Petra]?
Who will lead me to Edom?
11 Have You not rejected us,
O God?
And will You not go out,
O God, with our armies?

12 Give us help against the
adversary,
For deliverance by man is in
vain [a worthless hope].
13 With God we will do valiantly,
For it is He who will trample
down our enemies.
[Ps 60:5–12]

PSALM 109

Vengeance Invoked upon Adversaries.

To the Chief Musician.
A Psalm of David.

1 O GOD of my praise!
Do not keep silent,
2 For the mouth of the wicked
and the mouth of the
deceitful are opened against
me;
They have spoken against me
with a lying tongue.
3 They have also surrounded
me with words of hatred,
And have fought against me
without a cause.
4 In return for my love, they
attack me,
But I am in prayer.
5 They have repaid me evil for
good,
And hatred for my love.

6 Appoint a wicked man against
him,
And let an attacker stand at
his right hand [to kill him].
7 When he enters into dispute,
let wickedness come about.
Let his prayer [for help] result
[only] in sin.
8 Let his days be few;
And let another take his
office. [Acts 1:20]

⁹Let his children be fatherless
And his wife a widow.
¹⁰Let his children wander and
    beg;
Let them seek their food *and*
    be driven far from their
    ruined homes. [Gen 4:12]
¹¹Let the creditor seize all that
    he has,
And let strangers plunder the
    product of his labor.
¹²Let there be no one to extend
    kindness to him,
Nor let anyone be gracious to
    his fatherless children.
¹³Let his descendants be cut off,
And in the following
    generation let their name be
    blotted out.

¹⁴Let the wickedness of his
    fathers be remembered by
    the LORD;
And do not let the sin of his
    mother be blotted out.
¹⁵Let them be before the LORD
    continually,
That He may cut off their
    memory from the earth;
¹⁶Because the man did
    not remember to show
    kindness,
But persecuted the suffering
    and needy man,
And the brokenhearted, to
    put them to death.
¹⁷He also loved cursing, and it
    came [back] to him;
He did not delight in blessing,
    so it was far from him.
¹⁸He clothed himself with
    cursing as with his garment,
And it seeped into his inner
    self like water
And like [anointing] oil into
    his bones.

¹⁹Let it be to him as a robe
    with which he covers
    himself,
And as a sash with which he
    is constantly bound.
²⁰Let this be the reward of my
    attackers from the LORD,
And of those who speak evil
    against my life.

²¹But You, O GOD, the Lord,
    show *kindness* to me, for
    Your name's sake;
Because Your lovingkindness
    (faithfulness, compassion)
    is good, O rescue me;
²²For I am suffering and needy,
And my heart is wounded
    within me.
²³I am vanishing like a shadow
    when it lengthens *and*
    fades;
I am shaken off like the
    locust.
²⁴My knees are unsteady from
    fasting;
And my flesh is gaunt and
    without fatness.
²⁵I also have become a reproach
    and an object of taunting to
    others;
When they see me, they shake
    their heads [in derision].
    [Matt 26:39]

²⁶Help me, O LORD my God;
Save me according to Your
    lovingkindness—
²⁷And let them know that this is
    Your hand;
You, LORD, have done it.
²⁸Let them curse, but You bless.
When adversaries arise, let
    them be ashamed,
But let Your servant rejoice.

²⁹ Let my attackers be clothed
   with dishonor,
   And let them cover
      themselves with their own
      shame as with a robe.
³⁰ I will give great praise *and*
   thanks to the LORD with my
   mouth;
   And in the midst of many I
      will praise Him.
³¹ For He will stand at the right
   hand of the needy,

To save him from those who
   judge his soul.

PSALM 110

The LORD Gives Dominion
to the King.

A Psalm of David.

¹ THE LORD (Father) says to
   my Lord (the Messiah, His
   Son),
   "Sit at My right hand

healed healers

Psalm 109:22 speaks of a wounded heart. Is it wrong to have a wounded heart? No, a wounded heart is not wrong, but if you have one, I encourage you to receive God's healing and go on with your life.

In Old Testament days if a priest had a wound or a bleeding sore, he could not minister (Leviticus 21:1–16). I think we can learn from that today, because we have a lot of wounded people who are trying to minister and bring healing to others while they themselves still have unhealed wounds from the past. These people are still bleeding and hurting. They are what I call "wounded healers."

Am I saying such people cannot minister? No, but I am saying they need to be healed. Jesus said the blind cannot lead the blind because if they do, they will both fall into a pit (see Matthew 15:14). There is a message in that statement. What is the use of my trying to minister victory to others if I have no victory in my own life? How can I minister emotional healing to others if I am not dealing with my emotional problems from my past? In order to minister properly, we first need to go to God and let Him heal us.

I have found that when I have a relationship problem, when I get wounded or when someone hurts my feelings, I cannot minister properly until I get that situation worked out because it takes away my strength and affects my faith. When I have unresolved problems in my life, I am not as strong as I could be.

God loves to use people who have been hurt or wounded and then healed because nobody can minister to someone else better than a person who has had the same problem or been in the same situation as the person they are trying to help. Ask God to heal you everywhere you hurt so He can use you to help others. Ask Him to make you a healed healer!

Until I make Your enemies
a footstool for Your feet
[subjugating them into
complete submission]."
[Josh 10:24; Matt 26:64;
Acts 2:34; 1 Cor 15:25; Col 3:1;
Heb 12:2]
2 The LORD will send the
scepter of Your strength
from Zion, *saying,*
"Rule in the midst of Your
enemies." [Rom 11:26, 27]
3 Your people will offer
themselves willingly [to
participate in Your battle] in
the day of Your power;

In the splendor of holiness,
from the womb of the dawn,
Your young men are to You as
the dew.
4 The LORD has sworn [an oath]
and will not change His
mind:
"You are a priest forever
According to the order of
Melchizedek." [Heb 5:10;
7:11, 15, 21]
5 The LORD is at Your right
hand,
He will crush kings in the day
of His wrath.

your Provider

Do you need provision in an area of your life, and you are not really sure where it is going to come from? Be encouraged because, in Psalm 111:5, God promises to provide for "those who fear Him [with awe-inspired reverence]." As long as we worship God, we are going to have His provision.

Perhaps you have been told that you are going to lose your job or your housing. Maybe you are elderly and living on a pension or Social Security, and you wonder what is going to happen to you in the future. You see prices on everything rising all the time, and the devil whispers in your ear, "You are not going to have enough to live on." Or maybe the figures just do not add up; your income simply is not enough to support you, and yet you are doing all you know to do.

Whatever the reason for your concern about your provision, mark Psalm 111:5 in your Bible. Meditate on it and even memorize it, because it holds the key to having your needs met. That way when a need arises in your life, you will have hidden the Word of God in your heart, and it will strengthen you and help you remain in faith rather than in fear.

Believe God's Word when He says He gives food and provision to those who reverently fear Him and worship Him. Whatever your situation may be, God will provide for you as you continue to worship and magnify Him.

Worship is actually fun and energizing; worry makes our hearts heavy and causes a loss of joy. Do not worry; worship and see God provide for your every need.

6 He will execute judgment [in overwhelming punishment] among the nations;
He will fill them with corpses,
He will crush the chief men over a broad country. [Ezek 38:21, 22; 39:11, 12]
7 He will drink from the brook by the wayside;
Therefore He will lift up His head [triumphantly].

PSALM 111

The LORD Praised for His Goodness.

1 PRAISE THE LORD!
(Hallelujah!)
I will give thanks to the LORD with all my heart,
In the company of the upright and in the congregation.
2 Great are the works of the LORD,
Studied by all those who delight in them.
3 Splendid and majestic is His work,
And His righteousness endures forever.
4 He has made His wonderful acts to be remembered;
The LORD is gracious and merciful *and* full of loving compassion.
5 He has given food to those who fear Him [with awe-inspired reverence];
He will remember His covenant forever. [Deut 10:12; Ps 96:9]
6 He has declared *and* made known to His people the power of His works,
In giving them the heritage of the nations.

7 The works of His hands are truth and [absolute] justice;
All His precepts are sure (established, reliable, trustworthy).
8 They are upheld forever and ever;
They are done in [absolute] truth and uprightness.

life point

The Bible says that those who walk in wisdom will be successful and live long lives. They will be exceedingly happy. They will be blessed, so blessed that they will be admired (see Proverbs 3:1–18). But there is no such thing as wisdom without worship. Psalm 111:10 says that reverence for God is the beginning of wisdom. In other words, reverence is foundational to having a fruitful life.

Many people today are seeking knowledge, and knowledge is good, but wisdom is better. Wisdom is the right use of knowledge. Knowledge without wisdom can cause one to be puffed up or filled with pride, which will ultimately ruin his life. A wise person will always be knowledgeable, but not all knowledgeable people are wise.

God's Word tells us to cry out for wisdom, to seek it as we would silver and gold, to make it a vital necessity in life. There is nothing more important than wisdom, and wisdom starts with reverence toward God.

⁹He has sent redemption to His
   people;
He has ordained His covenant
   forever;
Holy and awesome is His
   name—[inspiring reverence
   and godly fear].
¹⁰The [reverent] fear of the
   LORD is the beginning (the
   prerequisite, the absolute
   essential, the alphabet) of
   wisdom;
A good understanding *and*
   a teachable heart are
   possessed by all those who
   do *the will of the LORD*;
His praise endures forever.
   [Job 28:28; Prov 1:7; Matt
   22:37, 38; Rev 14:7]

PSALM 112

Prosperity of the One
Who Fears the LORD.

¹PRAISE THE LORD!
   (Hallelujah!)
Blessed [fortunate,
   prosperous, and favored by
   God] is the man who fears
   the LORD [with awe-inspired
   reverence and worships
   Him with obedience],
Who delights greatly in His
   commandments. [Deut
   10:12]
²His descendants will be
   mighty on earth;
The generation of the upright
   will be blessed.
³Wealth and riches are in his
   house,
And his righteousness
   endures forever.
⁴Light arises in the darkness
   for the upright;

He is gracious and
   compassionate and
   righteous (upright—in right
   standing with God).
⁵It is well with the man who is
   gracious and lends;
He conducts his affairs with
   justice. [Ps 37:26; Luke 6:35;
   Col 4:5]
⁶He will never be shaken;
The righteous will be
   remembered forever.
   [Prov 10:7]

⁷He will not fear bad news;
His heart is steadfast,
   trusting [confidently
   relying on and believing]
   in the LORD.
⁸His heart is upheld, he will
   not fear
While he looks [with
   satisfaction] on his
   adversaries.
⁹He has given freely to the
   poor;
His righteousness endures
   forever;
His horn will be exalted in
   honor. [2 Cor 9:9]

¹⁰The wicked will see it and be
   angered,
He will gnash his teeth and
   melt away [in despair and
   death];
The desire of the wicked will
   perish *and* come to nothing.

PSALM 113

The LORD Exalts the Humble.

¹PRAISE THE LORD!
   (Hallelujah!)
Praise, O servants of the LORD,
Praise the name of the LORD.

² Blessed be the name of the
LORD
From this time forth and
forever.
³ From the rising of the sun to
its setting
The name of the LORD is to be
praised [with awe-inspired
reverence].
⁴ The LORD is high above all
nations,
And His glory above the
heavens.

⁵ Who is like the LORD our God,
Who is enthroned on high,
⁶ Who humbles Himself to
regard
The heavens and the earth?
[Ps 138:6; Is 57:15]
⁷ He raises the poor out of the
dust
And lifts the needy from the
ash heap,
⁸ That He may seat them with
princes,
With the princes of His
people.
⁹ He makes the barren woman
live in the house
As a joyful mother of
children.
Praise the LORD! (Hallelujah!)

PSALM 114

God's Rescue of Israel
from Egypt.

¹ WHEN ISRAEL came out of
Egypt,
The house of Jacob from a
people of strange language,
² Judah became His sanctuary,
And Israel His dominion.
[Ex 29:45, 46; Deut 27:9]

³ The [Red] Sea looked and
fled;
The Jordan turned back.
[Ex 14:21; Josh 3:13, 16;
Ps 77:16]
⁴ The mountains leaped like
rams,
The [little] hills, like lambs.
⁵ What ails you, O sea, that you
flee?
O Jordan, that you turn back?
⁶ O mountains, that you leap
like rams,
O [little] hills, like lambs?

⁷ Tremble, O earth, at the
presence of the Lord,
At the presence of the God of
Jacob (Israel),
⁸ Who turned the rock into a
pool of water,
The flint into a fountain of
water. [Ex 17:6; Num 20:11]

PSALM 115

Pagan Idols Contrasted
with the LORD.

¹ NOT TO us, O LORD, not to us,
But to Your name give glory
Because of Your
lovingkindness, because of
Your truth *and* faithfulness.
² Why should the nations say,
"Where, now, is their God?"
³ But our God is in heaven;
He does whatever He pleases.
⁴ The idols [of the nations] are
silver and gold,
The work of man's hands.
⁵ They have mouths, but they
cannot speak;
They have eyes, but they
cannot see;
⁶ They have ears, but they
cannot hear;

They have noses, but they
cannot smell;
[7] They have hands, but they
cannot feel;
They have feet, but they
cannot walk;
Nor can they make a sound
with their throats.
[8] Those who make them will
become like them,
Everyone who trusts in them.
[Ps 135:15–18]

[9] O Israel, trust *and* take refuge
in the LORD! [Be confident
in Him, cling to Him, rely
on His word!]
He is their help and their shield.
[10] O house of Aaron, trust in the
LORD;
He is their help and their shield.
[11] You who [reverently] fear the
LORD, trust in LORD;
He is their help and their shield.
[12] The LORD has been mindful of
us; He will bless,
He will bless the house of
Israel;
He will bless the house of
Aaron.
[13] He will bless those who fear
and worship the LORD [with
awe-inspired reverence and
submissive wonder],

Both the small and the great.
[Ps 103:11; Rev 11:18; 19:5]
[14] May the LORD give you [great]
increase,
You and your children.
[15] May you be blessed of the LORD,
Who made heaven and earth.

[16] The heavens are the heavens
of the LORD,
But the earth He has given to
the children of men.
[17] The dead do not praise the
LORD,
Nor do any who go down into
silence;
[18] But as for us, we will bless *and*
affectionately and gratefully
praise the LORD
From this time forth and
forever.
Praise the LORD! (Hallelujah!)

PSALM 116

Thanksgiving for Rescue
from Death.

[1] I LOVE the LORD, because He
hears [and continues to hear]
My voice and my supplications
(my pleas, my cries, my
specific needs).
[2] Because He has inclined His
ear to me,

confess the Word

When we speak what we believe, as the psalmist did in Psalm 116:1, 2,
we are making a "confession."

I recommend having a list of confessions—things that can be backed by
the Word of God—things that you speak aloud over your life, your family,
your circumstances, and your future. You can find a list of Scripture
verses to adapt as confessions in the section entitled, "The Word for Your
Everyday Life," in the back of this Bible.

Before learning to confess God's Word, I was terribly negative. I was a Christian and active in church work. My husband and I tithed and attended church regularly, but we did not know that we could do anything about any of our circumstances. God began teaching me that I should not think and say negative things. I felt He told me He could not work in my life until I stopped being so negative. I obeyed, and I became happier.

After some time had elapsed, I felt that my circumstances had not improved significantly. I asked the Lord about it, and He said, "You have stopped speaking negatively, but you are not saying anything positive." That was my first lesson in "call[ing] into being that which does not exist" (see Romans 4:17). No one had taught me this principle before; God was teaching me Himself, and it proved to be one of the major breakthroughs in my life. He showed me that confessing His Word helps establish His life-giving truths in our hearts.

I made a list of the things that I had been learning, which were rightfully mine according to the Word of God. I had scriptures to support them. I confessed those truths aloud twice a day for approximately six months. I did this in my house, alone. I was not talking to any human person; I was declaring the Word of God and speaking it into the atmosphere where I lived. To this day, almost twenty years later, when I am praying and confessing the Word, I still hear many of those early confessions come out of my mouth.

I would like to share a few confessions from my list with you:

"I am dead to sin but alive to God" (see Romans 6:11); "I will study the Word of God; I will pray" (see 2 Timothy 2:15; Luke 18:1); "I take every thought captive unto the obedience of Jesus Christ, casting down every imagination, and every exalted and proud thing that exalts itself against the knowledge of God" (see 2 Corinthians 10:5); "No weapon that is formed against me will succeed, but every tongue that rises against me in judgment, I will condemn" (see Isaiah 54:17); "I do not think more highly of myself than I ought to think" (see Romans 12:3); "I intend that my mouth will not transgress. I will speak forth the righteousness and praise of God all the day long" (see Psalm 17:3; 35:28); "I cry to God Most High, Who accomplishes all things on my behalf and completes my purpose in His plan" (see Psalm 57:2). "God has not given me a spirit of fear, but one of power, love, and a sound mind" (see 2 Timothy 1:7).

I can look at my list now, and I am absolutely amazed at how many of the things have come to pass, and how impossible they seemed, naturally speaking, at the time.

I encourage you to make your own list, tailored to your situation. As you begin to confess God's Word, you will notice major changes in your life.

Therefore I will call on Him
as long as I live.
³ The cords *and* sorrows of
death encompassed me,
And the terrors of Sheol came
upon me;
I found distress and sorrow.
⁴ Then I called on the name of
the LORD:
"O LORD, please save my life!"

⁵ Gracious is the LORD, and
[consistently] righteous;
Yes, our God is
compassionate.
⁶ The LORD protects the simple
(childlike);
I was brought low [humbled
and discouraged], and He
saved me.
⁷ Return to your rest, O my soul,
For the LORD has dealt
bountifully with you.
[Matt 11:29]
⁸ For You have rescued my life
from death,
My eyes from tears,
And my feet from stumbling
and falling.
⁹ I will walk [in submissive
wonder] before the LORD
In the land of the living.
¹⁰ I believed [and clung to my
God] when I said,
"I am greatly afflicted." [2 Cor
4:13]
¹¹ I said in my alarm,
"All men are liars."

¹² What will I give to the LORD
[in return]
For all His benefits toward me?
[How can I repay Him for His
precious blessings?]
¹³ I will lift up the cup of
salvation

And call on the name of the
LORD.
¹⁴ I will pay my vows to the
LORD,
Yes, in the presence of all His
people.
¹⁵ Precious [and of great
consequence] in the sight of
the LORD
Is the death of His godly ones
[so He watches over them].
¹⁶ O LORD, truly I am Your
servant;
I am Your servant, the son of
Your handmaid;
You have unfastened my
chains.
¹⁷ I will offer to You the sacrifice
of thanksgiving,
And will call on the name of
the LORD.
¹⁸ I will pay my vows to the LORD,
Yes, in the presence of all His
people,

life point

Notice that in Psalm 116:17, the
psalmist says that he will "call on
the name of the LORD," but only
after he has offered the sacrifice of
thanksgiving.

Many times I have attempted to call
on the power of the Name of Jesus
to help me, while at the same time
my life was filled with complaining—
not thankfulness. I have discovered
that there is no positive power in
complaining. Complaining is filled
with power, but it is negative (evil)
power. If we want God's power to be
released in our lives, we will have to
stop complaining and be thankful.

[19] In the courts of the LORD's
   house (temple) —
In the midst of you,
   O Jerusalem.
Praise the LORD! (Hallelujah!)

PSALM 117

A Psalm of Praise.

[1] O PRAISE the LORD, all you
   nations!
Praise Him, all you people!
   [Rom 15:11]
[2] For His lovingkindness
   prevails over us [and we
   triumph and overcome
   through Him],
And the truth of the LORD
   endures forever.
Praise the LORD! (Hallelujah!)

PSALM 118

Thanksgiving for the LORD's
Saving Goodness.

[1] O GIVE thanks to the LORD,
   for He is good;
For His lovingkindness
   endures forever.
[2] Oh let Israel say,
   "His lovingkindness endures
   forever."
[3] Oh let the house of Aaron say,
   "His lovingkindness endures
   forever."
[4] Oh let those who [reverently]
   fear the LORD, say,
   "His lovingkindness endures
   forever."

[5] Out of my distress I called on
   the LORD;
The LORD answered me and
   set me free.

[6] The LORD is on my side; I will
   not fear.
What can [mere] man do to
   me? [Heb 13:6]
[7] The LORD is on my side, He is
   among those who help me;
Therefore I will look [in
   triumph] on those who
   hate me.
[8] It is better to take refuge in the
   LORD
Than to trust in man.
[9] It is better to take refuge in the
   LORD
Than to trust in princes.

[10] All nations encompassed me;
In the name of the LORD I will
   surely cut them off.
[11] They encompassed me, yes,
   they surrounded me [on
   every side];
In the name of the LORD I will
   cut them off.
[12] They swarmed around me
   like bees;
They flare up *and* are
   extinguished like a fire of
   thorns;
In the name of the LORD I will
   surely cut them off. [Deut
   1:44]
[13] You [my enemy] pushed
   me violently so that I was
   falling,
But the LORD helped me.
[14] The LORD is my strength and
   song,
And He has become my
   salvation.

[15] The sound of joyful shouting
   and salvation is in the tents
   of the righteous:
The right hand of the LORD
   does valiantly.

the right kind of fear

The psalmist says in Psalm 118:4 that he will reverently fear the Lord by declaring that His loving-kindness endures forever. As he worships God and talks about some of His great attributes, his faith is being strengthened.

Notice something interesting in Psalm 118:5. The psalmist tells how, in his distress, he called upon the Lord. But he did not do that until *after* he had worshiped the Lord and praised Him in verse 4 for the very attributes he was calling upon Him to display in his distressing situation. He continues by declaring: "The Lord is on my side; I will not fear. What can [mere] man do to me?" (Psalm 118:6).

Why should we fear? If Almighty God is for us, *and He is*, then what can mere human beings do to us? We definitely need to realize how big God is and how small our enemies are when compared to Him.

You may be worried about what people are going to do to you. You may be worried that someone is going to take your job away, that someone is not going to give you what you need. A person may treat you unfairly or may reject you. You may be worried about what somebody is going to think or say about you. I encourage you to be more concerned about what God thinks of you than what people think of you.

The Bible tells us that we are not to fear people, but that we are to reverently and worshipfully fear the Lord. When we refuse to fear others, but instead reverently and worshipfully fear God, then He moves on our behalf so that nothing anyone tries to do to us ever harms us permanently. Evil people may come against us one way, but they will have to flee before us "seven ways" (see Deuteronomy 28:7).

For a period of time it may seem as if someone is taking advantage of you. But if you keep your eyes on God and continue to worship Him, keeping your conversation in line with His Word, in the end God will reward you and bring justice because He is a God of justice. He loves justice and hates wrongdoing. God is our Vindicator, and He always makes wrong things right if we keep trusting Him long enough.

We need to retire from self-care and cast our cares upon the Lord. If we place our trust in God, nobody is going to take advantage of us—at least not for long. God has thousands of ways to get His blessings to us. When a door closes, He opens another one. If there are no doors, He makes one!

Do you find yourself in distress or afraid of people? Then do what the psalmist did. First focus on God's loving-kindness, and then encourage yourself with the knowledge that God is on your side.

¹⁶The right hand of the Lᴏʀᴅ is
    exalted;
  The right hand of the Lᴏʀᴅ
    does valiantly.
¹⁷I will not die, but live,
  And declare the works *and*
    recount the illustrious acts
    of the Lᴏʀᴅ.
¹⁸The Lᴏʀᴅ has disciplined me
    severely,
  But He has not given me over
    to death. [2 Cor 6:9]

¹⁹Open to me the [temple] gates
    of righteousness;
  I shall enter through them,
    I shall give thanks to the
    Lᴏʀᴅ.
²⁰This is the gate of the Lᴏʀᴅ;
  The righteous will enter
    through it. [Ps 24:7]
²¹I will give thanks to You,
    for You have heard *and*
    answered me;
  And You have become my
    salvation [my Rescuer, my
    Savior].

²²The stone which the builders
    rejected
  Has become the chief corner
    stone.
²³This is from the Lᴏʀᴅ *and* is
    His doing;
  It is marvelous in our eyes.
    [Matt 21:42; Acts 4:11;
    1 Pet 2:7]
²⁴This [day in which God has
    saved me] is the day which
    the Lᴏʀᴅ has made;
  Let us rejoice and be glad in it.
²⁵O Lᴏʀᴅ, save now, we beseech
    You;
  O Lᴏʀᴅ, we beseech You, send
    now prosperity *and* give us
    success!

²⁶Blessed is the one who
    comes in the name of
    the Lᴏʀᴅ;
  We have blessed you from the
    house of the Lᴏʀᴅ [you who
    come into His sanctuary
    under His guardianship].
    [Mark 11:9, 10]
²⁷The Lᴏʀᴅ is God, and He has
    given us light [illuminating
    us with His grace and
    freedom and joy].
  Bind the festival sacrifices
    with cords to the horns of
    the altar.
²⁸You are my God, and I give
    thanks to You;
  [You are] my God, I extol You.
²⁹O give thanks to the Lᴏʀᴅ, for
    He is good;
  For His lovingkindness
    endures forever.

PSALM 119

Meditations and Prayers
Relating to the Law of God.

א
Aleph.

¹HOW BLESSED *and* favored
    by God are those whose
    way is blameless [those
    with personal integrity, the
    upright, the guileless],
  Who walk in the law [and
    who are guided by the
    precepts and revealed will]
    of the Lᴏʀᴅ.
²Blessed *and* favored by God
    are those who keep His
    testimonies,
  And who [consistently] seek
    Him *and* long for Him with
    all their heart.

life point

Psalm 119:1, 2 says that "those whose way is blameless," who are guided by the precepts of the Lord, and who keep His testimonies and seek Him consistently with all of their hearts can expect God's blessing and favor. This is true in life's good times and in its difficult seasons.

When you find yourself in a time of trial, try not to simply focus on where you are right now and what is happening to you at the moment, but see yourself and your circumstances through the eyes of faith. You may feel as though you are out in the middle of an ocean with a storm raging around you, but *you will get to the other side*. There are blessings waiting for you there, *so do not jump overboard!* Learn, as the psalmist did, to walk in a way that is blameless and to keep seeking God (see Psalm 119:1, 2). You will be blessed and favored as you do!

³ They do no unrighteousness;
They walk in His ways.
[1 John 3:9; 5:18]
⁴ You have ordained Your
precepts,
That we should follow
them with [careful]
diligence.
⁵ Oh, that my ways may be
established
To observe *and* keep Your
statutes [obediently
accepting and honoring
them]!
⁶ Then I will not be ashamed
When I look [with respect] to
all Your commandments [as
my guide].
⁷ I will give thanks to You with
an upright heart,
When I learn [through
discipline] Your righteous
judgments [for my
transgressions].
⁸ I shall keep Your statutes;
Do not utterly abandon me
[when I fail].

ב
Beth.
⁹ How can a young man keep
his way pure?
By keeping watch [on
himself] according to Your
word [conforming his life to
Your precepts].
¹⁰ With all my heart I have
sought You, [inquiring of
You and longing for You];
Do not let me wander from
Your commandments
[neither through
ignorance nor by willful
disobedience]. [2 Chr 15:15]
¹¹ Your word I have treasured
and stored in my heart,
That I may not sin against You.
¹² Blessed *and* reverently
praised are You, O Lᴏʀᴅ;

life point

I believe Psalm 119:6 says what we need to be saying in our hearts every day: "God, if I will simply read Your Book, respect Your Commandments, and do what You say, everything in my life will work out for the best."

Teach me Your statutes.
13 With my lips I have told of
All the ordinances of Your
mouth.
14 I have rejoiced in the way of
Your testimonies,
As much as in all riches.
15 I will meditate on Your precepts
And [thoughtfully] regard
Your ways [the path of
life established by Your
precepts]. [Ps 104:34]
16 I will delight in Your statutes;
I will not forget Your word.

ג
Gimel.

17 Deal bountifully with Your
servant,
That I may live and keep Your
word [treasuring it and
being guided by it day by
day]. [Ps 119:97–101]
18 Open my eyes [to spiritual
truth] so that I may behold
Wonderful things from Your
law.
19 I am a stranger on the earth;
Do not hide Your
commandments from me.
[Gen 47:9; 1 Chr 29:15; Ps
39:12; 2 Cor 5:6; Heb 11:13]
20 My soul is crushed with longing
For Your ordinances at all
times.
21 You rebuke the presumptuous
and arrogant, the cursed ones,
Who wander from Your
commandments.

22 Take reproach and contempt
away from me,
For I observe Your
testimonies.
23 Even though princes sit and
talk to one another against
me,
Your servant meditates on
Your statutes.
24 Your testimonies also are my
delight
And my counselors.

ד
Daleth.

25 My earthly life clings to the
dust;
Revive and refresh me
according to Your word.
[Ps 143:11]

putting the Word to work

Have you ever been lost? Do
you remember the relief you felt
when someone was able to give
you good directions? The best
directions we have for living an
abundant life that is pleasing
to God are found in the Bible.
Hide God's Word in your heart by
studying and even memorizing
Scripture verses and passages,
so you will not sin against Him
and will be able to live in His
blessings (see Psalm 119:9–11).

speak the Word

*Lord, I pray that You would open my eyes to spiritual truth so that
I may behold wonderful things in Your Word.*
—ADAPTED FROM PSALM 119:18

²⁶I have told of my ways, and
  You have answered me;
  Teach me Your statutes.
²⁷Make me understand the way
  of Your precepts,
  So that I will meditate (focus
  my thoughts) on Your
  wonderful works.
  [Ps 145:5, 6]
²⁸My soul dissolves because of
  grief;
  Renew *and* strengthen me
  according to [the promises
  of] Your word.
²⁹Remove from me the
  way of falsehood *and*
  unfaithfulness,
  And graciously grant me Your
  law.
³⁰I have chosen the faithful way;
  I have placed Your ordinances
  before me.
³¹I cling tightly to Your
  testimonies;
  O Lord, do not put me to
  shame!
³²I will run the way of Your
  commandments [with
  purpose],
  For You will give me a heart
  that is willing.

ה

He.

³³Teach me, O Lord, the way of
  Your statutes,
  And I will [steadfastly]
  observe it to the end.
³⁴Give me understanding [a
  teachable heart and the
  ability to learn], that I may
  keep Your law;
  And observe it with all my
  heart. [Prov 2:6; James 1:5]
³⁵Make me walk in the path of
  Your commandments,

For I delight in it.
³⁶Incline my heart to Your
  testimonies
  And not to *dishonest* gain *and*
  envy. [Ezek 33:31; Mark 7:21,
  22; 1 Tim 6:10; Heb 13:5]
³⁷Turn my eyes away from
  vanity [all those worldly,
  meaningless things that
  distract—let Your priorities
  be mine],
  And restore me [with renewed
  energy] in Your ways.
³⁸Establish Your word *and*
  confirm Your promise to
  Your servant,
  As that which produces [awe-
  inspired] reverence for You.
  [Deut 10:12; Ps 96:9]
³⁹Turn away my reproach
  which I dread,
  For Your ordinances are good.
⁴⁰I long for Your precepts;
  Renew me through Your
  righteousness.

ו

Vav.

⁴¹May Your lovingkindness also
  come to me, O Lord,
  Your salvation according to
  Your promise;
⁴²So I will have an answer for
  the one who taunts me,
  For I trust [completely]
  in Your word [and its
  reliability].
⁴³And do not take the word
  of truth utterly out of my
  mouth,
  For I wait for Your
  ordinances.
⁴⁴I will keep Your law
  continually,
  Forever and ever [writing
  Your precepts on my heart].

45 And I will walk at liberty,
For I seek *and* deeply long for
Your precepts.
46 I will also speak of Your
testimonies before kings
And shall not be ashamed.
[Ps 138:1; Matt 10:18, 19;
Acts 26:1, 2]
47 For I shall delight in Your
commandments,
Which I love.
48 And I shall lift up my hands
to Your commandments,
Which I love;
And I will meditate on Your
statutes.

ז
Zayin.

49 Remember [always] the
word *and* promise to Your
servant,
In which You have made me
hope.
50 This is my comfort in my
affliction,
That Your word has revived
me *and* given me life. [Rom
15:4]
51 The arrogant utterly ridicule
me,
Yet I do not turn away from
Your law.
52 I have remembered
[carefully] Your ancient
ordinances, O Lord,
And I have taken comfort.
53 Burning indignation has
seized me because of the
wicked,
Who reject Your law.
54 Your statutes are my songs
In the house of my
pilgrimage.
55 O Lord, I remember Your
name in the night,

And keep Your law.
56 This has become mine [as the
gift of Your grace],
That I observe Your precepts
[accepting them with loving
obedience].

ח
Heth.

57 The Lord is my portion;
I have promised to keep Your
words.
58 I sought Your favor with all
my heart;
Be merciful *and* gracious
to me according to Your
promise.
59 I considered my ways
And turned my feet to [follow
and obey] Your testimonies.
60 I hurried and did not delay
To keep Your
commandments.
61 The cords of the wicked have
encircled *and* ensnared me,
But I have not forgotten Your
law.
62 At midnight I will rise to give
thanks to You
Because of Your righteous
ordinances.
63 I am a companion of all who
[reverently] fear You,
And of those who keep *and*
honor Your precepts.
64 The earth, O Lord, is full of
Your lovingkindness *and*
goodness;
Teach me Your statutes.

ט
Teth.

65 You have dealt well with Your
servant,
O Lord, according to Your
promise.

66 Teach me good judgment
(discernment) and
knowledge,
For I have believed *and*
trusted *and* relied on Your
commandments.
67 Before I was afflicted I went
astray,
But now I keep *and* honor
Your word [with loving
obedience].
68 You are good and do good;
Teach me Your statutes.
69 The arrogant have forged a lie
against me,
But I will keep Your precepts
with all my heart.
70 Their heart is insensitive like
fat [their minds are dull and
brutal],
But I delight in Your law.
71 It is good for me that I have
been afflicted,
That I may learn Your
statutes.
72 The law from Your mouth is
better to me
Than thousands of gold and
silver *pieces*.

׳

Yodh.

73 Your hands have made me
and established me;
Give me understanding *and* a
teachable heart, that I may
learn Your commandments.
74 May those who [reverently]
fear You see me and be
glad,
Because I wait for Your word.
75 I know, O Lᴏʀᴅ, that Your
judgments are fair,
And that in faithfulness You
have disciplined me. [Heb
12:10]

76 O may Your lovingkindness
and graciousness comfort
me,
According to Your word
(promise) to Your servant.
77 Let Your compassion come to
me that I may live,
For Your law is my delight.
78 Let the arrogant be ashamed
and humiliated, for they
sabotage me with a lie;
But I will meditate on Your
precepts.
79 May those who fear You [with
submissive wonder] turn to
me,
Even those who have known
Your testimonies.
80 May my heart be blameless in
Your statutes,
So that I will not be ashamed.

כ

Kaph.

81 My soul languishes *and* grows
weak for Your salvation;
I wait for Your word.
82 My eyes fail [with longing,
watching] for [the
fulfillment of] Your
promise,
Saying, "When will You
comfort me?"
83 For I have become like a
wineskin [blackened and
shriveled] in the smoke [in
which it hangs],
Yet I do not forget Your
statutes.
84 How many are the days of
Your servant [which he
must endure]?
When will You execute
judgment on those who
persecute me? [Rev 6:10]

85 The arrogant (godless) have
   dug pits for me,
 Men who do not conform to
   Your law.
86 All Your commandments are
   faithful *and* trustworthy.
 They have persecuted me
   with a lie; help me [LORD]!
87 They had almost destroyed
   me on earth,
 But as for me, I did not turn
   away from Your precepts.
88 According to Your steadfast
   love refresh me *and* give me
   life,
 So that I may keep *and* obey
   the testimony of Your
   mouth.

ל

Lamedh.

89 Forever, O LORD,
 Your word is settled in
   heaven [standing firm
   and unchangeable].
   [Ps 89:2; Matt 24:34, 35;
   1 Pet 1:25]
90 Your faithfulness *continues*
   from generation to
   generation;
 You have established the
   earth, and it stands
   [securely].
91 They continue this day
   according to Your
   ordinances,
 For all things [all parts of the
   universe] are Your servants.
   [Jer 33:25]
92 If Your law had not been my
   delight,
 Then I would have perished
   in my time of trouble.
93 I will never forget Your
   precepts,

For by them You have
   revived me *and* given me
   life.
94 I am Yours, save me [as Your
   own];
 For I have [diligently] sought
   Your precepts *and* required
   them [as my greatest
   need]. [Ps 42:1]
95 The wicked wait for me to
   destroy me,
 But I will consider Your
   testimonies.
96 I have seen that all [human]
   perfection has its limits
   [no matter how grand and
   perfect and noble];
 Your commandment is
   exceedingly broad *and*
   extends without limits [into
   eternity]. [Rom 3:10–19]

מ

Mem.

97 Oh, how I love Your law!
 It is my meditation all the
   day. [Ps 1:2]
98 Your commandments make
   me wiser than my enemies,
 For Your words are always
   with me.
99 I have better understanding
   and deeper insight than all
   my teachers [because of
   Your word],
 For Your testimonies are my
   meditation. [2 Tim 3:15]
100 I understand more than
   the aged [who have not
   observed Your precepts],
 Because I have observed *and*
   kept Your precepts.
101 I have restrained my feet
   from every evil way,

That I may keep Your word.
[Prov 1:15]
102 I have not turned aside from
Your ordinances,
For You Yourself have
taught me.
103 How sweet are Your words to
my taste,
Sweeter than honey to my
mouth! [Ps 19:10; Prov 8:11]
104 From Your precepts I get
understanding;
Therefore I hate every false
way.

 נ

Nun.

105 Your word is a lamp to my
feet
And a light to my path. [Prov
6:23]
106 I have sworn [an oath] and
have confirmed it,
That I will keep Your
righteous ordinances. [Neh
10:29]
107 I am greatly afflicted;
Renew *and* revive me [giving
me life], O LORD, according
to Your word.

putting the Word to work

Wandering around in the dark can be scary and frustrating! Do you ever feel that you are wandering in life, not sure of which way to go? Learn God's Word; it is a lamp to your feet and a light to your path (see Psalm 119:105). God promises to use His Word to instruct you in the way you are to go, one step at a time!

108 Accept *and* take pleasure in
the freewill offerings of my
mouth, O LORD,
And teach me Your
ordinances. [Hos 14:2; Heb
13:15]
109 My life is continually in my
hand,
Yet I do not forget Your law.
110 The wicked have laid a snare
for me,
Yet I do not wander from
Your precepts.
111 I have taken Your testimonies
as a heritage forever,
For they are the joy of my
heart. [Deut 33:4]
112 I have inclined my heart to
perform Your statutes
Forever, even to the end.

ס

Samekh.

113 I hate those who are double-
minded,
But I love *and* treasure Your
law.
114 You are my hiding place and
my shield;
I wait for Your word. [Ps 32:7;
91:1]
115 Leave me, you evildoers,
That I may keep the
commandments of my God
[honoring and obeying
them]. [Ps 6:8; 139:19; Matt
7:23]
116 Uphold me according to Your
word [of promise], so that I
may live;
And do not let me be
ashamed of my hope
[in Your great goodness].
[Ps 25:2; Rom 5:5; 9:33;
10:11]
117 Uphold me that I may be safe,

That I may have regard for
Your statutes continually.
[118] You have turned Your back
on all those who wander
from Your statutes,
For their deceitfulness is
useless.
[119] You have removed all the
wicked of the earth like
dross [for they have no
value];
Therefore I love Your
testimonies.
[120] My flesh trembles in
[reverent] fear of You,
And I am afraid *and* in awe of
Your judgments.

ע
Ayin.

[121] I have done justice and
righteousness;
Do not leave me to those who
oppress me.
[122] Be the guarantee for Your
servant for good [as Judah
was the guarantee for
Benjamin];
Do not let the arrogant
oppress me. [Gen 43:9]
[123] My eyes fail [with longing,
watching] for [the
fulfillment of] Your
salvation,
And for [the fulfillment of]
Your righteous word.
[124] Deal with Your servant
according to Your
[gracious] lovingkindness,
And teach me Your statutes.
[125] I am Your servant; give me
understanding [the ability
to learn and a teachable
heart]
That I may know Your
testimonies.

[126] It is time for the Lord to act;
They have broken Your law.
[127] Therefore I love Your
commandments more than
gold,
Yes, more than refined gold.
[128] Therefore I esteem as right all
Your precepts concerning
everything;
I hate every false way.

פ
Pe.

[129] Your testimonies are
wonderful;
Therefore my soul keeps
them.
[130] The unfolding of Your
[glorious] words give light;
Their unfolding gives
understanding to the
simple (childlike).
[131] I opened my mouth and
panted [with anticipation],
Because I longed for Your
commandments.

life point

**According to Psalm 119:130, the
unfolding of God's Word brings
light, which is something we all
need. We do not always know or
see what we need to do, and many
times we do not recognize our own
problems. We need God's light to
understand ourselves and to see
how we need to change and how
we can cooperate with God to make
things better. Reading God's Word is
like looking in a mirror. It enables us
to see what needs to be cleaned up
in our lives.**

¹³²Turn to me and be gracious to me *and* show me favor,
As is Your way to those who love Your name.
¹³³Establish my footsteps in [the way of] Your word;
Do not let any human weakness have power over me [causing me to be separated from You].
¹³⁴Redeem me from the oppression of man;
That I may keep Your precepts. [Luke 1:74]
¹³⁵Make Your face shine [with pleasure] upon Your servant,
And teach me Your statutes. [Ps 4:6]
¹³⁶My eyes weep streams of water
Because people do not keep Your law.

צ
Tsadhe.

¹³⁷Righteous are You, O Lord,
And upright are Your judgments.
¹³⁸You have commanded Your testimonies in righteousness
And in great faithfulness.
¹³⁹My zeal has [completely] consumed me,
Because my enemies have forgotten Your words.
¹⁴⁰Your word is very pure (refined);
Therefore Your servant loves it.
¹⁴¹I am small and despised,
But I do not forget Your precepts.
¹⁴²Your righteousness is an everlasting righteousness,
And Your law is truth. [Ps 19:9; John 17:17]
¹⁴³Trouble and anguish have found me,
Yet Your commandments are my delight *and* my joy.
¹⁴⁴Your righteous testimonies are everlasting;
Give me understanding [the ability to learn and a teachable heart] that I may live.

ק
Qoph.

¹⁴⁵I cried with all my heart; answer me, O Lord!
I will observe Your statutes.
¹⁴⁶I cried to You; save me
And I will keep Your testimonies.
¹⁴⁷I rise before dawn and cry [in prayer] for help;
I wait for Your word.
¹⁴⁸My eyes anticipate the night watches *and* I awake before the call of the watchman,
That I may meditate on Your word.
¹⁴⁹Hear my voice according to Your [steadfast] lovingkindness;
O Lord, renew *and* refresh me according to Your ordinances.
¹⁵⁰Those who follow after wickedness approach;
They are far from Your law.
¹⁵¹You are near, O Lord,
And all Your commandments are truth.
¹⁵²Of old I have known from Your testimonies
That You have founded them forever. [Luke 21:33]

ר

Resh.

¹⁵³ Look upon my agony and
   rescue me,
   For I do not forget Your law.
¹⁵⁴ Plead my cause and redeem
   me;
   Revive me *and* give me life
   according to [the promise
   of] Your word.
¹⁵⁵ Salvation is far from the
   wicked,
   For they do not seek Your
   statutes.
¹⁵⁶ Great are Your tender
   mercies *and* steadfast love,
   O LORD;
   Revive me *and* give me
   life according to Your
   ordinances.
¹⁵⁷ Many are my persecutors and
   my adversaries,
   Yet I do not turn away from
   Your testimonies.
¹⁵⁸ I see the treacherous and
   loathe them,
   Because they do not respect
   Your law.
¹⁵⁹ Consider how I love Your
   precepts;
   Revive me *and* give me life,
   O LORD, according to Your
   lovingkindness.
¹⁶⁰ The sum of Your word is
   truth [the full meaning of
   all Your precepts],
   And every one of Your
   righteous ordinances
   endures forever.

ש

Shin.

¹⁶¹ Princes persecute me without
   cause,

But my heart stands in
   [reverent] awe of Your
   words [so I can expect You
   to help me]. [1 Sam 24:11,
   14; 26:18]
¹⁶² I rejoice at Your word,
   As one who finds great
   treasure.
¹⁶³ I hate and detest falsehood,
   But I love Your law.
¹⁶⁴ Seven times a day I praise You,
   Because of Your righteous
   ordinances.
¹⁶⁵ Those who love Your law
   have great peace;
   Nothing makes them
   stumble. [Prov 3:2; Is 32:17]
¹⁶⁶ I hope *and* wait [with
   complete confidence] for
   Your salvation, O LORD,
   And I do Your
   commandments. [Gen
   49:18]
¹⁶⁷ My soul keeps Your
   testimonies [hearing and
   accepting and obeying
   them];
   I love them greatly.
¹⁶⁸ I keep Your precepts and
   Your testimonies,
   For all my ways are [fully
   known] before You.

ת

Tav.

¹⁶⁹ Let my [mournful] cry come
   before You, O LORD;
   Give me understanding
   [the ability to learn and
   a teachable heart]
   according to Your word
   [of promise].
¹⁷⁰ Let my supplication come
   before You;

Deliver me according to Your word.

171 Let my lips speak praise [with thanksgiving],
For You teach me Your statutes.

172 Let my tongue sing [praise for the fulfillment] of Your word,
For all Your commandments are righteous.

173 Let Your hand be ready to help me,
For I have chosen Your precepts.

174 I long for Your salvation, O Lord,
And Your law is my delight.

175 Let my soul live that it may praise You,
And let Your ordinances help me.

176 I have gone astray like a lost sheep;
Seek Your servant, for I do not forget Your commandments. [Is 53:6; Luke 15:4; 1 Pet 2:25]

PSALM 120

Prayer for Breaking Away from the Treacherous.

A Song of Ascents.

1 IN MY trouble I cried to the Lord,
And He answered me.

2 Rescue my soul, O Lord, from lying lips,
And from a deceitful tongue.

3 What shall be given to you, and what more shall be done to you,
You deceitful tongue?—

4 Sharp arrows of the warrior,
With the burning coals of the broom tree.

seek God first

We should be mature enough in our faith that we do not run to somebody else every time we need to know what to do in a certain situation. I am not implying that it is wrong to go to people we feel are wiser than we are to ask for a word of counsel or advice. But I do believe it is wrong, and insulting to God, to go to people too often. Having someone give us advice is not necessarily a problem; the problem comes when we seek man rather than God. God is a jealous God (see James 4:5 and Deuteronomy 4:24), and He wants us to ask for His advice.

It is important to clearly establish in our hearts that we will seek God first, as David did in Psalm 121:1–2. God wants to guide each one of us, every person who truly trusts Him.

I encourage you to seek balance in this area and to wean yourself from seeking other people's opinions if you have a consistent habit of doing so. Discipline yourself to go to God first, and let Him choose whether He wants to speak to you Himself or use the counsel of other believers to clarify things for you.

5 Woe to me, for I sojourn in
   Meshech,
 and I live among the tents
   of Kedar [among hostile
   people]! [Gen 10:2; 25:13;
   Jer 49:28, 29]
6 Too long my soul has had its
   dwelling
 With those who hate peace.
7 I am for peace, but when I
   speak,
 They are for war.

PSALM 121

The Lord the Keeper
of Israel.

A Song of Ascents.

1 I WILL lift up my eyes to the
   hills [of Jerusalem]—
 From where shall my help
   come? [Jer 3:23]
2 My help comes from the Lord,
 Who made heaven and earth.
3 He will not allow your foot to
   slip;
 He who keeps you will not
   slumber. [1 Sam 2:9; Ps
   127:1; Prov 3:23, 26; Is 27:3]
4 Behold, He who keeps Israel
 Will neither slumber [briefly]
   nor sleep [soundly].

5 The Lord is your keeper;
 The Lord is your shade on
   your right hand. [Is 25:4]

6 The sun will not strike you by
   day,
 Nor the moon by night. [Ps
   91:5; Is 49:10; Rev 7:16]
7 The Lord will protect you
   from all evil;
 He will keep your life.
8 The Lord will guard your
   going out and your coming
   in [everything that you do]
 From this time forth and
   forever. [Deut 28:6; Prov
   2:8; 3:6]

PSALM 122

Prayer for the Peace
of Jerusalem.

A Song of Ascents. Of David.

1 I WAS glad when they said to
   me,
 "Let us go to the house of the
   Lord." [Is 2:3; Zech 8:21]
2 Our feet are standing
 Within your gates,
   O Jerusalem,
3 Jerusalem, that is built
 As a city that is firmly joined
   together;
4 To which the [twelve] tribes
   go up, even the tribes of the
   Lord,
 [As was decreed as] an
   ordinance for Israel,

speak the Word

God, I declare that my help comes from You. You will not allow my
foot to slip. You are my keeper and You do not slumber or sleep.
You are the shade on my right hand. You will protect me
from all evil. You will keep my life and guard
my going out and my coming in forever.
–ADAPTED FROM PSALM 121:2–8

To give thanks to the name of the LORD.

⁵For there the thrones of judgment were set,
The thrones of the house of David.

⁶Pray for the peace of Jerusalem:
"May they prosper who love you [holy city].
⁷"May peace be within your walls
And prosperity within your palaces."
⁸For the sake of my brothers and my friends,
I will now say, "May peace be within you."
⁹For the sake of the house of the LORD our God [which is Jerusalem],
I will seek your (the city's) good.

PSALM 123

Prayer for the LORD's Help.

A Song of Ascents.

¹UNTO YOU I lift up my eyes,
O You who are enthroned in the heavens!
²Behold, as the eyes of servants look to the hand of their master,
And as the eyes of a maid to the hand of her mistress,
So our eyes look to the LORD our God,
Until He is gracious *and* favorable toward us.

³Be gracious to us, O LORD, be gracious *and* favorable toward us,
For we are greatly filled with contempt.
⁴Our soul is greatly filled

With the scoffing of those who are at ease,
And with the contempt of the proud [who disregard God's law].

PSALM 124

Praise for Rescue from Enemies.

A Song of Ascents. Of David.

¹"IF IT had not been the LORD who was on our side,"
Let Israel now say,
²"If it had not been the LORD who was on our side
When men rose up against us,
³Then they would have [quickly] swallowed us alive,
When their wrath was kindled against us;
⁴Then the waters would have engulfed us,
The torrent would have swept over our soul;
⁵Then the raging waters would have swept over our soul."

⁶Blessed be the LORD,

life point

God is for us; He is on our side (see Psalm 118:6). The devil has one position: he is against us. But God is over us, under us, through us, for us, and He surrounds us. So like Mount Zion we should not be moved, because God is all around us (see Psalm 125:1, 2).

Who has not given us as
prey to be torn by their
teeth.
[7] We have escaped like a
bird from the snare of the
fowlers;

The trap is broken and we
have escaped.
[8] Our help is in the name of the
LORD,
Who made heaven and
earth.

fill your mouth with laughter

Psalm 126:2, 3 speak of laughter and joy. I once watched a Christian television talk show in which the participants were talking about a laughing revival that took place in various parts of the world at one time. Someone asked the host of the show if he thought it was of God.

"Does it offend your mind?" the host asked.

"Yes, it does," answered the person who had raised the question.

"Well, then," responded the host, "it is probably of God."

Have you ever noticed that Jesus offended people who were falsely religious? It sometimes seemed He did it on purpose. In Matthew 15:12 Jesus' disciples said to Him, "Do You know that the Pharisees were offended when they heard You say this?" Jesus' answer to them was: "Leave them alone; they are blind guides [leading blind followers]. If a blind man leads a blind man, both will fall into a pit" (Matthew 15:14). If we are going to follow God, we need to realize that our minds may not always understand everything He does. Stop checking with your mind and start asking if you bear witness in your spirit to what is happening. We often reject things and movements that are genuinely of God simply because we have never seen them and do not understand them in our minds.

We must guard against developing an attitude like the Pharisees' in our hearts and attitudes. If the truth were known, the church today is full of Pharisees. I used to be one of them. In fact, I was a chief Pharisee. I was rigid, legalistic, boring, out to impress others, humorless, critical, and judgmental. I was on my way to heaven, but I was not enjoying the trip.

It is okay for us to relax a bit. Jesus was sent into this world not to bind us up, but to set us free. We need to be free to laugh, enjoy life, love people, and not be afraid to step out and try new things.

Now, I do not mean we are to go through life trying to see how ridiculous we can act. I am not talking about weirdness and fanaticism; I am talking about freedom and joy. I am talking about freely following the leading of the Holy Spirit. Go ahead, laugh a little. God will not be offended; He wants you to be joyful!

PSALM 125

The LORD Surrounds His People.

A Song of Ascents.

[1] THOSE WHO trust in *and* rely on the LORD [with confident expectation]
Are like Mount Zion, which cannot be moved but remains forever.
[2] As the mountains surround Jerusalem,
So the LORD surrounds His people
From this time forth and forever.
[3] For the scepter of wickedness shall not rest on the land of the righteous,
So that the righteous will not reach out their hands to do wrong.

[4] Do good, O LORD, to those who are good
And to those who are upright in their hearts.
[5] But as for those who turn aside to their crooked ways [in unresponsiveness to God],
The LORD will lead them away with those who do evil.
Peace be upon Israel.

PSALM 126

Thanksgiving for Return from Captivity.

A Song of Ascents.

[1] WHEN THE LORD brought back the captives to Zion (Jerusalem),
We were like those who dream [it seemed so unreal]. [Ps 53:6; Acts 12:9]

[2] Then our mouth was filled with laughter
And our tongue with joyful shouting;
Then they said among the nations,
"The LORD has done great things for them."
[3] The LORD has done great things for us;
We are glad!

[4] Restore our captivity, O LORD,
As the stream-beds in the South (the Negev) [are restored by torrents of rain].
[5] They who sow in tears shall reap with joyful singing.
[6] He who goes back and forth weeping, carrying his bag of seed [for planting],
Will indeed come again with a shout of joy, bringing his sheaves with him.

PSALM 127

Prosperity Comes from the LORD.

A Song of Ascents.
Of Solomon.

[1] UNLESS THE LORD builds the house,
They labor in vain who build it;
Unless the LORD guards the city,
The watchman keeps awake in vain. [Ps 121:1, 3, 5]
[2] It is vain for you to rise early,
To retire late,
To eat the bread of anxious labors—
For He gives [blessings] to His beloved *even in his* sleep.

[3] Behold, children are a heritage *and* gift from the LORD,

life point

According to Psalm 127:1, unless the Lord builds the house, those who build it labor in vain. We may be able to build, but what we build will not last if God is not involved in it. He is our Partner in life, and as such, He desires to be a part of everything we do. God is interested in every facet of our lives. Believing that truth is the beginning of an exciting journey with Him.

The fruit of the womb a
  reward. [Deut 28:4]
4 Like arrows in the hand of a
  warrior,
So are the children of one's
  youth.
5 How blessed [happy and
  fortunate] is the man whose
  quiver is filled with them;
They will not be ashamed
When they speak with their
  enemies [in gatherings] at
  the [city] gate.

PSALM 128

Blessedness of the Fear of the LORD.

A Song of Ascents.

1 BLESSED [HAPPY and
  sheltered by God's favor]
  is everyone who fears the
  LORD [and worships Him
  with obedience],
Who walks in His ways *and*
  lives according to His
  commandments. [Ps 1:1, 2]
2 For you shall eat the fruit of
  [the labor of] your hands,

You will be happy *and* blessed
  and it will be well with you.
3 Your wife shall be like a
  fruitful vine
Within the innermost part of
  your house;
Your children will be like
  olive plants
Around your table.
4 Behold, for so shall the man
  be blessed *and* divinely
  favored
Who fears the LORD [and
  worships Him with
  obedience].

5 May the LORD bless you from
  Zion [His holy mountain],
And may you see the
  prosperity of Jerusalem all
  the days of your life;
6 Indeed, may you see your
  [family perpetuated in
  your] children's children.
Peace be upon Israel!

PSALM 129

Prayer for the Overthrow of Zion's Enemies.

A Song of Ascents.

1 "MANY TIMES they have
  persecuted me (Israel) from
  my youth,"
Let Israel now say,
2 "Many times they have
  persecuted me from my
  youth,
Yet they have not prevailed
  against me.
3 "The [enemies, like] plowers
  plowed on my back;
They made their furrows [of
  suffering] long [in Israel]."
4 The LORD is righteous;

He has cut in two the [thick] cords of the wicked [which enslaved the people of Israel].

⁵May all who hate Zion
Be put to shame and turned backward [in defeat].
⁶Let them be like the grass on the housetops,
Which withers before it grows up,
⁷With which the reaper does not fill his hand,
Nor the binder of sheaves his arms,
⁸Nor do those who pass by say, "The blessing of the LORD be upon you;
We bless you in the name of the LORD."

PSALM 130

Hope in the LORD's Forgiving Love.

A Song of Ascents.

¹OUT OF the depths [of distress] I have cried to You, O LORD.
²Lord, hear my voice!
Let Your ears be attentive
To the voice of my supplications.
³If You, LORD, should keep an account of our sins *and* treat us accordingly,
O Lord, who could stand [before you in judgment and claim innocence]? [Ps 143:2; Rom 3:20; Gal 2:16]

⁴But there is forgiveness with You,
That You may be feared *and* worshiped [with submissive wonder]. [Deut 10:12]

⁵I wait [patiently] for the LORD, my soul [expectantly] waits,
And in His word do I hope.
⁶My soul waits for the Lord
More than the watchmen for the morning;
More than the watchmen for the morning.
⁷O Israel, hope in the LORD;
For with the LORD there is lovingkindness,
And with Him is abundant redemption.
⁸And He will redeem Israel
From all his sins.

PSALM 131

Childlike Trust in the LORD.

A Song of Ascents. Of David.

¹LORD, MY heart is not proud, nor my eyes haughty;
Nor do I involve myself in great matters,
Or in things too difficult for me.
²Surely I have calmed and quieted my soul;
Like a weaned child [resting] with his mother,
My soul is like a weaned child within me [composed and freed from discontent].

speak the Word

*Lord, I wait patiently for You, and in Your Word
my soul expectantly waits.*
—ADAPTED FROM PSALM 130:5

3 O Israel, hope in the Lord
From this time forth and
  forever.

PSALM 132

Prayer for the Lord's Blessing Upon the Sanctuary.

A Song of Ascents.

1 O LORD, remember on
  David's behalf
All his hardship *and*
  affliction;
2 How he swore to the Lord
And vowed to the Mighty One
  of Jacob:
3 "I absolutely will not enter my
  house,
Nor get into my bed—
4 I certainly will not permit my
  eyes to sleep
Nor my eyelids to slumber,
5 Until I find a place for the
  Lord,
A dwelling place for the
  Mighty One of Jacob
  (Israel)." [Acts 7:46]

6 Behold, we heard of it at
  Ephrathah;
We found it in the field of
  Jaar. [1 Sam 6:21]
7 Let us go into His tabernacle;
Let us worship at His
  footstool.
8 Arise, O Lord, to Your resting
  place,
You and the ark [the symbol]
  of Your strength.
9 Let Your priests be clothed
  with righteousness (right
  living),
And let Your godly ones shout
  for joy.

10 For the sake of Your servant
  David,
Do not turn away the face of
  Your anointed.
11 The Lord swore to David
A truth from which He will
  not turn back:
"One of your descendants I
  will set upon your throne.
  [Ps 89:3, 4; Luke 1:69; Acts
  2:30, 31]
12 "If your children will keep My
  covenant
And My testimony which I
  will teach them,
Their children also shall sit
  upon your throne forever."

13 For the Lord has chosen
  Zion;
He has desired it for His
  dwelling place:
14 "This is My resting place
  forever" [says the Lord];
"Here will I dwell, for I have
  desired it.
15 "I will abundantly bless her
  provisions;
I will satisfy her poor with
  bread.
16 "Her priests also I will clothe
  with salvation,
And her godly ones will shout
  aloud for joy.
17 "There I will make the
  horn (strength) of David
  grow;
I have prepared a lamp
  for My anointed [fulfilling
  the promises]. [1 Kin 11:36;
  15:4; 2 Chr 21:7; Luke 1:69]
18 "His enemies I will clothe
  with shame,
But upon himself shall his
  crown shine."

getting rid of "what-if"

Our oldest son, David, and his wife once needed a place to live temporarily. They had just sold their mobile home, and their newly purchased house would not be ready for a month. Of course, my husband and I invited them to live with us, even though I was a bit wary. My son and I are alike in many ways; we are both strong-willed, which does not always mix well in close quarters. Nothing negative had happened between us, but in anticipation of this move my mind kept coming up with "what-ifs."

My husband and I would be driving down the road, and my mouth would want to start talking about negative things that could take place: "What if there is no hot water left for my shower in the morning after everyone else is finished? What if they leave messes for me to clean up?" David and his wife had not even moved in, and nothing bad had yet happened. But my mouth wanted to declare disaster ahead of time.

The enemy wanted me to prophesy my future. He wanted me to be critical of the situation in advance.

If the devil can get us to be negative, he can provide us with negative circumstances. Often we call for our own problems. We "call into being that which does not exist" (see Romans 4:17), only we do it in the negative sense by sowing negative seeds.

Look at it this way: My blender works regardless of what is placed in it. If I put ice cream and milk in it, I will get a milkshake. If I put in water and dirt, I will get mud. The blender works. It is created to work. It is up to me to decide what I will put in it. What I put in is what I will get out. The same is true with our minds and hearts and mouths. What goes in is what is going to come out—for good or for bad.

Our son and daughter-in-law did live with us for a month, and everything worked out fine. I knew enough biblical principles by then to resist the temptation to complain in advance, and I urge you to beware of this temptation also. When I was tempted to speak negative words, I would choose to say, "This will work out fine. I am sure everyone will cooperate and be sensitive to the needs of the others."

My son and I made a joke about our challenge of getting along for thirty days under the same roof. We both like to be right, so he said, "I'll tell you what, Mom. Let's take turns being right. During the thirty days we are together, you can be right fifteen days, and I will be right fifteen days." We both laughed and had a good time. But the point is that I learned to discard "what-if" and accepted the blessing of pleasant unity in my home (see Psalm 133:1).

PSALM 133

The Excellency of Brotherly Unity.

A Song of Ascents. Of David.

¹BEHOLD, HOW good and how
    pleasant it is
  For brothers to dwell together
    in unity!
²It is like the precious oil [of
    consecration] poured on the
    head,
  Coming down on the beard,
  Even the beard of Aaron,
  Coming down upon the
    edge of his [priestly] robes
    [consecrating the whole
    body]. [Ex 30:25, 30]
³It is like the dew of [Mount]
    Hermon
  Coming down on the hills of
    Zion;
  For there the LORD has
    commanded the blessing:
    life forevermore.

PSALM 134

Greetings of Night Watchers.

A Song of Ascents.

¹BEHOLD, BLESS *and* praise
    the LORD, all servants of the
    LORD (priests, Levites),
  Who stand *and* serve by night
    in the house of the LORD.
    [1 Chr 9:33]
²Lift up your hands to the
    sanctuary
  And bless the LORD.
³May the LORD bless you from
    Zion,
  He who made heaven and
    earth.

PSALM 135

Praise the LORD's Wonderful Works. Vanity of Idols.

¹PRAISE THE LORD!
    (Hallelujah!)
  Praise the name of the LORD;
  Praise Him, O servants of the
    LORD (priests, Levites),
²You who stand in the house of
    the LORD,
  In the courts of the house of
    our God,
³Praise the LORD, for the LORD is
    good;
  Sing praises to His name, for
    it is gracious *and* lovely.
⁴For the LORD has chosen [the
    descendants of] Jacob for
    Himself,
  Israel for His own special
    treasure *and* possession.
    [Deut 7:6]

⁵For I know that the LORD is
    great
  And that our Lord is above all
    gods.
⁶Whatever the LORD pleases, He
    does,
  In the heavens and on the
    earth, in the seas and all
    deeps—
⁷Who causes the clouds to rise
    from the ends of the earth;
  Who makes lightning for the
    rain,
  Who brings the wind from
    His storehouses;

⁸Who struck the firstborn of
    Egypt,
  Both of man and animal; [Ex
    12:12, 29; Ps 78:51; 136:10]
⁹Who sent signs and wonders
    into your midst, O Egypt,

Upon Pharaoh and all his
servants.
¹⁰Who struck many nations
And killed mighty kings,
¹¹Sihon, king of the Amorites,
Og, king of Bashan,
And all the kingdoms of
Canaan;
¹²And He gave their land as a
heritage,
A heritage to Israel His people.
¹³Your name, O Lord, endures
forever,
Your fame *and* remembrance,
O Lord, [endures]
throughout all generations.
¹⁴For the Lord will judge His
people
And He will have compassion
on His servants [revealing
His mercy]. [Heb 10:30]
¹⁵The idols of the nations are
silver and gold,
The work of men's hands.
¹⁶They have mouths, but they do
not speak;
They have eyes, but they do
not see;
¹⁷They have ears, but they do not
hear,
Nor is there any breath in
their mouths.
¹⁸Those who make idols are
like them [absolutely
worthless—spiritually
blind, deaf, and powerless];
So is everyone who trusts
in *and* relies on them.
[Ps 115:4–8]

¹⁹O house of Israel, bless *and*
praise the Lord [with
gratitude];
O house of Aaron, bless the
Lord;
²⁰O house of Levi, bless the
Lord;
You who fear the Lord
[and worship Him with
obedience], bless the Lord
[with grateful praise]! [Deut
6:5; Ps 31:23]
²¹Blessed be the Lord from
Zion,
Who dwells [with us] at
Jerusalem.
Praise the Lord! (Hallelujah!)

PSALM 136

Thanks for the Lord's
Goodness to Israel.

¹GIVE THANKS to the Lord,
for He is good;
For His lovingkindness
(graciousness, mercy,
compassion) endures
forever.
²Give thanks to the God of
gods,
For His lovingkindness
endures forever.
³Give thanks to the Lord of
lords,
For His lovingkindness
endures forever.
⁴To Him who alone does great
wonders,

speak the Word

*Thank You, Lord, that Your hand is strong and
Your arm is outstretched toward me.*
—ADAPTED FROM PSALM 136:12

For His lovingkindness
endures forever;
⁵ To Him who made the heavens
with skill,
For His lovingkindness
endures forever;
⁶ To Him who stretched out the
earth upon the waters,
For His lovingkindness
endures forever;
⁷ To Him who made the great
lights,
For His lovingkindness
endures forever;
⁸ The sun to rule over the day,
For His lovingkindness
endures forever;
⁹ The moon and stars to rule by
night,
For His lovingkindness
endures forever;

¹⁰ To Him who struck the
firstborn of Egypt,
For His lovingkindness
endures forever; [Ex 12:29]
¹¹ And brought Israel out from
among them,
For His lovingkindness endures
forever; [Ex 12:51; 13:3, 17]
¹² With a strong hand and with
an outstretched arm,
For His lovingkindness
endures forever;
¹³ To Him who divided the Red
Sea into parts,
For His lovingkindness endures
forever; [Ex 14:21, 22]
¹⁴ And made Israel pass through
the midst of it,
For His lovingkindness
endures forever;
¹⁵ But tossed Pharaoh and his
army into the Red Sea,
For His lovingkindness
endures forever;

¹⁶ To Him who led His people
through the wilderness,
For His lovingkindness
endures forever;
¹⁷ To Him who struck down
great kings,
For His lovingkindness
endures forever;
¹⁸ And killed mighty kings,
For His lovingkindness
endures forever;
[Deut 29:7]
¹⁹ Sihon, king of the Amorites,
For His lovingkindness
endures forever; [Num
21:21–24]
²⁰ And Og, king of Bashan,
For His lovingkindness
endures forever; [Num
21:33–35]
²¹ And gave their land as a
heritage,
For His lovingkindness
endures forever;
²² Even a heritage to Israel His
servant,
For His lovingkindness
endures forever; [Josh 12:1]

²³ Who [faithfully] remembered
us in our lowly condition,
For His lovingkindness
endures forever;
²⁴ And has rescued us from our
enemies,
For His lovingkindness
endures forever;
²⁵ Who gives food to all flesh,
For His lovingkindness
endures forever;
²⁶ Give thanks to the God of
heaven,
For His lovingkindness
(graciousness, mercy,
compassion) endures
forever.

PSALM 137

An Experience of the Captivity.

¹BY THE rivers of Babylon,
There we [captives] sat down and wept,
When we remembered Zion [the city God imprinted on our hearts].
²On the willow trees in the midst of Babylon
We hung our harps.
³For there they who took us captive demanded of us a song with words,
And our tormentors [who made a mockery of us demanded] amusement, *saying,*
"Sing us one of the songs of Zion."

⁴How can we sing the LORD's song
In a strange *and* foreign land?
⁵If I forget you, O Jerusalem,
Let my right hand forget [her skill with the harp].
⁶Let my tongue cling to the roof of my mouth
If I do not remember you,
If I do not prefer Jerusalem
Above my chief joy. [Ezek 3:26]

⁷Remember, O LORD, against the sons of Edom,
The day of [the fall of] Jerusalem,
Who said "Down, down [with her]

To her very foundation."
⁸O daughter of Babylon, you devastator,
How blessed will be the one
Who repays you [with destruction] as you have repaid us. [Is 13:1–22; Jer 25:12, 13]
⁹How blessed will be the one who seizes and dashes your little ones
Against the rock.

PSALM 138

Thanksgiving for the LORD's Favor.

A Psalm of David.

¹I WILL give You thanks with all my heart;
I sing praises to You before the [pagan] gods.
²I will bow down [in worship] toward Your holy temple
And give thanks to Your name for Your lovingkindness and Your truth;
For You have magnified Your word together with Your name.
³On the day I called, You answered me;
And You made me bold *and* confident with [renewed] strength in my life.

⁴All the kings of the land will give thanks *and* praise You, O LORD,

speak the Word

Lord, I declare that You will accomplish that which concerns me!
–ADAPTED FROM PSALM 138:8

When they have heard of the promises of Your mouth [which were fulfilled].
⁵ Yes, they will sing of the ways of the LORD [joyfully celebrating His wonderful acts],
For great is the glory *and* majesty of the LORD.
⁶ Though the LORD is exalted, He regards the lowly [and invites them into His fellowship];
But the proud *and* haughty He knows from a distance. [Prov 3:34; James 4:6; 1 Pet 5:5]

⁷ Though I walk in the midst of trouble, You will revive me; You will stretch out Your hand against the wrath of my enemies, And Your right hand will save me. [Ps 23:3, 4]
⁸ The LORD will accomplish that which concerns me; Your [unwavering] lovingkindness, O LORD, endures forever— Do not abandon the works of Your own hands. [Ps 57:2; Phil 1:6]

PSALM 139

God's Omnipresence and Omniscience.

To the Chief Musician.
A Psalm of David.

¹ O LORD, you have searched me [thoroughly] and have known me.
² You know when I sit down and when I rise up [my entire life, everything I do];

You understand my thought from afar. [Matt 9:4; John 2:24, 25]
³ You scrutinize my path and my lying down, And You are intimately acquainted with all my ways.
⁴ Even before there is a word on my tongue [still unspoken], Behold, O LORD, You know it all. [Heb 4:13]
⁵ You have enclosed me behind and before, And [You have] placed Your hand upon me.
⁶ Such [infinite] knowledge is too wonderful for me; It is too high [above me], I cannot reach it.

⁷ Where can I go from Your Spirit? Or where can I flee from Your presence?
⁸ If I ascend to heaven, You are there; If I make my bed in Sheol (the nether world, the place of the dead), behold, You are there. [Rom 11:33]
⁹ If I take the wings of the dawn, If I dwell in the remotest part of the sea,
¹⁰ Even there Your hand will lead me, And Your right hand will take hold of me.
¹¹ If I say, "Surely the darkness will cover me, And the night will be the only light around me,"
¹² Even the darkness is not dark to You *and* conceals nothing from You, But the night shines as bright as the day;

Darkness and light are alike
  to You. [Dan 2:22]

¹³ For You formed my innermost
  parts;
You knit me [together] in my
  mother's womb.
¹⁴ I will give thanks *and* praise
  to You, for I am fearfully
  and wonderfully made;
Wonderful are Your works,
And my soul knows it very
  well.

¹⁵ My frame was not hidden
  from You,
When I was being formed in
  secret,
And intricately *and* skillfully
  formed [as if embroidered
  with many colors] in the
  depths of the earth.
¹⁶ Your eyes have seen my
  unformed substance;
And in Your book were all
  written

God's good plan

God's plan for our lives has been established in the spiritual realm since before the foundation of the earth, and it is a good plan, as we see in Jeremiah 29:11: "'For I know the plans and thoughts that I have for you,' says the LORD, 'plans for peace and well-being and not for disaster to give you a future and a hope.'"

Psalm 139:16 tells us that before we were even born, God had planned our days. However, Satan has worked hard to destroy the Lord's good plan in many of us, and he has had a high success rate.

God sent His Son, Jesus, to redeem us and to restore all things to proper order. He has written down His will for our lives, and as we believe it and confess it, it literally begins to become reality.

Some people believe for a great number of things but see very little manifestation of them. Perhaps the reason is because they are believing but not speaking. They may see some results of their faith, but not the radical results they would experience if they would bring their mouths along with their hearts into God's service (see Romans 10:9, 10).

Some people are trying to live in the blessings of the Lord while still speaking in ungodly ways. We need to avoid making that mistake. We will not see positive results in our daily lives if we speak negative things. We should remember that what we are speaking, we are calling for. We are reaching into the spiritual realm and drawing out *something* according to our words. We can reach into Satan's realm, the realm of curses, and draw out evil, negative things, or we can reach into God's realm, the realm of blessings, and draw out good, positive things. Words are like containers; they carry creative or destructive power.

The choice is up to us.

The days that were appointed
for me,
When as yet there was not one
of them [even taking shape].

17 How precious also are Your
thoughts to me, O God!
How vast is the sum of them!
[Ps 40:5]
18 If I could count them, they
would outnumber the sand.
When I awake, I am still with
You.

19 O that You would kill the
wicked, O God;
Go away from me, therefore,
men of bloodshed. [Is 11:4]
20 For they speak against You
wickedly,
Your enemies take *Your name*
in vain. [Jude 15]
21 Do I not hate those who hate
You, O LORD?
And do I not loathe those who
rise up against You?
22 I hate them with perfect *and*
utmost hatred;
They have become my enemies.

23 Search me [thoroughly],
O God, and know my heart;
Test me and know my
anxious thoughts;
24 And see if there is any wicked
or hurtful way in me,
And lead me in the everlasting
way.

PSALM 140

Prayer for Protection
against the Wicked.

To the Chief Musician.
A Psalm of David.

1 RESCUE ME, O LORD, from
evil men;

Protect me from violent men.
2 They devise evil things in
their hearts;
They continually [gather
together and] stir up wars.
3 They sharpen their tongues
like a serpent's;
Poison of a viper is under
their lips. [Rom 3:13] *Selah.*

4 Keep me, O LORD, from the
hands of the wicked;
Protect me from violent men
Who intend to trip up my
steps.
5 The proud have hidden a trap
for me, and cords;
They have spread a net by the
wayside;
They have set traps for me.
Selah.

6 I said to the LORD, "You are my
God;
Listen to the voice of my
supplications, O LORD.
7 "O GOD the Lord, the strength
of my salvation,
You have covered my head in
the day of battle.
8 "Do not grant, O LORD, the
desires of the wicked;
Do not further their evil
device, that they not be
exalted. *Selah.*

9 "Those who surround me
raise their heads;
May the mischief of their own
lips come upon them.
10 "Let burning coals fall upon
them;
Let them be thrown into the
fire,
Into deep [water] pits from
which they cannot rise.

11 "Do not let a slanderer be
established in the earth;
Let evil quickly hunt the
violent man [to overthrow
him and stop his evil acts]."

12 I know [with confidence] that
the LORD will maintain the
cause of the afflicted,
And [will secure] justice for
the poor.
13 Surely the righteous will give
thanks to Your name;
The upright will dwell in Your
presence.

PSALM 141

An Evening Prayer
for Sanctification and
Protection.

A Psalm of David.

1 LORD, I call upon You; hurry
to me.
Listen to my voice when I call
to You.
2 Let my prayer be counted as
incense before You;
The lifting up of my hands as
the evening offering. [1 Tim
2:8; Rev 8:3, 4]
3 Set a guard, O LORD, over my
mouth;
Keep watch over the door of
my lips [to keep me from
speaking thoughtlessly].
4 Do not incline my heart to
[consent to or tolerate] any
evil thing,
Or to practice deeds of
wickedness
With men who plan *and* do evil;
And let me not eat of their
delicacies (be tempted by
their gain).

5 Let the righteous
[thoughtfully] strike
(correct) me—it is a
kindness [done to
encourage my spiritual
maturity].
It is [the choicest anointing]
oil on the head;
Let my head not refuse [to
accept and acknowledge
and learn from] it;
For still my prayer is against
their wicked deeds. [Prov
9:8; 19:25; 25:12; Gal 6:1]
6 Their [wicked, godless] judges
are thrown down the sides
of the rocky cliff,
And they [who followed them]
will hear my words, for they
are pleasant (just).
7 As when the one plows and
breaks open the ground
[and the soil scatters behind
him],
Our bones have been scattered
at the mouth of Sheol [by
the injustices of the wicked].
[2 Cor 1:9]

8 For my eyes are toward You,
O GOD, the Lord;

putting the Word to work

Have you ever heard the saying
"Sticks and stones will break my
bones, but words will never hurt
me"? We all know that is not true;
in fact, words can deeply wound
us. Heed the advice of Psalm 141:3
and ask God to set a guard over
your mouth, that your words will be
encouraging and full of blessing.

In You I take refuge; do not pour out my life *nor* leave me defenseless.

[9] Keep me from the jaws of the trap which they have set for me,

when your mouth gets you in trouble

I pray Psalm 141:3 often because I know that I need help with my mouth on a daily basis. I want the Holy Spirit to convict me when I am talking too much, when I am saying things I should not say, when I am speaking negatively, when I am complaining, or when I am sounding harsh or engaging in any of the other kinds of "evil speaking."

Anything that offends God in our conversation needs to be eliminated. That is why we need to pray continually: "Set a guard, O LORD, over my mouth; keep watch over the door of my lips [to keep me from speaking thoughtlessly]."

Another scripture on the importance of watching what we say is Psalm 17:3: "I intend that my mouth will not transgress." This says we need to plan to keep our mouths from speaking bad or negative things. We *purpose* not to speak them. Whatever we do in this life of faith, we must do it on purpose. Discipline is a choice. It is not necessarily easy, but it begins with a quality decision. During difficult times when the storm is raging, we will need to purpose to keep our mouths from transgressing.

A third scripture that I pray regularly on this subject is Psalm 19:14: "Let the words of my mouth and the meditation of my heart be acceptable and pleasing in Your sight, O LORD, my [firm, immovable] rock and my Redeemer."

Are you having difficulty with your mouth? Pray the Word. It is God's Word that carries the power of the Holy Spirit. Let the scriptures be the cry of your heart. Be sincere in your desire to gain victory in this area, and as you seek God for His help, you will begin to notice that you are changing. This is what the Lord has done for me, and He can do it for you too; He is not One to show partiality to anyone (see Acts 10:34). All those who follow God-ordained guidelines get God-ordained results.

Pray this prayer of commitment to exercise control over your mouth: "Lord, I pray that You will help me to develop sensitivity to the Holy Spirit concerning everything about my conversation. I do not want to be stubborn like a horse or mule that will not obey without a bridle and bit. I want to move in Your direction with only a gentle nudge from You. Place a guard over my lips and let all the words of my mouth be acceptable in Your sight, O Lord, my Strength and my Redeemer. In Jesus' name I pray. Amen."

And from the snares of those
who do evil.
¹⁰ Let the wicked fall into their
own nets,
While I pass by *and* safely
escape [from danger].

PSALM 142

Prayer for Help in Trouble.

A skillful song, *or* a didactic
or reflective poem, of David;
when he was in the cave.
A Prayer.

¹ I CRY aloud with my voice to
the LORD;
I make supplication with my
voice to the LORD.
² I pour out my complaint
before Him;
I declare my trouble before
Him.
³ When my spirit was
overwhelmed *and* weak
within me [wrapped in
darkness],
You knew my path.
In the way where I walk
They have hidden a trap
for me.
⁴ Look to the right [the point of
attack] and see;
For there is no one who has
regard for me [to act in my
favor].
Escape has failed me *and* I
have nowhere to run;
No one cares about my life.

⁵ I cried out to You, O LORD;
I said, "You are my refuge,
My portion in the land of the
living.
⁶ "Give attention to my cry,
For I am brought very low;
Rescue me from my
persecutors,
For they are stronger than I.
⁷ "Bring my soul out of prison
(adversity),
So that I may give thanks *and*
praise Your name;
The righteous will surround
me [in triumph],
For You will look after me."

PSALM 143

Prayer for Help and Guidance.

A Psalm of David.

¹ HEAR MY prayer, O LORD,
Listen to my supplications!
Answer me in Your
faithfulness, and in Your
righteousness.
² And do not enter into
judgment with Your
servant,
For in Your sight no man
living is righteous *or*
justified. [Ps 130:3; Rom
3:20–26; Gal 2:16]
³ For the enemy has persecuted
me,
He has crushed my life down
to the ground;

speak the Word

*Thank You, God, for bringing my soul out of adversity so that
I may give thanks and praise Your name.*
—ADAPTED FROM PSALM 142:7

He has made me dwell in dark places, like those who have been long dead.
4 Therefore my spirit is overwhelmed *and* weak within me [wrapped in darkness];
My heart grows numb within me.

5 I remember the days of old;
I meditate on all that You have done;

I ponder the work of Your hands.
6 I reach out my hands to You;
My throat *thirsts* for You, as a parched land [thirsts for water].   *Selah.*

7 Answer me quickly, O LORD, my spirit fails;

life point

David's response to his feelings of depression and gloom was not to meditate on his problem. Instead, he literally came against the problem by *choosing* to remember the good times of past days—pondering the doings of God and the works of His hands (see Psalm 143:5). In other words, he thought about something good, and it helped him overcome his battle of depression.

Never forget this: *your mind plays an important role in your victory.*

I know it is the power of the Holy Spirit working through the Word of God that brings victory into our lives. But a large part of the work that needs to be done is for us to line up our thinking with God and His Word. If we refuse to do this or choose to think it is unimportant, we will never experience victory. But we will win if we discipline ourselves to meditate on the good things God has done.

life point

What is David doing in Psalm 143:5–8? He is crying out to God for help. When you and I feel ourselves sinking into the pit of depression, we can do what David did here. We can remember the days of old. We can meditate on all of the Lord's doings on our behalf. We can ponder the mighty works of His hands. We can spread forth our hands in prayer and supplication to Him. We can call upon Him to answer us speedily because we are leaning on and trusting in Him. We can lift up our souls, our inner beings, to Him.

All these things constitute an act of faith, and the Lord has promised to always respond to faith. If we are under a minor attack, it may take only a few hours or days. But if we are under a major attack, it may take much longer. However long it may be, we must stand firm and continue to cry out to God, receiving the help and encouragement that only He can give. We need to be confident that the Lord will deliver us, just as He delivered David from all his woes.

a biblical prescription for depression

Psalm 143:3–10 gives a description of depression and how to overcome it. Let's look at this passage in detail to see the steps we can take to defeat this attack of the enemy:

Psalm 143:3: *Identify the nature and cause of the problem.* The psalmist says he feels that he is dwelling in "dark places, like those who have been long dead." This certainly sounds to me like a description of someone who is depressed. I believe that the source of the depression described here is our enemy, Satan, who attacks the soul.

Psalm 143:4: *Recognize that depression steals life and light.* Depression oppresses a person's spiritual freedom and power. Our spirits (empowered and encouraged by God's Spirit) are powerful and free. Therefore, Satan seeks to oppress our spirits' power and liberty by filling our minds with darkness and gloom. Please realize that it is vital to resist the feeling called "depression" immediately when we begin to sense it. The longer it is allowed to remain, the harder it becomes to resist.

Psalm 143:5: *Remember the good times.* In this verse we see the psalmist's response to his condition. Remembering, meditating, and pondering are all functions of the mind. He obviously knows that his thoughts will affect his feelings, so he gets busy thinking about the kinds of things that will help overcome the attack upon his mind. He thinks about God and the good things He does.

Psalm 143:6: *Praise the Lord in the midst of the problem.* The psalmist knows the importance of praise; he lifts his hands in worship. He declares what his needs truly are: he needs God. Far too often when people get depressed, it is because they are in need of something, and they seek it in the wrong place, which only adds to their problems. God alone can water a thirsty soul. Do not be deceived into thinking that anything else can satisfy you fully and completely. Chasing after the wrong thing will always leave you disappointed, and disappointment opens the door to depression.

Psalm 143:7: *Ask for God's help.* The psalmist asks for help. He is basically saying, "Hurry up, God, because I am not going to be able to hold on very much longer without You."

Psalm 143:8: *Listen to the Lord.* The psalmist knows that he needs to hear from God. He needs to be assured of God's love and kindness. He needs God's attention and direction.

Psalm 143:9: *Pray for deliverance.* Once again the psalmist declares that only God can help him. Please notice that throughout this discourse, he keeps his mind on God and not on the problem.

Psalm 143:10: *Seek God's wisdom, knowledge, and leadership.* Perhaps the psalmist is indicating that he has gotten out of God's will and thus opened the door to the attack on his soul. He wants to be in God's will because he realizes that it is the only safe place to be. Then he asks God to help him be stable. He wants his unsettled emotions to be level—not up and down.

I encourage you to meditate on God's Word and apply its principles to your life. Let it bring you freedom and peace.

life point

In the final verses of Psalm 143, David calls upon the Lord to deliver him from his enemies because he has run to Him for help and protection. He asks the Lord to teach him His will and to let His Spirit lead him "on level ground" (verse 10).

I believe that what David was asking for when he spoke of "level ground" was balanced emotions. Secure in who he was and in Whose he was, David was able to place himself into the hands of the Lord. David allowed God to bring his life out of trouble, free him from distress, punish his enemies, and cause him to win the victory over all those who were afflicting his soul, because he belonged to the Lord.

You and I are to place ourselves in God's hands. We need to withstand the devil's attempts to drag us down into the depths of depression and despair by allowing God to move on our behalf to win our victory.

Do not hide Your face from me,
Or I will become like those
who go down into the pit
(grave).

⁸Let me hear Your
lovingkindness in the
morning,
For I trust in You.
Teach me the way in which I
should walk,
For I lift up my soul to You.
⁹Rescue me, O LORD, from my
enemies;
I take refuge in You.

¹⁰Teach me to do Your will [so
that I may please You],
For You are my God;
Let Your good Spirit lead me
on level ground.
¹¹Save my life, O LORD, for Your
name's sake;
In Your righteousness bring
my life out of trouble.
¹²In your lovingkindness, silence
and destroy my enemies
And destroy all those who
afflict my life,
For I am Your servant.

PSALM 144

Prayer for Rescue and Prosperity.

A Psalm of David.

¹BLESSED BE the LORD, my
Rock *and* my great strength,
Who trains my hands for war
And my fingers for battle;

2 My [steadfast] lovingkindness and my fortress,
My high tower and my rescuer,
My shield and He in whom I take refuge,
Who subdues my people under me.
3 LORD, what is man that You take notice of him?
Or the son of man that You think of him? [Job 7:17; Ps 8:4; Heb 2:6]
4 Man is like a mere breath;
His days are like a shadow that passes away.

5 Bow Your heavens, O LORD, and come down;
Touch the mountains, and they will smoke.
6 Flash lightning and scatter my enemies;
Send out Your arrows and confuse *and* embarrass *and* frustrate them.
7 Stretch out Your hand from above;
Set me free and rescue me from great waters,
Out of the hands of [hostile] foreigners [who surround us]
8 Whose mouths speak deceit [without restraint],
And whose right hand is a right hand of falsehood.

9 I will sing a new song to You, O God;
Upon a harp of ten strings I will sing praises to You,
10 Who gives salvation to kings,
Who sets David His servant free from the evil sword.

11 Set me free and rescue me from the hand of [hostile] foreigners,
Whose mouth speaks deceit [without restraint],

life point

In the opening verses of Psalm 144, David praises the Lord with strong, compelling words—"my Rock and my great strength," "my [steadfast] loving-kindness and my fortress," "my high tower and my rescuer," and more (Psalm 144:1, 2). The Lord subdued his enemies under him, but David also did his part. We must always remember that we are partners with God. God has a part, and we have a part. We cannot do God's part, and He will not do our part. In verse 1, David said the Lord taught his hands to war and his fingers to fight. This is the key to conquering depression. We must do what David did. We must recognize depression, submit it to the Lord, call upon Him for His help, and then fight that depression in the strength and power of the Holy Spirit.

How do we fight depression? By spending time with God, by praying and by speaking His Word. We also fight by lifting our eyes, heads, hands, and hearts and offering the sacrifice of praise and thanksgiving to the Lord, our Rock and our Strength, our High Tower and our Rescuer, our Shield and the One in Whom we take refuge, the One Who subdues our enemies under us.

And whose right hand is a
   right hand of falsehood.
¹²Let our sons in their youth be
   like plants full grown,
   And our daughters like corner
   pillars fashioned for a
   palace;
¹³Let our barns be full,
   supplying every kind of
   produce,
   And our flocks bring
   forth thousands and ten
   thousands in our fields;
¹⁴Let our cattle bear
   Without mishap and without
   loss,
   And let there be no outcry in
   our streets!
¹⁵How blessed *and* favored
   are the people in such
   circumstance;
   How blessed [fortunate,
   prosperous, and favored]
   are the people whose God is
   the LORD!

PSALM 145

The LORD Extolled for His
Goodness.

A Psalm of praise. Of David.

¹I WILL exalt You, my God,
   O King,
   And [with gratitude and
   submissive wonder] I will
   bless Your name forever
   and ever.
²Every day I will bless You *and*
   lovingly praise You;
   Yes, [with awe-inspired
   reverence] I will praise
   Your name forever and ever.
³Great is the LORD, and highly
   to be praised,

And His greatness is [so
   vast and profound as
   to be] unsearchable
   [incomprehensible to man].
   [Job 5:9; 9:10; Rom 11:33]
⁴One generation shall praise
   Your works to another,
   And shall declare Your
   mighty *and* remarkable acts.
⁵On the glorious splendor of
   Your majesty
   And on Your wonderful
   works, I will meditate.
⁶People will speak of the power
   of Your awesome acts,
   And [with gratitude and
   submissive wonder] I will
   tell of Your greatness.
⁷They will overflow [like a
   fountain] when they speak
   of Your great *and* abundant
   goodness
   And will sing joyfully of Your
   righteousness.

⁸The LORD is gracious and full
   of compassion,
   Slow to anger and abounding
   in lovingkindness.
⁹The LORD is good to all,
   And His tender mercies are
   over all His works [the
   entirety of things created].
¹⁰All Your works shall give
   thanks to You *and* praise
   You, O LORD,
   And Your godly ones will
   bless You.
¹¹They shall speak of the glory
   of Your kingdom
   And talk of Your power,
¹²To make known to the sons of
   men Your mighty acts
   And the glorious majesty of
   Your kingdom.

13 Your kingdom is an
everlasting kingdom,
And Your dominion *endures*
throughout all generations.
[Dan 7:14, 27]

14 The LORD upholds all those [of
His own] who fall
And raises up all those who
are bowed down.
15 The eyes of all look to You [in
hopeful expectation],
And You give them their food
in due time.
16 You open Your hand
And satisfy the desire of
every living thing.

17 The LORD is [unwaveringly]
righteous in all His ways
And gracious *and* kind in all
His works.
18 The LORD is near to all who
call on Him,
To all who call on Him in
truth (without guile).
19 He will fulfill the desire of
those who fear *and* worship
Him [with awe-inspired
reverence and obedience];
He also will hear their cry
and will save them.
20 The LORD keeps all who love
Him,
But all the wicked He will
destroy.
21 My mouth will speak the
praise of the LORD,

And all flesh will bless *and*
gratefully praise His holy
name forever and ever.

PSALM 146

The LORD an Abundant Helper.

1 PRAISE THE LORD!
(Hallelujah!)
Praise the LORD, O my soul!
2 While I live I will praise the
LORD;
I will sing praises to my God
as long as I live.
3 Do not trust in princes,
In mortal man, in whom there
is no salvation (help).
4 When his spirit leaves him,
he returns to the earth;
In that very day his thoughts
and plans perish. [1 Cor 2:6]
5 How blessed *and* graciously
favored is he whose help is
the God of Jacob (Israel),
Whose hope is in the LORD his
God, [Gen 32:30]
6 Who made heaven and earth,
The sea, and all that is in
them,
Who keeps truth *and* is
faithful forever, [Gen 1:3]
7 Who executes justice for the
oppressed,
Who gives food to the hungry.
The LORD sets free the
prisoners.

speak the Word

*God, I am blessed and graciously favored because
my help and my hope are in You!*
–ADAPTED FROM PSALM 146:5

⁸The LORD opens *the eyes of* the
  blind;
  The LORD lifts up those who
  are bowed down;
  The LORD loves the righteous
  [the upright in heart]. [Luke
  13:13; John 9:7, 32]
⁹The LORD protects the
  strangers;
  He supports the fatherless and
  the widow;
  But He makes crooked the
  way of the wicked.
¹⁰The LORD shall reign forever,
  Your God, O Zion, to all
  generations.
  Praise the LORD! (Hallelujah!)
  [Ps 10:16; Rev 11:15]

PSALM 147

Praise for Jerusalem's
Restoration and Prosperity.

¹PRAISE THE LORD!
  For it is good to sing praises to
  our [gracious and majestic]
  God;
  Praise is becoming *and*
  appropriate.
²The LORD is building up
  Jerusalem;
  He is gathering [together] the
  exiles of Israel.
³He heals the brokenhearted
  And binds up their wounds
  [healing their pain and
  comforting their sorrow]. [Ps
  34:18; Is 57:15; 61:1; Luke 4:18]
⁴He counts the number of the
  stars;
  He calls them all by their
  names.
⁵Great is our [majestic and
  mighty] Lord and abundant
  in strength;

His understanding is
  inexhaustible [infinite,
  boundless].
⁶The LORD lifts up the humble;
  He casts the wicked down to
  the ground.

⁷Sing to the LORD with
  thanksgiving;
  Sing praises to our God with
  the lyre,
⁸Who covers the heavens with
  clouds,
  Who provides rain for the
  earth,
  Who makes grass grow on the
  mountains.
⁹He gives to the beast its food,
  And to the young ravens that
  for which they cry.
¹⁰He does not delight in the
  strength (military power) of
  the horse,
  Nor does He take pleasure in
  the legs (strength) of a man.
¹¹The LORD favors those who
  fear *and* worship Him [with
  awe-inspired reverence and
  obedience],
  Those who wait for His mercy
  and lovingkindness. [Ps
  145:20]

¹²Praise the LORD, O Jerusalem!
  Praise your God, O Zion!
¹³For He has strengthened the
  bars of your gates,
  He has blessed your children
  within you.
¹⁴He makes peace in your
  borders;
  He satisfies you with the
  finest of the wheat.
¹⁵He sends His command to the
  earth;
  His word runs very swiftly.

¹⁶He gives [to the earth] snow
like [a blanket of] wool;
He scatters the frost like
ashes.
¹⁷He casts out His ice like
fragments;
Who can stand before His cold?
¹⁸He sends out His word and
melts the ice;
He causes His wind to blow
and the waters to flow.
¹⁹He declares His word to Jacob,
His statutes and His
ordinances to Israel. [Mal 4:4]
²⁰He has not dealt this way with
any [other] nation;
They have not known
[understood, appreciated,
heeded, or cherished] His
ordinances.
Praise the LORD! (Hallelujah!)
[Ps 79:6; Jer 10:25]

PSALM 148

The Whole Creation Invoked
to Praise the LORD.

¹PRAISE THE LORD!
Praise the LORD from the
heavens;
Praise Him in the heights!
²Praise Him, all His angels;
Praise Him, all His hosts
(armies)!
³Praise Him, sun and moon:
Praise Him, all stars of light!
⁴Praise Him, highest heavens,
And the waters above the
heavens!
⁵Let them praise the name of
the LORD,
For He commanded and they
were created.
⁶He has also established them
forever and ever;

He has made a decree which
shall not pass away.
⁷Praise the LORD from the earth,
Sea monsters and all deeps;
⁸Lightning and hail, snow and
fog;
Stormy wind, fulfilling His
orders;
⁹Mountains and all hills;
Fruitful trees and all cedars;
¹⁰Beasts and all cattle;
Creeping things and winged
birds;
¹¹Kings of the earth and all
people;
Princes and all judges of the
earth;
¹²Both young men and virgins;
Old men and children.
¹³Let them praise the name of
the LORD,
For His name alone is exalted
and supreme;
His glory *and* majesty are
above earth and heaven.
¹⁴He has lifted up a horn for
His people [giving them
strength, prosperity,
dignity, and preeminence],
Praise for all His godly ones;
For the people of Israel, a
people near to Him.
Praise the LORD! (Hallelujah!)
[Ps 75:10; Eph 2:17]

PSALM 149

Israel Invoked to Praise
the LORD.

¹PRAISE THE LORD!
Sing to the LORD a new song,
And praise Him in the
congregation of His godly
ones (believers).

putting the Word to work

If you have ever been to a professional sporting event, you have seen and experienced exuberant enthusiasm of the fans. Do you praise God with that kind of intensity? While at times you may praise Him in the quietness of your heart, the psalmist tells us that we are also to praise God with instruments, with dancing, or with shouts of joy! He is worthy of your exuberant praise.

² Let Israel rejoice in their
   Maker;
   Let Zion's children rejoice in
   their King. [Zech 9:9; Matt
   21:5]
³ Let them praise His name
   with dancing;
   Let them sing praises to Him
   with the tambourine and
   lyre.
⁴ For the LORD takes pleasure in
   His people;
   He will beautify the humble
   with salvation.
⁵ Let the godly ones exult in
   glory;
   Let them sing for joy on their
   beds.
⁶ Let the high praises of God be
   in their throats,
   And a two-edged sword in
   their hands, [Heb 4:12; Rev
   1:16]
⁷ To execute vengeance on the
   nations

And punishment on the
   peoples,
⁸ To bind their kings with
   chains
   And their nobles with fetters
   of iron,
⁹ To execute on them the
   judgment written.
   This is the honor for all His
   godly ones.
   Praise the LORD! (Hallelujah!)

PSALM 150

A Psalm of Praise.

¹ PRAISE THE LORD!
   Praise God in His sanctuary;
   Praise Him in His mighty
   heavens.
² Praise Him for His mighty
   acts;
   Praise Him according to
   [the abundance of] His
   greatness. [Deut 3:24; Ps
   145:5, 6]

³ Praise Him with trumpet
   sound;
   Praise Him with harp and
   lyre.
⁴ Praise Him with tambourine
   and dancing;
   Praise Him with stringed
   instruments and flute.
⁵ Praise Him with resounding
   cymbals;
   Praise Him with loud
   cymbals.
⁶ Let everything that has
   breath *and* every breath of
   life praise the LORD!
   Praise the LORD! (Hallelujah!)

Proverbs

Author:
Solomon, with smaller portions by others

Date:
About 950 BC, with portions about 720 BC

Everyday Life Principles:
Whatever you do, seek wisdom.

Walking in wisdom means making decisions today that you will be happy with tomorrow.

Look to Proverbs to find godly, practical advice about many practical matters you face in your everyday life.

Proverbs was written by Solomon, who has been called the wisest man who ever lived, and is a book filled with wisdom and godly common sense about the practical matters of life. One of the most beneficial qualities we can seek in life is wisdom, which I like to define as "decisions you make now that you will be happy with later."

In the pages of Proverbs, you will find sound guidance and advice on a multitude of situations you face on a regular basis, including how to treat people, how to think, how to control your mouth, how to manage finances, how husbands and wives should behave, how to raise children, how children should relate to their parents, how to keep from being foolish and handle those who are, how to be a good friend, how to deal with employees, how to plan for the future, how to deal with offenses, and how to receive correction. It also teaches us that our words are carriers of either life or death, that a happy heart does us good like a medicine, and that the fear of the Lord is the beginning of wisdom.

Because Proverbs has 31 chapters, many people read one chapter of Proverbs per day, each month of the year. Whether you read a chapter per day or the entire book at once, I encourage you to read Proverbs often and let its wisdom saturate your heart and direct your life.

I encourage you to read the Psalms and read them often. Let them remind you to always tell God what is in your heart and receive comfort, strength, and direction from Him. Let them also remind you to praise and worship God with all your heart.

1 THE PROVERBS (truths obscurely expressed, maxims) of Solomon son of David, king of Israel:

2 To know [skillful and godly] wisdom and instruction;
To discern *and* comprehend the words of understanding *and* insight,
3 To receive instruction in wise behavior *and* the discipline of wise thoughtfulness,
Righteousness, justice, and integrity;
4 That prudence (good judgment, astute common sense) may be given to the naive *or* inexperienced [who are easily misled],
And knowledge and discretion (intelligent discernment) to the youth,
5 The wise will hear and increase their learning,
And the person of understanding will acquire wise counsel *and* the skill [to steer his course wisely and lead others to the truth], [Prov 9:9]
6 To understand a proverb and a figure [of speech] *or* an enigma with its interpretation,
And the words of the wise and their riddles [that require reflection].

7 The [reverent] fear of the Lord [that is, worshiping Him and regarding Him as truly awesome] is the beginning *and* the preeminent part of knowledge [its starting point and its essence];
But arrogant fools despise [skillful and godly] wisdom and instruction *and* self-discipline. [Ps 111:10]

8 My son, hear the instruction of your father,
And do not reject the teaching of your mother.
9 For they are a garland of grace on your head,
And chains *and* ornaments [of gold] around your neck.
10 My son, if sinners entice you,
Do not consent. [Ps 1:1; Eph 5:11]
11 If they say, "Come with us;
Let us lie in wait to *shed* blood,
Let us ambush the innocent without cause;

life point

Proverbs 1:1–4 says that wisdom involves prudence. *Prudence* means "good management." Prudent people do not operate in extremes. They are balanced and conduct themselves wisely. I encourage you to be prudent in every situation!

speak the Word

God, I pray that You will help me to be wise.
Help me to hear and increase in learning, to acquire wise counsel
and the skill to steer my course wisely and lead others to truth.
–ADAPTED FROM PROVERBS 1:5

¹²Let us swallow them alive like
  Sheol (the place of the dead),
Even whole, as those who go
  down to the pit [of death];
¹³We will find *and* take
  all kinds of precious
  possessions,
We will fill our houses with
  spoil;
¹⁴Throw in your lot with us
  [they insist];
We will all have one money
  bag [in common],"
¹⁵My son, do not walk on the
  road with them;
Keep your foot [far] away
  from their path,
¹⁶For their feet run to evil,
And they hurry to shed blood.
¹⁷Indeed, it is useless to spread
  the *baited* net
In the sight of any bird;
¹⁸But [when these people set a
  trap for others] they lie in
  wait for their own blood;
They set an ambush for their
  own lives [and rush to their
  destruction].
¹⁹So are the ways of everyone
  who is greedy for gain;
Greed takes away the lives of
  its possessors. [Prov 15:27;
  1 Tim 6:10]

²⁰Wisdom shouts in the street,
She raises her voice in the
  markets;
²¹She calls out at the head of
  the noisy streets [where
  large crowds gather];
At the entrance of the city
  gates she speaks her words:
²²"How long, O naive ones [you
  who are easily misled],
  will you love being simple-
  minded *and* undiscerning?

How long will scoffers [who
  ridicule and deride] delight
  in scoffing,
How long will fools [who
  obstinately mock truth] hate
  knowledge?
²³"If you will turn *and* pay
  attention to my rebuke,
Behold, I [Wisdom] will pour
  out my spirit on you;
I will make my words known
  to you. [Is 11:2; Eph 1:17–20]
²⁴"Because I called and you
  refused [to answer],
I stretched out my hand and
  no one has paid attention
  [to my offer]; [Is 65:11, 12;
  66:4; Jer 7:13, 14; Zech 7:11–
  13]
²⁵And you treated all my
  counsel as nothing

life point

Proverbs 1:23 says that wisdom will
make its words known to us if we
listen to it and pay attention to its
rebuke. If we follow wisdom, God
will open up wisdom to us, and
we will have more revelation and
understanding than we could ever
imagine.

All we need to do is be obedient to
what God has told us to do. He will
reveal to us treasures hidden in His
Word. We have not even scratched
the surface of the revelation that is
in the Word of God. If we obey Him,
He will make His will clearly known
to us. He will speak living words (His
rhema) to us, His personal words for
our lives.

understanding people

Proverbs 2:1–5 teaches us about the necessity and rewards of understanding. We need to seek understanding—of God's Word and will, of ourselves, and of other people.

I would like to focus for a moment on the importance of really understanding others. In order to minister to them we must have an understanding heart, and how can we do that if we have little understanding of their hurts and struggles?

One way to understand what people are going through is by going through it ourselves. We do not have to experience exactly the same circumstances, but I do not think anyone can understand a hurting person without having been hurt or having gone through a similar situation.

It is amazing how caring and compassionate we are when we have endured a few problems of our own, and how flippant and judgmental we can be if we have not had the same problem ourselves. How easily our answers can be: "Well, now, sister, you just need to believe God." How different it is when we have been hurting for months ourselves, and somebody comes to us with a problem. We throw our arms around that person and say, "Oh, I understand how you feel."

We all want understanding. It is one of the things for which we cry out to God when we are going through rough times. We just want to be understood. Jesus understands, as we see in Hebrews 4:15: "For we do not have a High Priest who is unable to sympathize and understand our weaknesses and temptations, but One who has been tempted [knowing exactly how it feels to be human] in every respect as we are, yet without [committing any] sin." Jesus can help us because He knows what we are going through. We can open up to Him without fear of judgment and rejection because He understands.

I am not sure that Jesus ever prayed for anybody until compassion was flowing in His heart. I recall an instance in the Bible in which a man came to Him asking for healing for his son, who was possessed by a demon that caused him terrible suffering. Jesus asked the man, "How long has this been happening to him?" (Mark 9:21). The answer did not affect whether or not Jesus would heal him. I believe Jesus asked the question because He wanted to have even more compassion than He already had for that father and for the boy.

We need to be concerned enough about people to ask them questions about their situations—"How long has this been happening? Where does it hurt? What gives you comfort?"

When some of us ask a person how they are doing and they say that they are having a rough time, we tend to answer, "Well, praise the Lord anyway!" But when we are hurting or in trouble, that is not how we want others to respond to us. We want them to show us some real heartfelt understanding and compassion.

Be a person who seeks understanding and desires to be compassionate—and you will find yourself acting wisely toward others.

And would not accept my
   reprimand,
26 I also will laugh at your
   disaster;
I will mock when your dread
   and panic come,
27 When your dread *and* panic
   come like a storm,
And your disaster comes like
   a whirlwind,
When anxiety and distress
   come upon you [as
   retribution].
28 "Then they will call upon me
   (Wisdom), but I will not
   answer;
They will seek me eagerly but
   they will not find me, [Job
   27:9; 35:12, 13; Is 1:15, 16; Jer
   11:11; Mic 3:4; James 4:3]
29 Because they hated
   knowledge
And did not choose the fear of
   the LORD [that is, obeying Him
   with reverence and awe-filled
   respect], [Prov 8:13]
30 They would not accept my
   counsel,
And they spurned all my
   rebuke.
31 "Therefore they shall eat
   of the fruit of their own
   [wicked] way
And be satiated with [the
   penalty of] their own devices.

32 "For the turning away of the
   naive will kill them,
And the careless ease of
   [self-righteous] fools will
   destroy them. [Is 32:6]
33 "But whoever listens to me
   (Wisdom) will live securely
   and in confident trust
And will be at ease, without
   fear *or* dread of evil."

2 MY SON, if you will
   receive my words
   And treasure my
   commandments within you,
2 So that your ear is attentive to
   [skillful and godly] wisdom,
And apply your heart to
   understanding [seeking it
   conscientiously and striving
   for it eagerly];
3 Yes, if you cry out for insight,
And lift up your voice for
   understanding;
4 If you seek skillful *and*
   godly wisdom as you would
   silver
And search for her as you
   would hidden treasures;
5 Then you will understand the
   [reverent] fear of the LORD
   [that is, worshiping Him
   and regarding Him as truly
   awesome]

And discover the knowledge of God. [Prov 1:7]

⁶For the Lᴏʀᴅ gives [skillful and godly] wisdom;
From His mouth come knowledge and understanding.

⁷He stores away sound wisdom for the righteous [those who are in right standing with Him];
He is a shield to those who walk in integrity [those of honorable character and moral courage],

⁸He guards the paths of justice;
And He preserves the way of His saints (believers). [1 Sam 2:9; Ps 66:8, 9]

⁹Then you will understand righteousness and justice [in every circumstance]
And integrity and every good path.

¹⁰For [skillful and godly] wisdom will enter your heart
And knowledge will be pleasant to your soul.

¹¹Discretion will watch over you,
Understanding *and* discernment will guard you,

¹²To keep you from the way of evil *and* the evil man,
From the man who speaks perverse things;

¹³From those who leave the paths of uprightness
To walk in the ways of darkness;

¹⁴Who find joy in doing evil
And delight in the perversity of evil,

¹⁵Whose paths are crooked,
And who are devious in their ways;

¹⁶To keep you from the immoral woman;
From the seductress with her flattering words, [Prov 2:11]

¹⁷Who leaves the companion (husband) of her youth,
And forgets the covenant of her God.

¹⁸For her house leads down to death
And her paths lead to the dead;

¹⁹None who go to her return again,
Nor do they regain the paths of life—

²⁰So you will walk in the way of good men [that is, those of personal integrity, moral courage and honorable character],
And keep to the paths of the righteous.

²¹For the upright [those who are in right standing with God] will live in the land
And those [of integrity] who are blameless [in God's sight] will remain in it;

²²But the wicked will be cut off from the land

speak the Word

Thank You, Lord, for giving me skillful and godly wisdom, knowledge, and understanding.
—ᴀᴅᴀᴘᴛᴇᴅ ꜰʀᴏᴍ Pʀᴏᴠᴇʀʙꜱ 2:6

And the treacherous shall be [forcibly] uprooted *and* removed from it.

3 MY SON, do not forget my teaching, But let your heart keep my commandments;

[2] For length of days and years of life [worth living] And tranquility *and* prosperity [the wholeness of life's blessings] they will add to you.

why not ask, *"why?"*

Proverbs 3:5, 6 is basically a passage that encourages us to have faith in God and not in our own thinking or reasoning. People who feel compelled to reason out everything have a hard time with faith because reasoning is not faith, and without faith it is impossible to please God (see Hebrews 11:6).

I can teach on reasoning because I used to be a "class A" chief "reasoner." I was the lady who had to have everything figured out. I had to have a plan. I had to know not only all about my own business but all about other people's business too—even God's. I was continually asking, "Why, God, why? When, God, when?"

In some respects, I had to reason everything out like the religious leaders of Jesus' day. We read about them in Mark 2:6–8: "But some of the scribes were sitting there debating in their hearts [the implication of what He had said], 'Why does this man talk that way? He is blaspheming; who can forgive sins [remove guilt, nullify sin's penalty, and assign righteousness] except God alone?' Immediately Jesus, being fully aware [of their hostility] and knowing in His spirit that they were thinking this, said to them, 'Why are you debating and arguing about these things in your hearts?'"

The Amplified Classic version of verse 6 says that the scribes were "holding a dialogue with themselves." Do you ever hold a dialogue with yourself? Realistically, you probably talk to yourself more than you talk to anybody else. I encourage you to examine what you are saying to yourself. These scribes were not saying those unkind things in Mark 2 aloud, but in their hearts. They were asking questions about Jesus within themselves. Immediately, He became aware of their arguing, debating, and reasoning and called it to their attention.

We need to be aware that trying to reason things out by ourselves is a problem. It is a serious matter that we need to deal with, just as Jesus dealt with it in the hearts of those who followed Him. Ask God to help you stop reasoning and begin to live by faith, trusting in and relying on Him, not on your own understanding.

³Do not let mercy *and* kindness and truth leave you [instead let these qualities define you];

Bind them [securely] around your neck,

Write them on the tablet of your heart. [Col 3:9–12]

⁴So find favor and high esteem In the sight of God and man. [Luke 2:52]

⁵Trust in *and* rely confidently on the LORD with all your heart

And do not rely on your own insight *or* understanding.

⁶In all your ways know *and* acknowledge *and* recognize Him,

And He will make your paths straight *and* smooth [removing obstacles that block your way].

⁷Do not be wise in your own eyes;

Fear the LORD [with reverent awe and obedience] and turn [entirely] away from evil. [Prov 8:13]

⁸It will be health to your body [your marrow, your nerves, your sinews, your muscles— all your inner parts]

life point

I believe what God meant when He said, "Do not be wise in your own eyes" (Proverbs 3:7), was "Do not even think that you can run your life and do a good job without My help and direction!" We need His help, wisdom, and guidance in every situation.

And refreshment (physical well-being) to your bones.

⁹Honor the LORD with your wealth

And with the first fruits of all your crops (income); [Deut 26:2; Mal 3:10; Luke 14:13, 14]

¹⁰Then your barns will be abundantly filled

And your vats will overflow with new wine. [Deut 28:8]

¹¹My son, do not reject *or* take lightly the discipline of the LORD [learn from your mistakes and the testing that comes from His correction through discipline];

Nor despise His rebuke, [Ps 94:12; Heb 12:5, 6; Rev 3:19]

¹²For those whom the LORD loves He corrects,

Even as a father *corrects* the son in whom he delights.

¹³Happy [blessed, considered fortunate, to be admired] is the man who finds [skillful and godly] wisdom,

And the man who gains understanding *and* insight [learning from God's word and life's experiences],

¹⁴For wisdom's profit is better than the profit of silver,

And her gain is better than fine gold.

¹⁵She is more precious than rubies;

And nothing you can wish for compares with her [in value]. [Job 28:12–18]

¹⁶Long life is in her right hand;

In her left hand are riches
and honor. [Prov 8:12–21;
1 Tim 4:8]
¹⁷ Her ways are highways of
pleasantness *and* favor,
And all her paths are peace.
¹⁸ She is a tree of life to those
who take hold of her,
And happy [blessed,
considered fortunate, to be
admired] is everyone who
holds her tightly.
¹⁹ The LORD by His wisdom has
founded the earth;
By His understanding He has
established the heavens.
[Col 1:16]
²⁰ By His knowledge the deeps
were broken up
And the clouds drip with
dew.
²¹ My son, let them not escape
from your sight,
But keep sound wisdom and
discretion,
²² And they will be life to your
soul (your inner self)

And a gracious adornment to
your neck (your outer self).
²³ Then you will walk on your
way [of life] securely
And your foot will not stumble.
[Ps 91:11, 12; Prov 10:9]
²⁴ When you lie down, you will
not be afraid;
When you lie down, your
sleep will be sweet.
²⁵ Do not be afraid of sudden
fear
Nor of the storm of the wicked
when it comes [since you
will be blameless];
²⁶ For the LORD will be your
confidence, firm *and* strong,
And will keep your foot from
being caught [in a trap].

²⁷ Do not withhold good from
those to whom it is due [its
rightful recipients],
When it is in your power to do
it. [Rom 13:7; Gal 6:10]

life point

As Christians, we should not place
our confidence in our education, our
looks, our position, our property,
our gifts, our talents, our abilities,
our accomplishments, or in other
people's opinions. Through Proverbs
3:26, our heavenly Father is basically
saying to us, "No more; it is time
to let go of all those fleshly things
to which you have been holding so
firmly for so long. It is time to put
your trust and confidence in Me, and
Me alone!"

life point

We can have good intentions and
still be disobedient. Procrastination
is very deceptive and Proverbs 3:27,
28 instructs us not to do it. Often,
we do not see putting things off as
disobedience because we *intend*
to obey God; it is just that we are
going to do it *when*—when we
have more money, when we are
not so busy, as soon as Christmas is
over, after school starts next year,
when we return from vacation, etc.
Remember, the best intentions do
not produce results. Ask God to help
you take action in a timely manner
in every situation.

28 Do not say to your neighbor,
   "Go, and come back,
   And tomorrow I will give it,"
   When you have it with you.
   [Lev 19:13; Deut 24:15]
29 Do not devise evil against
   your neighbor,
   Who lives securely beside you.
30 Do not quarrel with a man
   without cause,
   If he has done you no harm.
   [Rom 12:18]
31 Do not envy a man of violence
   And do not choose any of his
   ways. [Ps 37:1; 73:3; Prov 24:1]
32 For the devious are repulsive
   to the LORD;
   But His private counsel is
   with the upright [those
   with spiritual integrity and
   moral courage]. [Ps 25:14]
33 The curse of the LORD is on
   the house of the wicked,
   But He blesses the home of
   the just and righteous. [Ps
   37:22; Zech 5:4; Mal 2:2]
34 Though He scoffs at the
   scoffers and scorns the
   scorners,
   Yet He gives His grace [His
   undeserved favor] to the
   humble [those who give up
   self-importance]. [James 4:6;
   1 Pet 5:5]
35 The wise will inherit honor
   and glory,
   But dishonor and shame is
   conferred on fools. [Is 32:6]

4 HEAR, O children, the
   instruction of a father,
   And pay attention [and be
   willing to learn] so that you
   may gain understanding
   and intelligent discernment.

2 For I give you good doctrine;
   Do not turn away from my
   instruction.
3 When I was a son with my
   father (David),
   Tender and the only son in
   the sight of my mother
   (Bathsheba),
4 He taught me and said to me,
   "Let your heart hold fast my
   words;
   Keep my commandments and
   live. [1 Chr 28:9; Eph 6:4]
5 "Get [skillful and godly]
   wisdom! Acquire
   understanding [actively
   seek spiritual discernment,
   mature comprehension, and
   logical interpretation]!
   Do not forget nor turn away
   from the words of my mouth.
6 "Do not turn away from her
   (Wisdom) and she will
   guard and protect you;
   Love her, and she will watch
   over you.
7 "The beginning of wisdom
   is: Get [skillful and godly]
   wisdom [it is preeminent]!
   And with all your acquiring,
   get understanding [actively
   seek spiritual discernment,
   mature comprehension,
   and logical interpretation].
   [James 1:5]
8 "Prize wisdom [and exalt
   her], and she will exalt you;
   She will honor you if you
   embrace her.
9 "She will place on your head a
   garland of grace;
   She will present you with a
   crown of beauty and glory."

10 Hear, my son, and accept my
   sayings,

And the years of your life will
    be many.
[11]I have instructed you in the
    way of [skillful and godly]
    wisdom;
I have led you in upright paths.

[12]When you walk, your steps
    will not be impeded [for
    your path will be clear and
    open];
And when you run, you will
    not stumble.

the benefits of wisdom

Proverbs 4:5 instructs us to gain "understanding and spiritual discernment," which is a way of defining wisdom, and I would like to share some of the results you can expect as you apply wisdom in your life.

Wisdom will always lead you to God's best. Wisdom teaches that you will not keep friends if you try to control and dominate everything that goes on in your life and theirs. You will not keep friends if you talk about them behind their backs or tell their secrets. Wisdom says, "Do not say things about others that you would not want people saying about you."

Wisdom will guide you in money matters. You will not get into debt if you do not spend more money than you make. A lot of people never have fruitful ministries because they think they can run a ministry without good business principles. The Holy Spirit does not need to speak in an audible voice to tell us that we cannot have more money going out than we have coming in. Wisdom tells us that we will get in trouble if we do that.

Wisdom will not let us get overextended in our time commitments if we listen to her. No matter how anxious we may be to accomplish things, wisdom says we need to take time and wait on God to give us peace about what we are to do and not do. It has been very difficult for me over the years to learn to say no to certain speaking opportunities, but I have learned that it is not wise to wear myself out trying to do so much that I end up not doing a quality job.

To God, quality is more important than quantity. Many times wisdom leads us to say no to things to which we would like to say yes. Wisdom may also lead us to say yes to something when we would rather say no. For example, if a friend invites me to do something that is extremely important to her, and I have recently had to say no to her several times, even if I do not really want to accept the invitation, it might be wise for me to do so if I value her friendship and want to keep it.

Wisdom is our friend; it helps us not to live in regret. I think the saddest thing in the world would be to reach old age and look back at my life and feel nothing but regret about what I did or did not do. Wisdom helps us make choices now that we will be happy with later.

¹³ Take hold of instruction;
[actively seek it, grip it
firmly and] do not let go.
Guard her, for she is your life.
¹⁴ Do not enter the path of the
wicked,
And do not go the way of evil
men.
¹⁵ Avoid it, do not travel on it;
Turn away from it and
pass on.
¹⁶ For the wicked cannot sleep
unless they do evil;
And they are deprived of
sleep unless they make
someone stumble *and* fall.
¹⁷ For they eat the bread of
wickedness
And drink the wine of
violence.
¹⁸ But the path of the just
(righteous) is like the light
of dawn,
That shines brighter and
brighter until [it reaches its
full strength and glory in]
the perfect day. [2 Sam 23:4;
Matt 5:14; Phil 2:15]
¹⁹ The way of the wicked is like
[deep] darkness;
They do not know over what
they stumble. [John 12:35]
²⁰ My son, pay attention to my
words *and* be willing to learn;
Open your ears to my sayings.
²¹ Do not let them escape from
your sight;
Keep them in the center of
your heart.
²² For they are life to those who
find them,
And healing *and* health to all
their flesh.
²³ Watch over your heart with all
diligence,

life point

Proverbs 4:18 is so encouraging to
me! This verse says to me that God
is not angry with us because we
have not yet "arrived." He is pleased
that we are pressing on, that we are
staying on the path. If you and I will
just "keep on keeping on," God will
be pleased with our progress.

Keep walking the walk. A walk
is something taken one step at a
time. This is an important truth to
remember.

If I invited you to take a walk, you
would think I was crazy if I became
angry after the first few steps
because we had not yet arrived at
our destination. We can understand
ordinary things like this, and yet we
have a difficult time understanding that God expects our spiritual
growth to take some time.

We do not think there is something
wrong with one-year-old children
because they cannot walk perfectly.
They fall down frequently, but we pick
them up, love them, bandage them
if necessary, and keep working with
them. Surely our awesome God can do
even more for us than we do for our
children. He is patient and stays with
us until we reach our destination.

For from it *flow* the springs of
life.
²⁴ Put away from you a deceitful
(lying, misleading) mouth,
And put devious lips far from
you.

life point

Proverbs 4:23 exhorts us to guard our hearts "with all diligence." Practically, that means we need to examine our attitudes and our thoughts on a regular basis and make adjustments as needed.

Many people are deceived into believing they cannot help what they think, but we *can* choose our thoughts. We need to think about what we have been thinking about. When we do that, it doesn't take very long to discover the root cause of a bad attitude.

The enemy will always try to fill our minds with wrong thinking, but we do not have to receive everything he tries to give us. I would not take a spoonful of poison just because someone offered it to me, and neither would you. If we are smart enough not to swallow poison, we should also be smart enough not to allow Satan to poison our minds, attitudes, and, ultimately, our lives.

Guard your heart aggressively. Let your thoughts be good thoughts. Think about things that are true and honorable (see Philippians 4:8), and watch your heart attitude change.

25 Let your eyes look directly ahead [toward the path of moral courage]
And let your gaze be fixed straight in front of you [toward the path of integrity].

26 Consider well *and* watch carefully the path of your feet,
And all your ways will be steadfast *and* sure.
27 Do not turn away to the right nor to the left [where evil may lurk];
Turn your foot from [the path of] evil.

5 MY SON, be attentive to my wisdom [godly wisdom learned by costly experience],
Incline your ear to my understanding; [1 Kin 4:29]
2 That you may exercise discrimination *and* discretion (good judgment),
And your lips may reserve knowledge *and* answer wisely [to temptation].
3 For the lips of an immoral woman drip honey [like a honeycomb]
And her speech is smoother than oil; [Ezek 20:30; Col 2:8–10; 2 Pet 2:14–17]
4 But in the end she is bitter like [the extract of] wormwood,
Sharp as a two-edged sword.
5 Her feet go down to death;
Her steps take hold of Sheol (the nether world, the place of the dead),
6 So that she does not think [seriously] about the path of life;
Her ways are aimless *and* unstable; you cannot know where her path leads.
7 Now then, my sons, listen to me

And do not depart from (forget) the words of my mouth.
⁸Let your way [in life] be far from her,
And do not go near the door of her house [avoid even being near the places of temptation], [Prov 4:15; Rom 16:17; 1 Thess 5:19–22]
⁹Or you will give your honor to others,
And your years to the cruel one,
¹⁰And strangers will be filled with your strength
And your hard-earned wealth will go to the house of a foreigner [who does not know God];
¹¹And you will groan when your *life is* ending,
When your flesh and your body are consumed;
¹²And you say, "How I hated instruction *and* discipline,
And my heart despised correction *and* reproof!
¹³"I have not listened to the voice of my teachers,
Nor have I inclined my ear to those who instructed me.
¹⁴"I was almost in total ruin
In the midst of the assembly and congregation."

¹⁵Drink water from your own cistern [of a pure marriage relationship]
And fresh running water from your own well.
¹⁶Should your springs (children) be dispersed,
As streams of water in the streets?

life point

As believers, you and I should not hate instruction, as we read about in Proverbs 5:12, but we should be teachable. If we ever reach the point where we think we know everything, then we can be assured that we know nothing! We need to stop hating and despising things—even little things. People use the words *hate* and *despise* quite casually, making comments such as: "I hate going to the grocery store," or "I hate traffic," or "I despise my job." We are not supposed to hate anything but sin.

We all are tempted to hate certain things, just as we are prone to dread certain things. Dread is a close relative of fear. We do not need to dread doing the dishes, getting up, going to work, exercising, or anything else. Satan uses those feelings of dread and our feelings of hatred to deceive us. We simply are not to have hearts that despise anyone or anything. If you have hatred in your heart, repent and then ask God to replace any despising attitude with His love and grace.

¹⁷[Confine yourself to your own wife.]
Let *your children* be yours alone,
And not *the children* of strangers with you.
¹⁸Let your fountain (wife) be blessed [with the rewards of fidelity],

And rejoice in the wife of
your youth. [Song 4:12, 15]
¹⁹ *Let her be as* a loving hind
and graceful doe,
Let her breasts refresh *and*
satisfy you at all times;
Always be exhilarated *and*
delight in her love.
²⁰ Why should you, my son,
be exhilarated with an
immoral woman
And embrace the bosom of an
outsider (pagan)?
²¹ For the ways of man are
directly before the eyes of
the LORD,
And He carefully watches
all of his paths [all of his
comings and goings]. [2 Chr
16:9; Job 31:4; 34:21; Prov
15:3; Jer 16:17; Hos 7:2;
Heb 4:13]
²² The iniquities done by a
wicked man will trap him,
And he will be held with the
cords of his sin.
²³ He will die for lack of
instruction (discipline),
And in the greatness of his
foolishness he will go astray
and be lost.

6 MY SON, if you
have become surety
(guaranteed a debt
or obligation) for your
neighbor,
If you have given your pledge
for [the debt of] a stranger
or another [outside your
family],
² If you have been snared with
the words of your lips,
If you have been trapped by
the speech of your mouth,

³ Do this now, my son, and
release yourself [from the
obligation];
Since you have come into the
hand of your neighbor,
Go humble yourself, and
plead with your neighbor
[to pay his debt and release
you].
⁴ Give no [unnecessary] sleep
to your eyes,
Nor slumber to your eyelids;
⁵ Tear yourself away like a
gazelle from the hand of *the
hunter*
And like a bird from the hand
of the fowler.

⁶ Go to the ant, O lazy one;
Observe her ways and be
wise, [Job 12:7]
⁷ Which, having no chief,
Overseer or ruler,
⁸ She prepares her food in the
summer
And brings in her provisions
[of food for the winter] in
the harvest.
⁹ How long will you lie down,
O lazy one?
When will you arise from
your sleep [and learn
self-discipline]? [Prov
24:33, 34]
¹⁰ "Yet a little sleep, a little
slumber,
A little folding of the hands to
lie down *and* rest"—
¹¹ So your poverty will come
like an *approaching* prowler
who walks [slowly, but
surely]
And your need [will come]
like an armed man [making
you helpless]. [Prov 10:4;
13:4; 20:4]

¹²A worthless person, a wicked man,

Is one who walks with a perverse (corrupt, vulgar) mouth.

¹³Who winks with his eyes [in mockery], who shuffles his feet [to signal],

Who points with his fingers [to give subversive instruction];

¹⁴Who perversely in his heart plots trouble *and* evil continually;

Who spreads discord *and* strife.

¹⁵Therefore [the crushing weight of] his disaster will come suddenly *upon him;*

Instantly he will be broken, and there will be no healing *or* remedy [because he has no heart for God].

¹⁶These six things the LORD hates;

Indeed, seven are repulsive to Him:

¹⁷A proud look [the attitude that makes one overestimate oneself and discount others], a lying tongue,

And hands that shed innocent blood, [Ps 120:2, 3]

¹⁸A heart that creates wicked plans,

Feet that run swiftly to evil,

¹⁹A false witness who breathes out lies [even half-truths],

And one who spreads discord (rumors) among brothers.

²⁰My son, be guided by your father's [God-given] commandment (instruction)

And do not reject the teaching of your mother; [Eph 6:1–3]

²¹Bind them continually upon your heart (in your thoughts),

And tie them around your neck. [Prov 3:3; 7:3]

²²When you walk about, they (the godly teachings of your parents) will guide you;

When you sleep, they will keep watch over you;

And when you awake, they will talk to you.

²³For the commandment is a lamp, and the teaching [of the law] is light,

And reproofs (rebukes) for discipline are the way of life, [Ps 19:8; 119:105]

²⁴To keep you from the evil woman,

From [the flattery of] the smooth tongue of an immoral woman.

²⁵Do not desire (lust after) her beauty in your heart,

Nor let her capture you with her eyelashes.

²⁶For on account of a prostitute one is reduced to a piece of bread [to be eaten up],

And the immoral woman hunts [with a hook] the precious life [of a man].

²⁷Can a man take fire to his chest

And his clothes not be burned?

²⁸Or can a man walk on hot coals

And his feet not be scorched?

²⁹So is the one who goes in to his neighbor's wife;

Whoever touches her will
not be found innocent *or* go
unpunished.
30 People do not despise a thief
if he steals
To satisfy himself when he is
hungry;
31 But when he is found, he must
repay seven times [what he
stole];
He must give all the property
of his house [if necessary to
meet his fine].
32 But whoever commits
adultery with a woman
lacks common sense *and*
sound judgment *and* an
understanding [of moral
principles];
He who would destroy his
soul does it.
33 Wounds and disgrace he will
find,
And his reproach (blame) will
not be blotted out.
34 For jealousy enrages the
[wronged] husband;
He will not spare [the
guilty one] on the day of
vengeance.
35 He will not accept any
ransom [offered to buy him
off from demanding full
punishment];
Nor will he be satisfied
though you offer him many
gifts (bribes).

7 MY SON, keep my words
And treasure my
commandments within
you [so they are readily
available to guide you].
2 Keep my commandments and
live,

And keep my teaching *and*
law as the apple of your eye.
3 Bind them [securely] on your
fingers;
Write them on the tablet of
your heart.
4 Say to [skillful and godly]
wisdom, "You are my sister,"
And regard understanding
and intelligent insight as
your intimate friends;
5 That they may keep you from
the immoral woman,
From the foreigner [who does
not observe God's laws
and] who flatters with her
[smooth] words.

6 For at the window of my
house
I looked out through my
lattice.
7 And among the naive
[the inexperienced and
gullible],
I saw among the youths
A young man lacking [good]
sense,
8 Passing through the street
near her corner;
And he took the path to her
house
9 In the twilight, in the
evening;
In the black and dark night.
10 And there a woman met him,
Dressed as a prostitute and
sly *and* cunning of heart.
11 She was boisterous and
rebellious;
She would not stay at home.
12 At times *she was* in the
streets, at times in the
market places,
Lurking *and* setting her
ambush at every corner.

13 So she caught him and kissed him
And with a brazen *and* impudent face she said to him:
14 "I have peace offerings with me;
Today I have paid my vows.
15 "So I came out to meet you [that you might share with me the feast of my offering],
Diligently I sought your face and I have found you.
16 "I have spread my couch with coverings *and* cushions of tapestry,
With colored fine linen of Egypt.
17 "I have perfumed my bed With myrrh, aloes, and cinnamon.
18 "Come, let us drink our fill of love until morning;
Let us console *and* delight ourselves with love.
19 "For my husband is not at home. He has gone on a long journey;
20 He has taken a bag of money with him,
And he will come home on the appointed day."
21 With her many persuasions she caused him to yield;
With her flattering lips she seduced him.
22 Suddenly he went after her, as an ox goes to the slaughter [not knowing the outcome],
Or as one in stocks going to the correction [to be given] to a fool,
23 Until an arrow pierced his liver [with a mortal wound];
Like a bird fluttering straight into the net,

He did not know that it *would cost* him his life.

24 Now therefore, my sons, listen to me,
And pay attention to the words of my mouth.
25 Do not let your heart turn aside to her ways,
Do not stray into her [evil, immoral] paths.
26 For she has cast down many [mortally] wounded;
Indeed, all who were killed by her were strong. [Neh 13:26]
27 Her house is the way to Sheol,
Descending to the chambers of death. [1 Cor 6:9]

8 DOES NOT wisdom call,
And understanding lift up her voice?
2 On the top of the heights beside the way,
Where the paths meet, wisdom takes her stand;
3 Beside the gates, at the entrance to the city,
At the entrance of the doors, she cries out:
4 "To you, O men, I call,
And my voice is directed to the sons of men.
5 "O you naive *or* inexperienced [who are easily misled],
understand prudence *and* seek astute common sense;
And, O you [closed-minded, self-confident] fools,
understand wisdom [seek the insight and self-discipline that leads to godly living]. [Is 32:6]
6 "Listen, for I will speak excellent *and* noble things;

And the opening of my lips
will reveal right things.
7 "For my mouth will utter truth,
And wickedness is repulsive
and loathsome to my lips.
8 "All the words of my mouth
are in righteousness (upright,
in right standing with God);
There is nothing contrary to
truth or perverted (crooked)
in them.
9 "They are all straightforward
to him who understands [with
an open and willing mind],
And right to those who find
knowledge *and* live by it.

life point

Proverbs 8:6–9 describes what should be our confession, our testimony, and our reputation. Our reputation involves not only what we say about ourselves, but also what others say about us.

Unfortunately, many of us have learned to speak in circles, and often when we finish speaking, others do not have the slightest idea what we have just said. We need to learn how to engage in plain, straightforward, honest, truthful communication.

James 3:10 tells us that we should not let both blessings and cursings issue from our mouths. Instead, we ought to be like the virtuous woman in Proverbs 31:26, on whose tongue is the teaching of kindness. As children of God, we need to be excellent in our speech and speak words that are righteous and true.

10 "Take my instruction rather
than [seeking] silver,
And take knowledge rather
than choicest gold,
11 "For wisdom is better than
rubies;
And all desirable things
cannot compare with her.
[Job 28:15; Ps 19:10; 119:127]
12 "I, [godly] wisdom, reside
with prudence [good
judgment, moral courage
and astute common sense],
And I find knowledge and
discretion. [James 1:5]
13 "The [reverent] fear *and*
worshipful awe of the LORD
includes the hatred of evil;
Pride and arrogance and the
evil way,
And the perverted mouth,
I hate.
14 "Counsel is mine and sound
wisdom;
I am understanding, power
and strength are mine.
15 "By me kings reign
And rulers decide *and* decree
justice. [Dan 2:21; Rom 13:1]
16 "By me princes rule, and
nobles,
All who judge *and* govern
rightly.
17 "I love those who love me;
And those who seek me early
and diligently will find me.
[1 Sam 2:30; Ps 91:14; John
14:21; James 1:5]
18 "Riches and honor are with me,
Enduring wealth and
righteousness (right
standing with God).
[Prov 3:16; Matt 6:33]
19 "My fruit is better than gold,
even pure gold,

a little common sense goes a long way

In Proverbs 8:15, 16, wisdom is speaking, and she says that through her, leaders rule. Wisdom brings us to places of leadership, and if we want to be good leaders, we need wisdom and something else with it—common sense!

People often ask me, "How were you able to build a ministry like yours?" I share with them a ministry success principle, one of the most positive aspects of our ministry, the thing that has brought us to where we are today: "Use common sense!"

My husband, Dave, and I use common sense in everything we do in our ministry. You might call it "sanctified common sense." It is not merely reason or logic. The mind of the flesh is sense and reason without the Holy Spirit. Dave and I strive not to walk according to the mind of the flesh, because we are aware that sense and reason alone can cause a lot of trouble. We seek godly, Spirit-filled, sanctified common sense. We believe common sense leads us to present a balanced gospel. We do not buy things we do not have the money to pay for. We do not hire people if we cannot afford to pay their salaries. We know that we cannot try to control our friends if we want to keep them. We have enough common sense to know what to do to stay out of trouble.

Living by common sense really is not difficult; just do what you would want others to do to you. Pay your bills on time; communicate properly; mix encouragement with correction so a person's spirit is not broken— these are just a few examples of good common sense.

As you use more and more common sense, things will get better and better for you. Do not do things that are foolish; do ask God for wisdom. While you are at it, ask Him to help you also use your good, sanctified common sense in every situation.

And my yield is better than choicest silver.
20 "I, [Wisdom, continuously] walk in the way of righteousness,
In the midst of the paths of justice,
21 That I may cause those who love me to inherit wealth *and* true riches,
And that I may fill their treasuries.

22 "The LORD created *and* possessed me at the beginning of His way,
Before His works of old [were accomplished].
23 "From everlasting I was established *and* ordained,
From the beginning, before the earth existed,
[I, godly wisdom, existed]. [John 1:1; 1 Cor 1:24]

24 "When there were no ocean
   depths I was born,
   When there were no
   fountains *and* springs
   overflowing with water.
25 "Before the mountains were
   settled,
   Before the hills, I was born;
   [Job 15:7, 8]
26 While He had not yet
   made the earth and the
   fields,
   Or the first of the dust of the
   earth.
27 "When He established the
   heavens, I [Wisdom] was
   there;
   When He drew a circle upon
   the face of the deep,
28 When He made firm the skies
   above,
   When the fountains and
   springs of the deep became
   fixed *and* strong,
29 When He set for the sea its
   boundary
   So that the waters would not
   transgress [the boundaries
   set by] His command,
   When He marked out the
   foundations of the earth—
   [Job 38:10, 11; Ps 104:6–9;
   Jer 5:22]
30 Then I was beside Him, as a
   master craftsman;
   And I was daily His delight;
   Rejoicing before Him
   always, [Matt 3:17;
   John 1:2, 18]
31 Rejoicing in the world, His
   inhabited earth,
   And having my delight in the
   sons of men. [Ps 16:3]
32 "Now therefore, O sons, listen
   to me,

For blessed [happy, prosperous,
   to be admired] are they who
   keep my ways. [Ps 119:1, 2;
   128:1, 2; Luke 11:28]
33 "Heed (pay attention to)
   instruction and be wise,
   And do not ignore *or* neglect it.
34 "Blessed [happy, prosperous,
   to be admired] is the man
   who listens to me,

life point

We can miss God by being in a hurry
to get what we want. If we do not
wait, especially in important areas,
we can bring trouble into our lives
(see Proverbs 8:34–36). I am "fine-
tuning" patience in my life all the
time.

I am a natural-born confronter.
In the past, if I wanted a problem
solved, I confronted the issue and
forced a solution. It took me years
to learn that sometimes it was not
good for me to deal with issues so
directly. I learned that I could make
matters worse, or get in God's way
and end up having to go through the
same situation again because I did
not wait for God's timing. Because I
was impatient, I did not give God a
chance to solve things for me.

I have learned that when I feel overly
anxious to handle something, I should
let it rest for at least twenty-four
hours. It is amazing how we can
change our minds if we will just let
things settle for a few hours. We can
save ourselves so much trouble if we
will learn to wait on God.

Watching daily at my gates,
Waiting at my doorposts.
35 "For whoever finds me
(Wisdom) finds life
And obtains favor *and* grace
from the LORD.
36 "But he who fails to find me
or sins against me injures
himself;
All those who hate me love
and court death."

9 WISDOM HAS built her
[spacious and sufficient]
house;
She has hewn out *and* set up
her seven pillars.
2 She has prepared her food,
she has mixed her wine;
She has also set her table.
[Matt 22:2–4]
3 She has sent out her maidens,
she calls
From the highest places of the
city:
4 "Whoever is naive *or*
inexperienced, let him turn
in here!"
As for him who lacks
understanding, she says,
5 "Come, eat my food
And drink the wine I have
mixed [and accept my gifts].
[Is 55:1; John 6:27]
6 "Leave [behind] your
foolishness [and the foolish]
and live,
And walk in the way of
insight *and* understanding."

7 He who corrects *and* instructs
a scoffer gets dishonor for
himself,
And he who rebukes a
wicked man gets insults for
himself.

8 Do not correct a scoffer [who
foolishly ridicules and takes
no responsibility for his
error] or he will hate you;
Correct a wise man [who
learns from his error], and
he will love you. [Ps 141:5]
9 Give *instruction* to a wise man
and he will become even
wiser;
Teach a righteous man and he
will increase his learning.
10 The [reverent] fear of the LORD
[that is, worshiping Him
and regarding Him as truly
awesome] is the beginning
and the preeminent part of
wisdom [its starting point
and its essence],
And the knowledge of the
Holy One is understanding
and spiritual insight.
11 For by me (wisdom from
God) your days will be
multiplied,
And years of life shall be
increased.
12 If you are wise, you are wise
for yourself [for your own
benefit];
If you scoff [thoughtlessly
ridicule and disdain], you
alone will pay the penalty.
13 The foolish woman is restless
and noisy;
She is naive *and* easily misled
and thoughtless, and knows
nothing at all [of eternal
value].
14 She sits at the doorway of her
house,
On a seat by the high *and*
conspicuous places of the
city,
15 Calling to those who pass by,

Who are making their paths
straight:
16 "Whoever is naive *or*
inexperienced, let him turn
in here!"
And to him who lacks
understanding (common
sense), she says,
17 "Stolen waters (pleasures)
are sweet [because they are
forbidden];
And bread *eaten* in secret is
pleasant." [Prov 20:17]
18 But he does not know that
the spirits of the dead are
there,
And that her guests are
[already] in the depths of
Sheol (the nether world, the
place of the dead).

10 THE PROVERBS of Solomon:

A wise son makes a father
glad,
But a foolish [stubborn] son
[who refuses to learn] is a
grief to his mother.
2 Treasures of wickedness
and ill-gotten gains do not
profit,
But righteousness *and* moral
integrity in daily life
rescues from death.
3 The LORD will not allow
the righteous to hunger
[God will meet all his
needs],

But He will reject *and* cast
away the craving of the
wicked. [Ps 34:9, 10; 37:25]
4 Poor is he who works
with a negligent *and*
idle hand,
But the hand of the diligent
makes *him* rich.
5 He who gathers during
summer *and* takes
advantage of his
opportunities is a son who
acts wisely,
But he who sleeps during
harvest *and* ignores the
moment of opportunity
is a son who acts
shamefully.
6 Blessings are on the head of
the righteous [the upright,
those in right standing with
God],
But the mouth of the wicked
conceals violence.
7 The memory of the righteous
[person] is a [source of]
blessing,
But the name of the wicked
will [be forgotten and] rot
[like a corpse]. [Ps 112:6;
9:5]
8 The wise in heart [are willing
to learn so they] will
accept *and* obey commands
(instruction),
But the babbling fool
[who is arrogant and
thinks himself wise]
will come to ruin.

speak the Word

*Thank You, God, that blessings are on the heads of the righteous
and that I am righteous through Your Son!*
–ADAPTED FROM PROVERBS 10:6

9 He who walks in integrity *and* with moral character walks securely,
But he who takes a crooked way will be discovered *and* punished.

10 He who [maliciously] winks the eye [of evil intent] causes trouble;
And the babbling fool [who is arrogant and thinks himself wise] will come to ruin.

11 The mouth of the righteous is a fountain of life *and* his words of wisdom are a source of blessing,
But the mouth of the wicked conceals violence *and* evil.

12 Hatred stirs up strife,
But love covers *and* overwhelms all transgressions [forgiving and overlooking another's faults].

13 On the lips of the discerning, [skillful and godly] wisdom is found,
But discipline *and* the rod are for the back of the one who is without common sense *and* understanding.

14 Wise men store up *and* treasure knowledge [in mind and heart],
But with the mouth of the foolish, ruin is at hand.

15 The rich man's wealth is his fortress;
The ruin of the poor is their poverty. [Ps 52:7; 1 Tim 6:17]

16 The wages of the righteous [the upright, those in right standing with God] is [a worthwhile, meaningful] life,
The income of the wicked, punishment. [Rom 6:21–23; 1 Tim 6:10]

17 He who learns from instruction *and* correction is on the [right] path of life [and for others his example is a path toward wisdom and blessing],
But he who ignores *and* refuses correction goes off course [and for others his example is a path toward sin and ruin].

18 He who hides hatred has lying lips,
And he who spreads slander is a fool. [Prov 26:24–26]

19 When there are many words, transgression *and* offense are unavoidable,
But he who controls his lips *and* keeps thoughtful silence is wise.

20 The tongue of the righteous is like precious silver (greatly valued);
The heart of the wicked is worth little.

21 The lips of the righteous feed *and* guide many,
But fools [who reject God and His wisdom] die for lack of understanding.

speak the Word

Thank You, God, that Your blessing brings true riches and that You add no sorrow to it.
—ADAPTED FROM PROVERBS 10:22

22 The blessing of the LORD
brings [true] riches,
And He adds no sorrow to it
[for it comes as a blessing
from God].
23 Engaging in evil is like sport
to the fool [who refuses
wisdom and chases sin],
But to a man of
understanding [skillful and
godly] wisdom *brings joy.*
24 What the wicked fears will
come upon him,
But the desire of the righteous
[for the blessings of God]
will be granted.
25 When the whirlwind passes,
the wicked is no more,
But the righteous has an
everlasting foundation.
[Ps 125:1; Matt 7:24–27]
26 Like vinegar to the teeth and
smoke to the eyes,
So is the lazy one to those
who send him *to work.*
27 The [reverent] fear of the
LORD [worshiping, obeying,
serving, and trusting Him
with awe-filled respect]
prolongs one's life,
But the years of the wicked
will be shortened.
28 The hope of the righteous
[those of honorable character
and integrity] is joy,
But the expectation of the
wicked [those who oppose
God and ignore His
wisdom] comes to nothing.
29 The way of the LORD is a
stronghold to the upright,
But it is ruin to those who do
evil.
30 The [consistently] righteous
will never be shaken,

But the wicked will not inhabit
the earth. [Ps 37:22; 125:1]
31 The mouth of the righteous
flows with [skillful and
godly] wisdom,
But the perverted tongue will
be cut out.
32 The lips of the righteous
know (speak) what is
acceptable,
But the mouth of the wicked
knows (speaks) what is
perverted (twisted).

11

A FALSE balance
and dishonest
business practices are
extremely offensive to the
LORD,
But an accurate scale is
His delight. [Lev 19:35, 36;
Prov 16:11]
2 When pride comes [boiling up
with an arrogant attitude of
self-importance], then come
dishonor *and* shame,
But with the humble [the
teachable who have been
chiseled by trial and who
have learned to walk
humbly with God] there is
wisdom *and* soundness of
mind.
3 The integrity *and* moral
courage of the upright will
guide them,
But the crookedness of the
treacherous will destroy
them.
4 Riches will not provide
security in the day of wrath
and judgment,
But righteousness rescues
from death. [Prov 10:2;
Zeph 1:18]

⁵The righteousness of the blameless will smooth their way *and* keep it straight,
But the wicked will fall by his own wickedness.

⁶The righteousness of the upright will rescue them,
But the treacherous will be caught by their own greed.

⁷When the wicked man dies, his expectation will perish;
And the hope of [godless] strong men perishes.

⁸The righteous is rescued from trouble,
And the wicked takes his place.

⁹With his mouth the godless man destroys his neighbor,
But through knowledge *and* discernment the righteous will be rescued.

¹⁰When it goes well for the righteous, the city rejoices,
And when the wicked perish, there are shouts of joy.

putting the Word to work

Proverbs 11:14 teaches us that there is safety in a multitude of wise and godly counselors. Do you have wise, godly people who can provide sound counsel in your life? If so, consult them often. Never put them ahead of God, and do not let them make your final decisions, because those should be made between you and God. However, wise counselors are very valuable, and if you do not have such people in your life, ask God to send them.

¹¹By the blessing [of the influence] of the upright the city is exalted,
But by the mouth of the wicked it is torn down.

¹²He who despises his neighbor lacks sense,
But a man of understanding keeps silent.

¹³He who goes about as a gossip reveals secrets,
But he who is trustworthy *and* faithful keeps a matter hidden.

¹⁴Where there is no [wise, intelligent] guidance, the people fall [and go off course like a ship without a helm],
But in the abundance of [wise and godly] counselors there is victory.

¹⁵He who puts up security *and* guarantees a debt for an outsider will surely suffer [for his foolishness],
But he who hates (declines) being a guarantor is secure [from its penalties].

¹⁶A gracious *and* good woman attains honor,
And ruthless men attain riches [but not respect].

¹⁷The merciful *and* generous man benefits his soul [for his behavior returns to bless him],
But the cruel *and* callous man does himself harm.

¹⁸The wicked man earns deceptive wages,

But he who sows righteousness
and lives his life with integrity
will have a true reward
[that is both permanent and
satisfying]. [Hos 10:12; Gal
6:8, 9; James 3:18]
¹⁹ He who is steadfast in
righteousness *attains* life,
But he who pursues evil
attains his own death.
²⁰ The perverse in heart are
repulsive *and* shamefully
vile to the Lord,
But those who are blameless
and above reproach in their
walk are His delight!
²¹ Assuredly, the evil man will
not go unpunished,
But the descendants of the
righteous will be freed.
²² As a ring of gold in a swine's
snout,
So is a beautiful woman who
is without discretion [her
lack of character mocks her
beauty].
²³ The desire of the righteous
brings only good,
But the expectation of the
wicked brings wrath.
²⁴ There is the one who
[generously] scatters
[abroad], and yet increases
all the more;

putting the Word to work

Proverbs 11:25 says that people who
are generous will be prosperous and
enriched and that when we "water" others, we will be "watered"
in return. In what ways can you be
generous to someone today?

And there is the one who
withholds what is justly due,
but it results only in want *and*
poverty.
²⁵ The generous man [is a
source of blessing and]
shall be prosperous *and*
enriched,
And he who waters will
himself be watered
[reaping the generosity he
has sown]. [2 Cor 9:6–10]
²⁶ The people curse him who
holds back grain [when the
public needs it],
But a blessing [from God and
man] is upon the head of
him who sells it.
²⁷ He who diligently seeks
good seeks favor *and*
grace,
But he who seeks evil, evil
will come to him.
²⁸ He who leans on *and* trusts in
and is confident in his riches
will fall,
But the righteous [who trust
in God's provision] will
flourish like a *green* leaf.
²⁹ He who troubles
(mismanages) his own
house will inherit the wind
(nothing),
And the foolish will be a
servant to the wise-hearted.
³⁰ The fruit of the [consistently]
righteous is a tree of life,
And he who is wise captures
and wins souls [for God—he
gathers them for eternity].
[Matt 4:19; 1 Cor 9:19; James
5:20]
³¹ If the righteous will be
rewarded on the earth [with
godly blessings],

How much more [will] the wicked and the sinner [be repaid with punishment]!

12 WHOEVER LOVES instruction *and* discipline loves knowledge,
But he who hates reproof *and* correction is stupid.
2 A good man will obtain favor from the LORD,
But He will condemn a man who devises evil.
3 A man will not be established by wickedness,
But the root of the [consistently] righteous will not be moved.
4 A virtuous *and* excellent wife [worthy of honor] is the crown of her husband,
But she who shames him [with her foolishness] is like rottenness in his bones. [Prov 31:23; 1 Cor 11:7]
5 The thoughts *and* purposes of the [consistently] righteous are just (honest, reliable),
But the counsels *and* schemes of the wicked are deceitful.
6 The [malevolent] words of the wicked lie in wait for [innocent] blood [to slander],
But the mouth of the upright will rescue *and* protect them.
7 The wicked are overthrown [by their evil] and are no more,
But the house of the [consistently] righteous will stand [securely].
8 A man will be commended according to his insight *and* sound judgment,

But the one who is of a perverse mind will be despised.
9 Better is he who is lightly esteemed and has a servant,
Than he who [boastfully] honors himself [pretending to be what he is not] and lacks bread.
10 A righteous man has kind regard for the life of his animal,
But even the compassion of the wicked is cruel. [Deut 25:4]
11 He who tills his land will have plenty of bread,
But he who follows worthless *things* lacks common sense *and* good judgment.
12 The wicked desire the plunder of evil men,
But the root of the righteous yields *richer* fruit.
13 An evil man is [dangerously] ensnared by the transgression of his lips,
But the righteous will escape from trouble.
14 A man will be satisfied with good from the fruit of his words,
And the deeds of a man's hands will return to him [as a harvest].
15 The way of the [arrogant] fool [who rejects God's wisdom] is right in his own eyes,
But a wise *and* prudent man is he who listens to counsel. [Prov 3:7; 9:9; 21:2]
16 The [arrogant] fool's anger is quickly known [because he lacks self-control and common sense],

But a prudent man ignores an insult.

17 He who speaks truth [when he testifies] tells what is right,
But a false witness utters deceit [in court].
18 There is one who speaks rashly like the thrusts of a sword,
But the tongue of the wise brings healing.
19 Truthful lips will be established forever,
But a lying tongue is [credited] only for a moment.
20 Deceit is in the heart of those who devise evil,
But counselors of peace have joy.
21 No harm befalls the righteous,
But the wicked are filled with trouble. [Job 5:19; Ps 91:3; Prov 12:13; Is 46:4; Jer 1:8; Dan 6:27; 2 Tim 4:18]
22 Lying lips are extremely disgusting to the LORD,
But those who deal faithfully are His delight. [Prov 6:17; 11:20; Rev 22:15]
23 A shrewd man is reluctant to display his knowledge [until the proper time],
But the heart of [over-confident] fools proclaims foolishness. [Is 32:6]
24 The hand of the diligent will rule,
But the negligent and lazy will be put to forced labor.
25 Anxiety in a man's heart weighs it down,
But a good (encouraging) word makes it glad. [Ps 50:4; Prov 15:13]

life point

I believe all of us Christians should keep our hearts light. The King James Version of Proverbs 12:25 says, "Heaviness in the heart of man maketh it stoop: but a good word maketh it glad."

We do not have to go around with troubled, heavy hearts or with a spirit of heaviness on us. In John 14:1 Jesus told His disciples, "Do not let your hearts be troubled (afraid, cowardly)." Isaiah 61:3 gives a wonderful promise to those who need the Lord to lift the heaviness from them. It says that God wants to "grant to those who mourn in Zion the following: . . . the oil of joy instead of mourning, the garment [expressive] of praise instead of a disheartened spirit . . ."

The Lord does not want us to have heavy or troubled hearts. The next time things are not going right for you, remember to release your burdens and anxieties to the Lord. He wants you to be lighthearted and to enjoy life.

26 The righteous man is a guide to his neighbor,
But the way of the wicked leads them astray.
27 The lazy man does not catch and roast his prey,
But the precious possession of a [wise] man is diligence [because he recognizes opportunities and seizes them].

²⁸In the way of righteousness is life,
And in its pathway there is no death [but immortality—eternal life]. [John 3:36; 4:36; 8:51; 11:26; 1 Cor 15:54; Gal 6:8]

13

A WISE son heeds *and* accepts [and is the result of] his father's discipline *and* instruction,
But a scoffer does not listen to reprimand *and* does not learn from his errors.

²From the fruit of his mouth a [wise] man enjoys good,
But the desire of the treacherous is for violence.

³The one who guards his mouth [thinking before he speaks] protects his life;
The one who opens his lips wide [and chatters without thinking] comes to ruin.

⁴The soul (appetite) of the lazy person craves and gets nothing [for lethargy overcomes ambition],
But the soul (appetite) of the diligent [who works willingly] is rich *and* abundantly supplied. [Prov 10:4]

⁵A righteous man hates lies,
But a wicked man is loathsome, and he acts shamefully.

⁶Righteousness (being in right standing with God) guards the one whose way is blameless,
But wickedness undermines *and* overthrows the sinner.

⁷There is one who pretends to be rich, yet has nothing at all;
Another pretends to be poor, yet has great wealth. [Prov 12:9; Luke 12:20, 21]

⁸The ransom for a man's life is his wealth,
But the poor man does not even have to listen to a rebuke *or* threats [from the envious].

⁹The light of the righteous [within him—grows brighter and] rejoices,
But the lamp of the wicked [is a temporary light and] goes out.

¹⁰Through pride *and* presumption come nothing but strife,
But [skillful and godly] wisdom is with those who welcome [well-advised] counsel.

¹¹Wealth *obtained* by fraud dwindles,
But he who gathers gradually by [honest] labor will increase [his riches].

¹²Hope deferred makes the heart sick,
But when desire is fulfilled, it is a tree of life.

¹³Whoever despises the word *and* counsel [of God] brings destruction upon himself,
But he who [reverently] fears *and* respects the commandment [of God] will be rewarded.

¹⁴The teaching of the wise is a fountain *and* source of life,
So that one may avoid the snares of death.

¹⁵Good understanding wins favor [from others],

But the way of the unfaithful
is hard [like barren, dry
soil].
¹⁶Every prudent *and* self-
disciplined man acts with
knowledge,

But a [closed-minded] fool
[who refuses to learn]
displays his foolishness [for
all to see].
¹⁷A wicked messenger falls into
hardship,

from disappointment to reappointment

Proverbs 13:12 says that "hope deferred makes the heart sick." What is "hope deferred"? I believe it is what we call disappointment.

We all are disappointed when things do not work out the way we would like. We become disappointed when we have a plan that fails, a hope that does not materialize, or a goal that we do not reach. We are disappointed by everything from a picnic that is rained out to the loss of a job. We are disappointed when the new watch we were given will not keep time correctly, or when the child we had hoped would grow into a mature adult shows no signs of doing so.

When such things happen, for a certain period of time we experience a letdown, one that can lead to depression if not handled properly. That is when we have to make the decision to adapt and adjust, to take a new approach and just keep going despite our feelings. That is when we must remember that we have the Greater One residing within us, so that no matter what may happen to frustrate us, or how long it may take for our dreams and goals to become realities, we are not going to give up and quit just because of our emotions.

That is when we must remember what God once impressed on me in such a moment: *"When you get disappointed, you can always make the decision to get reappointed!"*

Disappointment often leads to discouragement, which is even more of a "downer." We have all experienced the depressing feeling that comes after we have tried our very best to do something and either nothing happens or it all falls totally apart.How disappointing and discouraging it is to see the things we love senselessly destroyed by others or, even worse, by our own neglect or failure. Regardless of how it may happen or who may be responsible, it is hard to go on when everything we have counted on falls down around us. That is when those of us who have the creative power of the Holy Spirit on the inside can get a new vision, a new direction, and a new goal to help us overcome the frustrating, downward pull of disappointment. Hope deferred does make the heart sick, but hope can be rekindled, and our hearts can be made whole again by the power of the Holy Spirit.

life point

People who are prudent and self-disciplined are balanced; they avoid extremes in the management of their lives and of their faith. It seems to me, after many years of observation in the kingdom of God, that people have a difficult time with balance. Ideas concerning the power of words, the mouth, confession, calling those things that do not exist as though they do, and speaking things into existence, is one example of an area in which I have seen people move into extremes. It seems that the flesh wants to live in the ditch on one side of the road or the other, but it has a difficult time staying in the middle of the highway between the lines of safety. We should speak positively about our lives and our futures. We should agree with what God says about us in His Word. Our confession does have a lot to do with our possession, but we should not ever think that we can have whatever we want just because we say it. We are to speak forth God's Word, not our carnal desires.

Extremes are actually the devil's playground. If he cannot get believers to totally ignore a truth and live in deception, his next tactic will be to get them so one-sided and out of balance with the truth that they are no better off than they were before. Sometimes they end up even worse off than they were previously.

Wisdom is a central theme of God's Word. As a matter of fact, there is no real victory without it, and we are wise to remain balanced in our everyday lives.

But a faithful ambassador
   brings healing.
18 Poverty and shame will
   come to him who refuses
   instruction *and* discipline,
But he who accepts *and* learns
   from reproof *or* censure is
   honored.
19 Desire realized is sweet to the
   soul;
But it is detestable to fools to
   turn away from evil [which
   they have planned].
20 He who walks [as a
   companion] with wise men
   will be wise,
But the companions of
   [conceited, dull-witted]
   fools [are fools themselves
   and] will experience harm.
   [Is 32:6]
21 Adversity pursues sinners,
But the [consistently] upright
   will be rewarded with
   prosperity.
22 A good man leaves an
   inheritance to his children's
   children,
And the wealth of the sinner
   is stored up for [the hands
   of] the righteous.
23 Abundant food is in the fallow
   (uncultivated) ground of the
   poor,
But [without protection] it is
   swept away by injustice.
24 He who withholds the rod
   [of discipline] hates his
   son,

But he who loves him disciplines *and* trains him diligently *and* appropriately [with wisdom and love]. [Prov 19:18; 22:15; 23:13; 29:15, 17; Eph 6:4]

25 The [consistently] righteous has enough to satisfy his appetite,
But the stomach of the wicked is in need [of bread].

14 THE WISE woman builds her house [on a foundation of godly precepts, and her household thrives],
But the foolish one [who lacks spiritual insight] tears it down with her own hands [by ignoring godly principles].

2 He who walks in uprightness [reverently] fears the LORD [and obeys and worships Him with profound respect],
But he who is devious in his ways despises Him.

3 In the mouth of the [arrogant] fool [who rejects God] is a rod for his back,
But the lips of the wise [when they speak with godly wisdom] will protect them.

4 Where there are no oxen, the manger is clean,
But much revenue [because of good crops] comes by the strength of the ox.

5 A faithful *and* trustworthy witness will not lie,
But a false witness speaks lies.

6 A scoffer seeks wisdom and finds none [for his ears are closed to wisdom],
But knowledge is easy for one who understands [because he is willing to learn].

7 Leave the presence of a [shortsighted] fool,
For you will not find knowledge *or* hear godly wisdom from his lips.

8 The wisdom of the sensible is to understand his way,
But the foolishness of [shortsighted] fools is deceit.

9 Fools mock sin [but sin mocks the fools],
But among the upright there is good will *and* the favor *and* blessing of God. [Prov 10:23]

10 The heart knows its own bitterness,
And no stranger shares its joy.

speak the Word

Help me, Lord, to speak wisely, because wise words will protect me.
—ADAPTED FROM PROVERBS 14:3

Thank You, God, for making me upright and giving me Your favor and Your blessing.
—ADAPTED FROM PROVERBS 14:9

11 The house of the wicked will be overthrown,

But the tent of the upright will thrive.

free from bitterness

Proverbs 14:10 speaks of bitterness in our hearts. Bitterness (harboring unforgiveness) in our hearts is extremely dangerous because the Bible tells us very plainly that if we will not forgive other people, then God will not forgive us (see Mark 11:26). If we do not forgive others, our faith will not work. And everything that comes from God comes by faith. If our faith does not work, we cannot receive from God and we are in trouble.

When I preach on the subject of forgiveness, I often ask members of the audience to stand if they have been offended and need to forgive someone. I have never seen fewer than 80 percent of the congregation stand.

It does not take a genius to figure out why we are lacking the power we need in the body of Christ. Power comes from love, not from hatred, bitterness, and unforgiveness.

"But you don't know what was done to me," people say when trying to excuse their bitterness, resentment, and unforgiveness. Based on what the Bible says, it really does not matter how great the offense was. We serve a God Who is greater, and if we will handle the offense in the right way, He will bring us justice and recompense if we allow Him to do so.

In Isaiah 61:7 the Lord promises us, "Instead of your [former] shame you will have a double portion." A double portion is a reward. It is a payback for past hurts. It is like workmen's compensation. The Lord once told me, "Joyce, you work for Me, and as long as you do, if you get hurt on the job, I will pay you back."

In Romans 12:19 we are told, "Beloved, never avenge yourselves, but leave the way open for God's wrath [and His judicial righteousness]; for it is written [in Scripture], 'Vengeance is Mine, I will repay,' says the Lord." Do not try to get people back for what they have done to you. Leave it in God's hands.

Jesus taught us that we are to forgive those who hurt us, bless and show kindness to those who curse us, and pray for those who mistreat us (Luke 6:28). That is hard. But there is something harder: being full of hatred, bitterness, and resentment.

Quite often people do not even know that they have hurt us. Do not spend your life hating someone who is probably out having a good time while you are all upset! Rather, choose to allow God to work forgiveness in you so you can be released from your bitterness and set free to enjoy life.

¹²There is a way *which seems*
   right to a man *and* appears
   straight before him,
   But its end is the way of
   death.
¹³Even in laughter the heart
   may be in pain,
   And the end of joy may be
   grief.
¹⁴The backslider in heart will
   have his fill with his own
   [rotten] ways,
   But a good man will *be
   satisfied* with his ways [the
   godly thought and action
   which his heart pursues and
   in which he delights].
¹⁵The naive *or* inexperienced
   person [is easily misled
   and] believes every word he
   hears,
   But the prudent man [is
   discreet and astute and]
   considers well where he is
   going.
¹⁶A wise man suspects danger
   and cautiously avoids evil,
   But the fool is arrogant and
   careless.
¹⁷A quick-tempered man acts
   foolishly *and* without self-
   control,
   And a man of wicked schemes
   is hated.
¹⁸The naive [are
   unsophisticated and easy
   to exploit and] inherit
   foolishness,
   But the sensible [are
   thoughtful and far-sighted
   and] are crowned with
   knowledge.
¹⁹The evil will bow down
   before the good,

life point

**Think of it: a person who has a calm
and undisturbed mind has health
for his or her body. But as we see
in Proverbs 14:30, envy, passion,
and anger can actually destroy
the physical body. Keeping these
negative emotions far from you is
good for your health!**

   And the wicked [will bow
   down] at the gates of the
   righteous.
²⁰The poor man is hated even
   by his neighbor,
   But those who love the rich
   are many.
²¹He who despises his neighbor
   sins [against God and his
   fellow man],
   But happy [blessed and
   favored by God] is he who is
   gracious *and* merciful to the
   poor.
²²Do they not go astray who
   devise evil *and* wander from
   the way of righteousness?
   But kindness and truth will
   be to those who devise
   good.
²³In all labor there is profit,
   But mere talk leads only to
   poverty.
²⁴The crown of the wise is their
   wealth [of wisdom],
   But the foolishness of [closed-
   minded] fools is [nothing
   but] folly.
²⁵A truthful witness saves lives,
   But he who speaks lies is
   treacherous.

26 In the [reverent] fear of
the LORD there is strong
confidence,
And His children will
[always] have a place of
refuge.
27 The [reverent] fear of
the LORD [that leads to
obedience and worship] is a
fountain of life,
So that one may avoid the
snares of death. [John 4:10,
14]
28 In a multitude of people is a
king's glory,
But in a lack of people is a
[pretentious] prince's ruin.
29 He who is slow to anger
has great understanding
[and profits from his self-
control],
But he who is quick-tempered
exposes *and* exalts his
foolishness [for all to see].
[Prov 16:32; James 1:19]
30 A calm *and* peaceful *and*
tranquil heart is life *and*
health to the body,
But passion *and* envy are like
rottenness to the bones.
31 He who oppresses the poor
taunts *and* insults his
Maker,
But he who is kind *and*
merciful *and* gracious to the
needy honors Him. [Prov
17:5; Matt 25:40, 45]
32 The wicked is overthrown
through his wrongdoing,
But the righteous has
hope *and* confidence
and a refuge [with God]
even in death.
33 Wisdom rests [silently] in
the heart of one who has
understanding,
But what is in the heart of
[shortsighted] fools is made
known. [Is 32:6]
34 Righteousness [moral and
spiritual integrity and
virtuous character] exalts a
nation,
But sin is a disgrace to any
people.
35 The king's favor *and* good will
are toward a servant who
acts wisely *and* discreetly,
But his anger *and* wrath
are toward him who acts
shamefully. [Matt 24:45, 47]

life point

The Bible teaches us in Proverbs
15:1 that a "soft and gentle and
thoughtful answer turns away
wrath." In other words, if someone
is angry and yelling, then responding
to that person calmly and gently
will change the situation and stop
an argument. How awesome! The
next time angry words seem to be
flying around you, respond with soft,
gentle words. That's the best way to
diffuse a tense conversation.

speak the Word

*Thank You, God, that I have strong confidence as I reverently
fear You. In You, I will always have a place of refuge.*
—ADAPTED FROM PROVERBS 14:26

15

A SOFT *and* gentle *and* thoughtful answer turns away wrath,
But harsh *and* painful *and* careless words stir up anger. [Prov 25:15]
² The tongue of the wise speaks knowledge that is pleasing *and* acceptable,
But the [babbling] mouth of fools spouts folly.
³ The eyes of the LORD are in every place,

Watching the evil and the good [in all their endeavors]. [Job 34:21; Prov 5:21; Jer 16:17; 32:19; Heb 4:13]
⁴ A soothing tongue [speaking words that build up and encourage] is a tree of life,
But a perversive tongue [speaking words that overwhelm and depress] crushes the spirit.
⁵ A [flippant, arrogant] fool rejects his father's instruction *and* correction,
But he who [is willing to learn and] regards *and* keeps in mind a reprimand acquires good sense.
⁶ Great *and* priceless treasure is in the house of the [consistently] righteous one [who seeks godly instruction and grows in wisdom],
But trouble is in the income of the wicked one [who rejects the laws of God].

life point

Throughout the Word of God we are told to be careful how we use our mouths. We are to pay attention to our words. We are never to speak things that will make people want to give up or quit. We are not to pollute one another or ourselves with negative words from our lips.

Proverbs 15:4 tells us that "a perversive tongue [speaking words that overwhelm and depress] crushes the spirit." Notice that the word *spirit* is spelled with a small *s*. This verse is not talking about the Holy Spirit; it is referring to our own human spirits. Depression of the human spirit is another problem created and magnified by wrong thoughts and words—our own or those of others.

We are not to use our mouths to hurt, break down, or depress, but rather to heal, restore, and uplift. The tongue has healing power, and we need to use it to bring healing.

life point

Those who are wise use their lips to spread knowledge (see Proverbs 15:7), but those who are foolish in heart speak whatever comes to mind. I believe one of the biggest problems with people is that they do not use wisdom when they think and thus do foolish things. Ask God to help you identify and correct any foolishness in your life and to enable you to use wisdom in everything to do.

7 The lips of the wise spread
knowledge [sifting it as
chaff from the grain];
But the hearts of
[shortsighted] fools are
not so.

8 The sacrifice of the wicked
is hateful *and* exceedingly
offensive to the LORD,
But the prayer of the upright
is His delight! [Is 1:11; Jer
6:20; Amos 5:22]

9 The way [of life] of the wicked
is hateful *and* exceedingly
offensive to the LORD,
But He loves one who pursues
righteousness [personal
integrity, moral courage and
honorable character].

10 There is severe discipline for
him who turns from the
way [of righteousness];
And he who hates correction
will die.

11 Sheol (the nether world,
the place of the dead)
and Abaddon (the abyss,
the place of eternal
punishment) *lie open* before
the LORD—
How much more the hearts
and inner motives of the
children of men. [Job 26:6;
Ps 139:8; Rev 9:2; 20:1, 2]

12 A scoffer [unlike a wise man]
resents one who rebukes
him *and* tries to teach him;
Nor will he go to the wise [for
counsel and instruction].

13 A heart full of joy *and*
goodness makes a cheerful
face,
But when a heart is full
of sadness the spirit is
crushed. [Prov 17:22]

life point

Proverbs 15:13 says that "a heart full of joy and goodness makes a cheerful face." In the Amplified Classic version of the Bible, where I first learned this verse, it says that a happy heart makes a "cheerful countenance." The Bible uses the word *countenance* in many places, so I think we should pay attention to it. Your countenance is your face, the way you look. God is concerned about how we look because either we are walking advertisements for Jesus or we are walking advertisements for the enemy. That is why it is important that we learn how to have a cheerful countenance and a pleasant look on our faces.

My husband has a secretary who is always smiling. Everything he asks her to do, she does with a smile. I think that is the way God wants all of us to be. When we smile, it puts other people at ease. It gives them freedom and liberty and a sense of confidence.

It is amazing how much more comfortable and secure we are when we smile at one another and how much discomfort and insecurity we cause one another when we go around with sour looks on our faces.

Sometimes our problems are not caused by the devil as we might like to assume; they are the results of the way we feel and act. We need to cheer up. When we relax and smile, it makes us (and everyone around us) feel better.

[14] The mind of the intelligent
   and discerning seeks
   knowledge *and* eagerly
   inquires after it,
 But the mouth of the
   [stubborn] fool feeds on
   foolishness. [Is 32:6]
[15] All the days of the afflicted
   are bad,
 But a glad heart has a
   continual feast [regardless
   of the circumstances].
[16] Better is a little with the
   [reverent, worshipful] fear
   of the Lord
 Than great treasure and
   trouble with it. [Ps 37:16;
   Prov 16:8; 1 Tim 6:6]
[17] Better is a dinner of
   vegetables *and* herbs where
   love is present
 Than a fattened ox served
   with hatred. [Prov 17:1]
[18] A hot-tempered man stirs up
   strife,
 But he who is slow to anger
   and patient calms disputes.
[19] The way of the lazy is like a
   hedge of thorns [it pricks,
   lacerates, and entangles
   him],
 But the way [of life] of the
   upright is smooth *and* open
   like a highway.
[20] A wise son makes a father glad,
 But a foolish man despises his
   mother.
[21] Foolishness is joy to him who
   is without heart *and* lacks
   [intelligent, common] sense,
 But a man of understanding
   walks uprightly [making his
   course straight]. [Eph 5:15]
[22] Without consultation *and* wise
   advice, plans are frustrated,

But with many counselors
   they are established and
   succeed.
[23] A man has joy in giving an
   appropriate answer,
 And how good *and* delightful
   is a word spoken at the right
   moment—how good it is!
[24] The [chosen] path of life leads
   upward for the wise,
 That he may keep away from
   Sheol (the nether world, the
   place of the dead) below.
   [Phil 3:20; Col 3:1, 2]
[25] The Lord will tear down the
   house of the proud *and*
   arrogant (self-righteous),
 But He will establish *and*
   protect the boundaries [of
   the land] of the [godly]
   widow.
[26] Evil plans *and* thoughts of the
   wicked are exceedingly vile
   and offensive to the Lord,
 But pure words are pleasant
   words to Him.
[27] He who profits unlawfully
   brings suffering to his own
   house,
 But he who hates bribes [and
   does not receive nor pay
   them] will live. [Is 5:8; Jer
   17:11]
[28] The heart of the righteous
   thinks carefully about how
   to answer [in a wise and
   appropriate and timely
   way],
 But the [babbling] mouth
   of the wicked pours out
   malevolent things. [1 Pet
   3:15]
[29] The Lord is far from the
   wicked [and distances
   Himself from them],

But He hears the prayer of
the [consistently] righteous
[that is, those with spiritual
integrity and moral courage].
³⁰The light of the eyes rejoices
the hearts of others,
And good news puts fat on the
bones.
³¹The ear that listens to *and*
learns from the life-giving
rebuke (reprimand, censure)
Will remain among the wise.
³²He who neglects *and* ignores
instruction *and* discipline
despises himself,
But he who learns
from rebuke acquires
understanding [and grows
in wisdom].
³³The [reverent] fear of the Lord
[that is, worshiping Him
and regarding Him as truly
awesome] is the instruction
for wisdom [its starting
point and its essence];
And before honor comes
humility.

16 THE PLANS *and*
reflections of the
heart belong to man,
But the [wise] answer of the
tongue is from the Lord.
²All the ways of a man are
clean *and* innocent in his
own eyes [and he may see
nothing wrong with his
actions],

life point

Proverbs 16:2 says that all our ways
are "clean and innocent," or pure, in
our own eyes. In other words, most
of us do not see our own faults.

It would do us good to choose about
three of our most trusted friends,
sit down with them several times
a year, and ask them, "How do you
see me?" This is because we see
ourselves a whole lot differently
than others see us. Ask this question of mature, trustworthy, honest
people. Take their answers seriously
and pray about them, asking God to
help you in your weaknesses.

But the Lord weighs *and*
examines the motives *and*
intents [of the heart and
knows the truth]. [1 Sam
16:7; Heb 4:12]
³Commit your works to the
Lord [submit and trust them
to Him],
And your plans will succeed
[if you respond to His will
and guidance].
⁴The Lord has made
everything for its own
purpose,
Even the wicked [according
to their role] for the day of
evil.

speak the Word

*Thank You, God, that as I submit my works to You and
trust You, You will cause my plans to succeed if I respond
to Your will and guidance.*
–ADAPTED FROM Proverbs 16:3

the wise answer of the tongue

Sometimes the Lord gives us "the [wise] answer of the tongue" (Proverbs 16:1) from our very own lips. I learned this truth when I was in a situation where I did not know what to do and my own thoughts left me confused. I was not getting anywhere with my circumstances until I took a walk with a friend.

I was facing a major decision that needed a godly answer, but I could not find God's leading. My friend and I discussed the issue for about an hour as we walked together, enjoying the fresh air and each other's company. That is when I learned that sometimes wisdom comes out of our own mouths as we begin to talk to someone about a situation.

We talked about the circumstance and discussed several different possible solutions and their potential outcomes. We talked about how good it might be if we handled the situation one way and how bad it might be if we handled it another way. Suddenly one particular answer settled in my heart.

What I decided I needed to do was not something I naturally wanted to do. A stubborn mind-set is a great enemy of peace. Some of my struggle was because I wanted to convince God my situation should be dealt with differently from the way He was leading me. His voice was difficult to discern because my mind was already set against His plan.

It's important for us to be willing to lay aside our own desires or we may miss a clear word from God. Our natural inclination is to manipulate things to work the way we want them to work. Some of our best childhood toys taught us that square pegs will not fit into round holes, and we must remember that our plans do not always fit God's ways—no matter how forcefully we try to make the two work together.

While my friend and I considered the situation together, a wise answer came out of my mouth that I knew was from the Lord. It did not come from my mind, but it rose from my inner being. God promises that if we seek Him, He will fill our mouths (see Psalm 81:10), and Jesus promises to give us words and wisdom that none of our "opponents will be able to resist or refute" (Luke 21:15).

⁵Everyone who is proud
  and arrogant in heart is
  disgusting *and* exceedingly
  offensive to the LORD;
Be assured he will not go
  unpunished. [Prov 8:13;
  11:20, 21]

⁶By mercy *and*
  lovingkindness and truth
  [not superficial ritual]
  wickedness is cleansed
  from the heart,
And by the fear of the LORD
  one avoids evil.

humble people are happy people

People who are proud are hard to deal with because they refuse correction and good advice. In fact, Proverbs 16:5 says they are "disgusting and exceedingly offensive to the Lord." They cannot be told anything because they think they already know everything. Since they are so opinionated, they are always on the defensive, which makes it hard for them to receive correction because to them that would seem to be an admission that they are wrong—and that is something they find almost impossible to do.

In my ministry, the Lord uses me to bring correction from His Word. Generally, the flesh does not care for that, but it is what makes us grow up in the Lord. Although I try to do it in a loving way, sometimes it still causes people to react against me because, being proud, they resist the truth. Yet Jesus told us that it is the truth that sets us free (see John 8:32). Remember: free people are happy people.

It was good for me to learn that when the Lord does lead me to correct people, it is not my job to convince them. That is the job of the Holy Spirit. He is the One Who convicts and convinces people of the truth. That means you and I do not have to try to "play God" in other people's lives.

Proud people feel they have to convince others that they are right and everyone else is wrong. They try to tell people how they need to change or what they need to do. As this verse from Proverbs tells us, that kind of domineering, superior approach is not pleasing to God, Who wants His children to walk in kindness and humility, not arrogance and pride.

Proud people are also usually very rigid, which explains why they are often such strict disciplinarians. They have their own way of doings things, and if anyone does not do it their way, they react strongly, sometimes even violently: "This is it! This is the way it has to be done—or else!"

Finally, proud people are often complicated people. Although the Bible calls us to a life of simplicity, proud people feel that they have to make a big deal out of everything, to make a mountain out of every molehill. Part of the reason for this is that they think they have to figure out everything, that they have to know the "ins and outs" of every situation and know the reason behind everything that happens in life. To put it simply, they want to be in control because deep down inside they feel nobody can handle things as well as they can!

All these things help to explain why proud people are usually not very happy people. And unhappy people do not make very many other people happy either. Cultivate humility in your life so you can be happy and bring joy to others.

7 When a man's ways please the LORD,
He makes even his enemies to be at peace with him.
8 Better is a little with righteousness
Than great income [gained] with injustice. [Ps 37:16; Prov 15:16]
9 A man's mind plans his way [as he journeys through life],
But the LORD directs his steps and establishes them. [Ps 37:23; Prov 20:24; Jer 10:23]
10 A divine decision [given by God] is on the lips of the king [as His representative];
His mouth should not be unfaithful or unjust in judgment. [Deut 17:18–20; 2 Sam 14:17–20; 1 Kin 3:9–12; Is 11:2]
11 A just balance and [honest] scales are the LORD's;
All the weights of the bag are His concern [established by His eternal principles].
12 It is repulsive [to God and man] for kings to behave wickedly,
For a throne is established on righteousness (right standing with God).
13 Righteous lips are the delight of kings,
And he who speaks right is loved.
14 The wrath of a king is like a messenger of death,
But a wise man will appease it.
15 In the light of the king's face is life,
And his favor is like a cloud bringing the spring rain.

16 How much better it is to get wisdom than gold!
And to get understanding is to be chosen above silver. [Prov 8:10, 19]
17 The highway of the upright turns away and departs from evil;
He who guards his way protects his life (soul).
18 Pride goes before destruction,
And a haughty spirit before a fall.
19 It is better to be humble in spirit with the lowly
Than to divide the spoil with the proud (haughty, arrogant).
20 He who pays attention to the word [of God] will find good,
And blessed (happy, prosperous, to be admired) is he who trusts [confidently] in the LORD.
21 The wise in heart will be called understanding,
And sweet speech increases persuasiveness and learning [in both speaker and listener].
22 Understanding (spiritual insight) is a [refreshing and boundless] wellspring of life to those who have it,
But to give instruction and correction to fools is foolishness.
23 The heart of the wise instructs his mouth [in wisdom]
And adds persuasiveness to his lips.
24 Pleasant words are like a honeycomb,

Sweet *and* delightful to the soul and healing to the body.

25 There is a way which seems right to a man *and* appears straight before him,
But its end is the way of death.

26 The appetite of a worker works for him,
For his hunger urges him on.

27 A worthless man devises *and* digs up evil,
And the words on his lips are like a scorching fire.

28 A perverse man spreads strife,
And one who gossips separates intimate friends. [Prov 17:9]

29 A violent *and* exceedingly covetous man entices his neighbor [to sin],
And leads him in a way that is not good.

30 He who [slyly] winks his eyes does so to plot perverse things;
And he who compresses his lips [as if in a secret signal] brings evil to pass.

31 The silver-haired head is a crown of splendor *and* glory;
It is found in the way of righteousness. [Prov 20:29]

32 He who is slow to anger is better *and* more honorable than the mighty [soldier],
And he who rules *and* controls his own spirit, than he who captures a city.

33 The lot is cast into the lap,
But its every decision is from the LORD.

17 BETTER IS a dry morsel [of food served] with quietness *and* peace
Than a house full of feasting [served] with strife *and* contention.

2 A wise servant will rule over the [unworthy] son who acts shamefully *and* brings disgrace [to the family]
And [the worthy servant] will share in the inheritance among the brothers.

3 The refining pot is for silver and the furnace for gold,
But the LORD tests hearts. [Ps 26:2; Prov 27:21; Jer 17:10; Mal 3:3]

4 An evildoer listens closely to wicked lips;
And a liar pays attention to a destructive *and* malicious tongue.

5 Whoever mocks the poor taunts his Maker,
And he who rejoices at [another's] disaster will not go unpunished. [Job 31:29; Prov 14:31; Obad 12]

6 Grandchildren are the crown of aged men,
And the glory of children is their fathers [who live godly lives]. [Ps 127:3; 128:3]

7 Excellent speech does not benefit a fool [who is spiritually blind],
Much less do lying lips *benefit* a prince.

8 A bribe is like a bright, precious stone in the eyes of its owner;
Wherever he turns, he prospers.

⁹He who covers *and* forgives an offense seeks love,
But he who repeats *or* gossips about a matter separates intimate friends.

¹⁰A reprimand goes deeper into one who has understanding *and* a teachable spirit
Than a hundred lashes into a fool. [Is 32:6]

¹¹A rebellious man seeks only evil;
Therefore a cruel messenger will be sent against him.

¹²Let a man meet a [ferocious] bear robbed of her cubs
Rather than the [angry, narcissistic] fool in his folly. [Hos 13:8]

¹³Whoever returns evil for good,

people who laugh, last

We need to enjoy life while we work and perform the things we think we are supposed to do each day. Proverbs 17:22 teaches us that happiness in our hearts is like a good medicine.

Because my childhood was stolen from me through abuse, I never learned to be childlike. I never learned to "lighten up" and "live a little." I was so serious that I thought I should not have anything to do with things I considered to be "frivolous." I was always uptight about everything, and I rarely laughed because I was so busy working and taking life seriously. On the other hand, my husband, Dave, is the type who enjoys life regardless of what is going on around him. Although I may never have the ability to be just like he is because of the differences in our personalities, I have learned I can be much happier and more lighthearted than I used to be.

As a minister of the gospel, I have a huge responsibility. I have to work hard at what I have been called to do, and I love it. I really do enjoy my work. But if I am not careful, I can become stressed and burned out. That is why I have to make an effort to apply to my life verses such as Proverbs 17:22 and develop a happy heart and a cheerful mind.

You and I need a balance of fun and responsibility. If we are not emotionally balanced, our entire lives will be affected. I truly believe if we do not learn to laugh more, we will get into trouble because, as the Bible teaches, a happy heart is like medicine. There have been many articles written in recent years stating that medical science now confirms that laughter can be instrumental in bringing healing to the body. Laughter is like internal jogging—it exercises our souls, bringing health to them.

We need to find more humor in our everyday lives. We ought to laugh at ourselves, not take ourselves too seriously. We all need to laugh more—and sometimes we need to do it on purpose. Remember, a happy heart is good medicine!

Evil will not depart from his house. [Ps 109:4, 5; Jer 18:20]

14 The beginning of strife is like letting out water [as from a small break in a dam; first it trickles and then it gushes];

Therefore abandon the quarrel before it breaks out *and* tempers explode.

15 He who justifies the wicked, and he who condemns the righteous

Are both repulsive to the Lord. [Ex 23:7; Prov 24:24; Is 5:23]

16 Why is there money in the hand of a fool to buy wisdom,

When he has no common sense *or* even a heart for it?

17 A friend loves at all times, And a brother is born for adversity.

18 A man lacking common sense gives a pledge

And becomes guarantor [for the debt of another] in the presence of his neighbor.

19 He who loves transgression loves strife *and* is quarrelsome;

He who [proudly] raises his gate seeks destruction [because of his arrogant pride].

20 He who has a crooked mind finds no good,

And he who is perverted in his language falls into evil. [James 3:8]

21 He who becomes the parent of a fool [who is spiritually blind] does so to his sorrow,

And the father of a fool [who is spiritually blind] has no joy.

22 A happy heart is good medicine *and* a joyful mind causes healing,

But a broken spirit dries up the bones. [Prov 12:25; 15:13, 15]

23 A wicked man receives a bribe from the [hidden] pocket

To pervert the ways of justice.

24 [Skillful and godly] wisdom is in the presence of a person of understanding [and he recognizes it],

But the eyes of a [thickheaded] fool are on the ends of the earth.

25 A foolish son is a grief *and* anguish to his father

And bitterness to her who gave birth to him.

26 It is also not good to fine the righteous,

Nor to strike the noble for their uprightness.

27 He who has knowledge restrains *and* is careful with his words,

And a man of understanding *and* wisdom has a cool spirit (self-control, an even temper). [James 1:19]

28 Even a [callous, arrogant] fool, when he keeps silent, is considered wise;

When he closes his lips he is regarded as sensible (prudent, discreet) *and* a man of understanding.

18 HE WHO [willfully] separates himself [from God and man] seeks his own desire,

He quarrels against all sound wisdom.

² A [closed-minded] fool does
    not delight in understanding,
But only in revealing
    his personal opinions
    [unwittingly displaying
    his self-indulgence and his
    stupidity].
³ When the wicked man comes
    [to the depth of evil],
    contempt [of all that is pure
    and good] also comes,
And with inner baseness
    (dishonor) comes outer
    shame (scorn).
⁴ The words of a man's mouth
    are like deep waters [copious
    and difficult to fathom];
The fountain of [mature,
    godly] wisdom is like a
    bubbling stream [sparkling,
    fresh, pure, and life-giving].
⁵ To show respect to the wicked
    person is not good,
Nor to push aside *and* deprive
    the righteous of justice.
⁶ A fool's lips bring contention
    and strife,
And his mouth invites a
    beating.
⁷ A fool's mouth is his ruin,
And his lips are the snare of
    his soul.
⁸ The words of a whisperer
    (gossip) are like dainty
    morsels [to be greedily eaten];
They go down into the
    innermost chambers of the
    body [to be remembered
    and mused upon].

⁹ He who is careless in his work
    Is a brother to him who
    destroys.
¹⁰ The name of the Lᴏʀᴅ is a
    strong tower;
The righteous runs to it and
    is safe *and* set on high [far
    above evil].
¹¹ The rich man's wealth is his
    strong city,
And like a high wall [of
    protection] in his own
    imagination *and* conceit.
¹² Before disaster the heart of a
    man is haughty *and* filled
    with self-importance,
But humility comes before
    honor.
¹³ He who answers before he
    hears [the facts]—
It is folly and shame to him.
    [John 7:51]
¹⁴ The spirit of a man sustains
    him in sickness,
But as for a broken spirit, who
    can bear it?
¹⁵ The mind of the prudent
    [always] acquires
    knowledge,
And the ear of the wise
    [always] seeks knowledge.
¹⁶ A man's gift [given in love or
    courtesy] makes room for
    him
And brings him before great
    men. [Gen 32:20; 1 Sam
    25:27; Prov 17:8; 21:14]
¹⁷ The first one to plead his case
    seems right,

speak the Word

God, I declare that Your name is a strong tower.
I can run into it and be safe!
    —ᴀᴅᴀᴘᴛᴇᴅ ꜰʀᴏᴍ Pʀᴏᴠᴇʀʙs 18:10

strengthen the weak

Do you realize what Proverbs 18:14 is saying? Regardless of what comes into people's lives, they can bear up under it if they have a strong spirit within to sustain them in those times of trouble. But if their spirit is weak or wounded, they will have a hard time bearing anything in life.

Do you know what is wrong with many in the body of Christ today, why they cannot seem to handle their problems? It is not because their problems are any worse than those of anybody else. It is because they are weak in spirit. The Bible says that we are to bear with the weaknesses of people who are not strong (see Romans 15:1). We are to lift them up and support them.

Romans 12:8 tells us that one of the ministry gifts God gives to the church is that of the encourager. Such people are usually easy to recognize because every time we get around them, they make us feel better by the things they say and do. It just seems to come naturally to them to uplift, encourage, and strengthen others by their very presence and personality.

If you are like I am and would not call yourself a naturally gifted encourager, then form a habit of being more encouraging. That is what I have done, and it not only makes others feel better, it increases my joy level also. We all can give compliments, and we all can say, "Thank you." We all can refuse to be slanderers. We all can refuse to allow evil things to come out of our mouths that tear people down. We all can build up, edify, lift up, and speak life to others.

Until another comes
and cross-examines
him.
¹⁸ To cast lots puts an end to
quarrels
And decides between
powerful contenders.
¹⁹ A brother offended *is harder
to win* over than a fortified
city,
And contentions [separating
families] are like the bars of
a castle.
²⁰ A man's stomach will
be satisfied with
the fruit of his
mouth;

He will be satisfied with the
consequence of his words.
²¹ Death and life are in the
power of the tongue,

life point

Proverbs 18:21 teaches us that "death and life are in the power of the tongue." I do not believe we can overestimate the importance of our words, because they truly can make the difference between life and death. Determine today to use the power of your words to speak life everywhere you go!

power in your mouth

Proverbs 18:21 is a verse I have known for years and am very familiar with, but I am blessed every time I read it. I do not think we can read it too often, know it too well, or apply it too much. As you can tell by reading this verse, it teaches us that death and life are in the power of the tongue, and those who indulge in it will eat its fruit, either for death or for life.

Basically, the writer of Proverbs is saying in this verse: "Every time you open your mouth, you are ministering death or life, and whatever you dish out is what you are going to eat."

We have heard the phrase "You're going to have to eat your words," and Proverbs 18:21 confirms this truth. The words we speak have power to influence our lives. In fact, you may be eating your words right now, and that may be why you are not happy with your life. Your mouth may be getting you in trouble with yourself!

Proverbs 18:21 teaches us that words are so awesome. They are containers for power; they carry either a life-giving force or a destructive force.

For example, in my conferences I speak words, and those who hear those words receive life—life in their relationships, in their ministries, in their thoughts, and in all the areas that God uses me to speak to them about.

I have written a book called *Me and My Big Mouth!*, which deals with the words we speak and how to make them work for us instead of against us. The subtitle of the book is "Your Answer Is Right Under Your Nose." Perhaps you are desperately looking for an answer to what is happening in your life. Do you believe it is even remotely possible that your answer could be found in changing the way you talk? Go ahead and try it. I know the truth of Proverbs 18:21 and have experienced it many times in my own life. I believe if you will begin to speak positive, encouraging words of life and blessing, you will see blessing in your life!

And those who love it *and* indulge it will eat its fruit *and* bear the consequences of their words. [Matt 12:37]

22 He who finds a [true and faithful] wife finds a good thing
And obtains favor *and* approval from the LORD. [Prov 19:14; 31:10]

23 The poor man pleads,

But the rich man answers roughly.

life point

Jesus is a friend who sticks closer than a brother (see Proverbs 18:24). Let Him be your best friend. If you do, you will be blessed, and your relationships will be more peaceful and balanced.

24 The man of *too many* friends
[chosen indiscriminately]
will be broken in pieces *and*
come to ruin,
But there is a [true, loving]
friend who [is reliable and]
sticks closer than a brother.

19 BETTER IS a poor
man who walks in his
integrity
Than a [rich] man who is
twisted in his speech and is
a [shortsighted] fool.
2 Also it is not good for a person
to be without knowledge,
And he who hurries with his
feet [acting impulsively
and proceeding without
caution or analyzing the
consequences] sins (misses
the mark).
3 The foolishness of man
undermines his way
[ruining whatever he
undertakes];
Then his heart is resentful
and rages against the LORD
[for, being a fool, he blames
the LORD instead of himself].
4 Wealth makes many friends,
But a poor man is separated
from his friend. [Prov 14:20]
5 A false witness will not go
unpunished,
And he who breathes out lies
will not escape. [Ex 23:1;
Deut 19:16–19; Prov 6:19;
21:28]
6 Many will seek the favor of a
generous *and* noble man,
And everyone is a friend to
him who gives gifts.
7 All the brothers of a poor man
hate him;

How much more do his
friends abandon him!
He pursues *them with* words,
but they are gone.
8 He who gains wisdom
and good sense loves
(preserves) his own soul;
He who keeps understanding
will find good *and* prosper.
9 A false witness will not go
unpunished,
And he who breathes lies will
perish.
10 Luxury is not fitting for a fool;
Much less for a slave to rule
over princes.
11 Good sense *and* discretion
make a man slow to anger,
And it is his honor *and* glory
to overlook a transgression
or an offense [without
seeking revenge and
harboring resentment].
12 The king's wrath *terrifies* like
the roaring of a lion,
But his favor is as [refreshing
and nourishing as] dew on
the grass. [Hos 14:5]
13 A foolish (ungodly) son is
destruction to his father,
And the contentions of a
[quarrelsome] wife are
like a constant dripping [of
water].
14 House and wealth are the
inheritance from fathers,
But a wise, understanding,
and sensible wife is [a gift
and blessing] from the LORD.
[Prov 18:22]
15 Laziness casts one into a deep
sleep [unmindful of lost
opportunity],
And the idle person will
suffer hunger.

¹⁶He who keeps *and* obeys the commandment [of the LORD] keeps (guards) his own life,

But he who is careless of his ways *and* conduct will die. [Prov 13:13; 16:17; Luke 10:28; 11:28]

¹⁷He who is gracious *and* lends a hand to the poor lends to the LORD,

And the LORD will repay him for his good deed. [Prov 28:27; Eccl 11:1; Matt 10:42; 25:40; 2 Cor 9:6–8; Heb 6:10]

¹⁸Discipline *and* teach your son while there is hope,

And do not [indulge your anger or resentment by imposing inappropriate punishment nor] desire his destruction.

¹⁹*A man of* great anger will bear the penalty [for his quick temper and lack of self-control];

For if you rescue him [and do not let him learn from the consequences of his action], you will only have to rescue him over and over again.

²⁰Listen to counsel, receive instruction, *and* accept correction,

That you may be wise in the time to come.

²¹Many plans are in a man's mind,

But it is the LORD's purpose for him that will stand (be carried out). [Job 23:13; Ps 33:10, 11; Is 14:26, 27; 46:10; Acts 5:39; Heb 6:17]

²²That which is desirable in a man is his loyalty *and* unfailing love,

But it is better to be a poor man than a [wealthy] liar.

²³The fear of the LORD *leads* to life,

So that one may sleep satisfied, untouched by evil. [Job 5:19; Ps 91:3; Prov 12:13; Is 46:4; Jer 1:8; Dan 6:27; 2 Tim 4:8]

²⁴The lazy man buries his hand in the [food] dish,

But will not even bring it to his mouth again.

²⁵Strike a scoffer [for refusing to learn], and the naive may [be warned and] become prudent;

Reprimand one who has understanding *and* a teachable spirit, and he will gain knowledge *and* insight.

²⁶He who assaults his father and chases away his mother

Is a son who brings shame and disgrace. [1 Tim 5:8]

²⁷Cease listening, my son, to instruction *and* discipline

And you will stray from the words of knowledge.

²⁸A wicked *and* worthless witness mocks justice,

speak the Word

Thank You, Lord, that no matter what plans may be in my mind, Your purpose for me is what will stand.
–ADAPTED FROM PROVERBS 19:21

And the mouth of the wicked
spreads iniquity.
²⁹ Judgments are prepared for
scoffers,
And beatings for the backs
of [thickheaded] fools.
[Is 32:6]

20 WINE IS a mocker,
strong drink a riotous
brawler;
And whoever is intoxicated
by it is not wise. [Prov 23:29,
30; Is 28:7; Hos 4:11]
² The terror of a king is like the
roaring of a lion;
Whoever provokes him to
anger forfeits his own life.
³ It is an honor for a man to
keep away from strife [by
handling situations with
thoughtful foresight],
But any fool will [start a]
quarrel [without regard for
the consequences].
⁴ The lazy man does not plow
when the winter [planting]
season arrives;
So he begs at the [next]
harvest and has nothing [to
reap].
⁵ A plan (motive, wise counsel)
in the heart of a man is like
water in a deep well,
But a man of understanding
draws it out. [Prov 18:4]
⁶ Many a man proclaims
his own loyalty *and*
goodness,
But who can find a faithful
and trustworthy man?
⁷ The righteous man who walks
in integrity *and* lives life
in accord with his [godly]
beliefs—

How blessed [happy and
spiritually secure] are his
children after him [who
have his example to follow].
⁸ A [discerning] king who sits
on the throne of judgment
Sifts all evil [like chaff] with
his eyes [and cannot be
easily fooled].
⁹ Who can say, "I have cleansed
my heart,
I am pure from my sin?"
[1 Kin 8:46; 2 Chr 6:36;
Job 9:30; 14:4; Ps 51:5;
1 John 1:8]
¹⁰ Differing weights [one for
buying and another for
selling] and differing
measures,
Both of them are detestable
and offensive to the Lord.
[Deut 25:13; Mic 6:10, 11]
¹¹ Even a boy is known *and*
distinguished by his acts,
Whether his conduct is pure
and right.
¹² The hearing ear and the
seeing eye,
The [omnipotent] Lord has
made both of them.
¹³ Do not love [excessive] sleep,
or you will become poor;
Open your eyes [so that
you can do your work] and
you will be satisfied with
bread.
¹⁴ "It is [almost] worthless, it is
[almost] worthless," says the
buyer [as he negotiates the
price];
But when he goes his way,
then he boasts [about his
bargain].
¹⁵ There is gold, and an
abundance of pearls,

But the lips of knowledge are
a vessel of preciousness
[the most precious of all].
[Job 28:12, 16–19; Prov 3:15;
8:11]

¹⁶ [The judge tells the creditor],
"Take the clothes of one
who is surety for a stranger;
And hold him in pledge
[when he guarantees a loan]
for foreigners." [Prov 27:13]

¹⁷ Food gained by deceit is sweet
to a man,
But afterward his mouth will
be filled with gravel [just
as sin may be sweet at first,
but later its consequences
bring despair].

¹⁸ Plans are established by
counsel;
So make war [only] with wise
guidance.

¹⁹ He who goes about as a gossip
reveals secrets;
Therefore do not associate
with a gossip [who talks
freely or flatters].
[Rom 16:17, 18]

²⁰ Whoever curses his father or
his mother,
His lamp [of life] will be
extinguished in time of
darkness.

²¹ An inheritance hastily gained
[by greedy, unjust means] at
the beginning
Will not be blessed in the end.
[Prov 28:20; Hab 2:6]

²² Do not say, "I will repay evil";

Wait [expectantly] for the
LORD, and He will rescue
and save you. [Deut 32:35;
2 Sam 16:12; Rom 12:17–19;
1 Thess 5:15; 1 Pet 3:9]

²³ Differing weights are
detestable *and* offensive to
the LORD,
And fraudulent scales are not
good.

²⁴ Man's steps are ordered *and*
ordained by the LORD.
How then can a man [fully]
understand his way?

²⁵ It is a trap for a man to [speak
a vow of consecration and]
say rashly, "It is holy!"
And [not until] afterward
consider [whether he can
fulfill it].

²⁶ A wise king sifts out the
wicked [from among the
good]
And drives the [threshing]
wheel over them [to
separate the chaff from the
grain].

²⁷ The spirit (conscience) of
man is the lamp of the LORD,
Searching *and* examining all
the innermost parts of his
being. [1 Cor 2:11]

²⁸ Loyalty *and* mercy, truth *and*
faithfulness, protect the
king,
And he upholds his throne by
lovingkindness.

²⁹ The glory of young men is
their [physical] strength,

speak the Word

Lord, I wait expectantly for You. I know that You will
rescue and save me.
—ADAPTED FROM PROVERBS 20:22

And the honor of aged
men is their gray head
[representing wisdom and
experience].
30 Blows that wound cleanse
away evil,
And strokes reach to the
innermost parts.

21 THE KING'S heart is
like channels of water
in the hand of the
LORD;
He turns it whichever way
He wishes. [Ex 10:1, 2; Ezra
6:22]
2 Every man's way is right in
his own eyes,
But the LORD weighs *and*
examines the hearts [of
people and their motives].
[Prov 24:12; Luke 16:15]
3 To do righteousness and
justice
Is more acceptable to the LORD
than sacrifice [for wrongs
repeatedly committed].
[1 Sam 15:22; Prov 15:8; Is
1:11; Hos 6:6; Mic 6:7, 8]
4 Haughty *and* arrogant eyes
and a proud heart,
The lamp of the wicked [their
self-centered pride], is sin
[in the eyes of God].
5 The plans of the diligent lead
surely to abundance *and*
advantage,
But everyone who acts in
haste comes surely to
poverty.
6 Acquiring treasures by a
lying tongue
Is a fleeting vapor, the
seeking *and* pursuit of
death.

7 The violence of the wicked
will [return to them and]
drag them away [like fish
caught in a net],
Because they refuse to act
with justice.
8 The way of the guilty is
[exceedingly] crooked,
But as for the pure, his conduct
is upright.
9 It is better to live in a corner
of the housetop [on the
flat roof, exposed to the
weather]
Than in a house shared with
a quarrelsome (contentious)
woman.
10 The soul of the wicked desires
evil [like an addictive
substance];
His neighbor finds no
compassion in his eyes.
[James 2:16]
11 When the scoffer is punished,
the naive [observes the
lesson and] becomes wise;
But when the wise *and*
teachable person is
instructed, he receives
knowledge. [Prov 19:25]
12 The righteous one keeps an
eye on the house of the
wicked—
How the wicked are cast
down to ruin.
13 Whoever shuts his ears at the
cry of the poor
Will cry out himself and not
be answered. [Matt 18:30–
34;
James 2:13]
14 A gift in secret subdues
anger,
And a bribe [hidden] in the
pocket, strong wrath.

¹⁵ When justice is done, it is a
joy to the righteous (the
upright, the one in right
standing with God),
But to the evildoers it is
disaster.

¹⁶ A man who wanders from
the way of understanding
(godly wisdom)
Will remain in the assembly
of the dead.

¹⁷ He who loves [only selfish]
pleasure *will become* a poor
man;
He who loves *and* is devoted
to wine and [olive] oil will
not become rich.

¹⁸ The wicked become a ransom
for the righteous,
And the treacherous in the
place of the upright [for
they fall into their own
traps].

¹⁹ It is better to dwell in a desert
land
Than with a contentious and
troublesome woman.

²⁰ There is precious treasure
and oil in the house of the
wise [who prepare for the
future],
But a short-sighted *and*
foolish man swallows it up
and wastes it.

²¹ He who earnestly seeks
righteousness and loyalty
Finds life, righteousness, and
honor. [Prov 15:9; Matt 5:6]

²² A wise man scales the city
[walls] of the mighty
And brings down the
stronghold in which they
trust.

²³ He who guards his mouth and
his tongue
Guards himself from troubles.
[Prov 12:13; 13:3; 18:21;
James 3:2]

²⁴ "Proud," "Haughty," "Scoffer,"
are his names
Who acts with overbearing
and insolent pride.

²⁵ The desire of the lazy kills him,
For his hands refuse to labor;

²⁶ He craves all the day long
[and does no work],
But the righteous [willingly]
gives and does not withhold
[what he has]. [2 Cor 9:6–10]

²⁷ The sacrifice of the wicked is
detestable *and* offensive [to
the LORD].
How much more
[unacceptable and insulting
can it be] when he brings it
with evil intention?

²⁸ A false witness will perish,
But a man who listens *to the
truth* will speak forever *and*
go unchallenged.

²⁹ A wicked man puts on a bold
face,
But as for the upright, he
considers, directs, *and*
establishes his way [with
the confidence of integrity].

speak the Word

*God, I declare that no human wisdom, understanding,
or counsel can prevail against You. Deliverance and victory
belong to You alone.*
–ADAPTED FROM PROVERBS 21:30, 31

30 There is no [human] wisdom
  or understanding
  Or counsel [that can prevail]
  against the LORD.
31 The horse is prepared for the
  day of battle,
  But deliverance *and* victory
  belong to the LORD.

22

A *GOOD* name
[earned by honorable
behavior, godly
wisdom, moral courage, and
personal integrity] is more
desirable than great riches;
  And favor is better than silver
  and gold.
2 The rich and poor have a
  common bond;
  The LORD is the Maker of
  them all. [Job 31:15; Prov
  14:31]
3 A prudent *and* far-sighted
  person sees the evil [of sin]
  and hides himself [from it],
  But the naive continue on and
  are punished [by suffering
  the consequences of sin].
4 The reward of humility [that
  is, having a realistic view of
  one's importance] and the
  [reverent, worshipful] fear
  of the LORD
  Is riches, honor, and life. [Prov
  21:21]

putting the Word
to work

**Proverbs 22:6 teaches that children
will not depart from good training.
If you are a parent, how can you
train your children in godly ways?
Ask God to help you. He will!**

5 Thorns and snares are in the
  way of the obstinate [for
  their lack of honor and their
  wrong-doing traps them];
  He who guards himself
  [with godly wisdom] will
  be far from them *and* avoid
  the consequences they
  suffer.
6 Train up a child in the way
  he should go [teaching him
  to seek God's wisdom and
  will for his abilities and
  talents],
  Even when he is old he will
  not depart from it. [Eph 6:4;
  2 Tim 3:15]
7 The rich rules over the poor,
  And the borrower is servant
  to the lender.
8 He who sows injustice will
  reap [a harvest of] trouble,
  And the rod of his wrath
  [with which he oppresses
  others] will fail.
9 He who is generous will be
  blessed,
  For he gives some of his food
  to the poor. [2 Cor 9:6–10]
10 Drive out the scoffer, and
  contention will go away;
  Even strife and dishonor will
  cease.
11 He who loves purity of heart
  And whose speech is gracious
  will have the king as his
  friend.
12 The eyes of the LORD keep
  guard over knowledge *and*
  the one who has it,
  But He overthrows the words
  of the treacherous.
13 The lazy one [manufactures
  excuses and] says, "There is
  a lion outside!

I will be killed in the streets
[if I go out to work]!"
¹⁴ The mouth of an immoral
woman is a deep pit [deep
and inescapable];
He who is cursed by the Lord
[because of his adulterous
sin] will fall into it.
¹⁵ Foolishness is bound up in
the heart of a child;
The rod of discipline
[correction administered
with godly wisdom and
lovingkindness] will
remove it far from him.
¹⁶ He who oppresses *or* exploits
the poor to get more for
himself
Or who gives to the rich
[to gain influence and favor],
will only come to poverty.

¹⁷ Listen carefully and hear the
words of the wise,
And apply your mind to my
knowledge;
¹⁸ For it will be pleasant if
you keep them in mind
[incorporating them as
guiding principles];
Let them be ready on your lips
[to guide and strengthen
yourself and others].
¹⁹ So that your trust *and* reliance
and confidence may be in
the Lord,
I have taught these things to
you today, even to you.
²⁰ Have I not written to you
excellent things
In counsels and knowledge,
²¹ To let you know the certainty
of the words of truth,
That you may give a correct
answer to him who sent you?
[Luke 1:3, 4]

²² Do not rob the poor
because he is poor
[and defenseless],
Nor crush the afflicted
[by legal proceedings]
at the gate [where the city
court is held], [Ex 23:6; Job
31:16, 21]
²³ For the Lord will plead their
case
And take the life of those
who rob them. [Zech 7:10;
Mal 3:5]

²⁴ Do not even associate with
a man given to angry
outbursts;
Or go [along] with a hot-
tempered man,
²⁵ Or you will learn his
[undisciplined] ways
And get yourself trapped [in
a situation from which it is
hard to escape].

²⁶ Do not be among those who
give pledges [involving
themselves in others'
finances],
Or among those who
become guarantors for
others' debts.
²⁷ If you have nothing with
which to pay [another's debt
when he defaults],
Why should his creditor
take your bed from under
you?

²⁸ Do not move the ancient
landmark [at the boundary
of the property]
Which your fathers have set.

²⁹ Do you see a man skillful
and experienced in his
work?

He will stand [in honor]
before kings;
He will not stand before
obscure men.

23 WHEN YOU sit down
to dine with a ruler,
Consider carefully
what is [set] before you;
²For you will put a knife to
your throat
If you are a man of *great*
appetite.
³Do not desire his delicacies,
For it is deceptive food
[offered to you with
questionable motives].

⁴Do not weary yourself [with
the overwhelming desire] to
gain wealth;
Cease from your own
understanding of it. [Prov
28:20; 1 Tim 6:9, 10]
⁵When you set your eyes on
wealth, it is [suddenly] gone.
For *wealth* certainly makes
itself wings
Like an eagle that flies to the
heavens.

⁶Do not eat the bread of a
selfish man,
Or desire his delicacies;

life point

**Proverbs 23:7 lets us know how
crucial it is for us to think properly.
Thoughts are powerful, and they
have creative ability. If our thoughts
are going to affect what we become
(and they will), then thinking right
thoughts should be a high priority
in our lives.**

⁷For as he thinks in his heart,
so is he [in behavior—one
who manipulates].
He says to you, "Eat and
drink,"
Yet his heart is not with you
[but it is begrudging the
cost].
⁸The morsel which you have
eaten you will vomit up,
And you will waste your
compliments.

⁹Do not speak in the ears of a
fool,
For he will despise the [godly]
wisdom of your words. [Is
32:6]

¹⁰Do not move the ancient
landmark [at the boundary
of the property]
And do not go into the fields
of the fatherless [to take
what is theirs], [Deut 19:14;
27:17; Prov 22:28]
¹¹For their Redeemer is strong
and mighty;
He will plead their case
against you.
¹²Apply your heart to
discipline
And your ears to words of
knowledge.

¹³Do not withhold discipline
from the child;
If you swat him with a *reed-
like* rod [applied with godly
wisdom], he will not die.
¹⁴You shall swat him with the
reed-like rod
And rescue his life from Sheol
(the nether world, the place
of the dead).

¹⁵My son, if your heart is wise,
My heart will also be glad;

think as God thinks

Proverbs 23:7 teaches us that we become what we think, and I have certainly learned this truth over the years. Indeed, "where the mind goes, the man follows." One of the first principles believers must learn if we intend to walk in real victory is that our minds must be renewed according to the Word of God. We must learn to think like God!

Sadly, we believe many things that simply are not true. For example, some people believe they have no worth and value because people have said they do not or have treated them in a way that made them feel worthless and devalued. However, the Bible makes clear that we are so valuable to God that He sent His only Son, Jesus Christ, to die and suffer in our place in order that we might be redeemed from our sins and have an intimate relationship with Him (see John 3:16, 17).

As we learn to think as God thinks, we exchange depression and hopelessness for joyful expectation. We believe God has a wonderful future planned for us, no matter what our past has been like. We believe God wants to bless us.

When we have negative thoughts, we end up with negative results. But positive thoughts open the door for God to work in our lives. If we think we are unable to do certain things, we will be rendered unable—even though God's Word says that we can do anything God asks us to do because of His ability in us (see Philippians 4:13). Our thoughts are *that* powerful.

If we really want our lives to change, we must first change our way of thinking. Romans 12:2 says we are not to conform to the world and its ways, but that we are to completely renew our minds and attitudes so we can prove for ourselves the good, acceptable, and perfect will of God. In other words, God has good plans for us, but we will not experience them if we cling to old ways of thinking.

It is vital that we cast down wrong thinking and replace it with thinking God approves of. The mind is the battlefield on which our war with Satan is won or lost. Satan is a liar and a deceiver. His lies become our reality only when we believe them. Stop allowing your mind to be a garbage dump for Satan's trash and instead make it available for God's ideas. Then you will enjoy a life worth living and have the testimony of bearing good fruit for God's glory.

[16] Yes, my heart will
    rejoice
When your lips speak
    right things.

[17] Do not let your heart envy
    sinners [who live godless
    lives and have no hope of
    salvation],

But [continue to] live in the
[reverent, worshipful] fear
of the LORD day by day.
¹⁸Surely there is a future [and a
reward],
And your hope *and* expectation
will not be cut off.
¹⁹Listen, my son, and be wise,
And direct your heart in the
way [of the LORD].
²⁰Do not associate with heavy
drinkers of wine,
Or with gluttonous eaters of
meat, [Is 5:22; Luke 21:34;
Rom 13:13; Eph 5:18]
²¹For the heavy drinker and the
glutton will come to poverty,
And the drowsiness [of
overindulgence] will clothe
one with rags.

²²Listen to your father, who sired
you,
And do not despise your
mother when she is old.
²³Buy truth, and do not sell it;
Get wisdom and instruction
and understanding.

²⁴The father of the righteous
will greatly rejoice,
And he who sires a wise child
will have joy in him.
²⁵Let your father and your
mother be glad,
And let her who gave birth
to you rejoice [in your wise
and godly choices].

²⁶My son, give me your heart
And let your eyes delight in
my ways,
²⁷For a prostitute is a deep pit,
And an immoral woman is a
narrow well.
²⁸She lurks *and* lies in wait like a
robber [who waits for prey],

And she increases the
faithless among men.

²⁹Who has woe? Who has
sorrow?
Who has strife? Who has
complaining?
Who has wounds without
cause?
Whose eyes are red *and* dim?
³⁰Those who linger long over
wine,
Those who go to taste mixed
wine. [Prov 20:1; Eph 5:18]
³¹Do not look at wine when it is
red,
When it sparkles in the glass,
When it goes down smoothly.
³²At the last it bites like a
serpent
And stings like a viper.
³³Your [drunken] eyes will see
strange things
And your mind will utter
perverse things [untrue
things, twisted things].
³⁴And you will be [as unsteady]
as one who lies down in the
middle of the sea,
And [as vulnerable to
disaster] as one who lies
down on the top of a ship's
mast, *saying,*
³⁵"They struck me, but I was not
hurt!
They beat me, but I did not
feel it!
When will I wake up?
I will seek more wine."

24

DO NOT be envious of
evil men,
Nor desire to be with
them;
²For their minds plot violence,

And their lips talk of trouble
[for the innocent].

3 Through [skillful and godly]
wisdom a house [a life, a
home, a family] is built,
And by understanding it is
established [on a sound and
good foundation],
4 And by knowledge its rooms
are filled
With all precious and
pleasant riches.

5 A wise man is strong,
And a man of knowledge
strengthens his power;
[Prov 21:22; Eccl 9:16]
6 For by wise guidance you can
wage your war,
And in an abundance of
[wise] counselors there is
victory *and* safety.

7 Wisdom is too exalted for a
[hardened, arrogant] fool;
He does not open his mouth
in the gate [where the city's
rulers sit in judgment].

life point

Proverbs 24:10 tells us that our
strength is limited if we become
careless or slack when we encounter
hard times or difficult situations.
The Bible never promises that we
will not face adversities; it promises
us the strength and grace we need
in order to overcome those adversities. With God's strength, we never
have to become fainthearted or give
up, no matter what trials or tribula-
tions come our way.

8 He who plans to do evil
Will be called a schemer *or*
deviser of evil.
9 The devising of folly is sin,
And the scoffer is repulsive to
men.

10 If you are slack (careless) in
the day of distress,
Your strength is limited.

11 Rescue those who are being
taken away to death,
And those who stagger to the
slaughter, Oh hold them
back [from their doom]!
12 If you [claim ignorance and]
say, "See, we did not know
this,"
Does He not consider it who
weighs *and* examines the
hearts *and* their motives?
And does He not know it who
guards your life *and* keeps
your soul?
And will He not repay [you
and] every man according
to his works?

13 My son, eat honey, because it
is good,
And the drippings of the
honeycomb are sweet to
your taste.
14 Know that [skillful and godly]
wisdom is [so very good] for
your life *and* soul;
If you find wisdom, then
there will be a future *and* a
reward,
And your hope *and*
expectation will not be cut
off.

15 Do not lie in wait, O wicked
man, against the dwelling
of the righteous;

Do not destroy his resting place;
¹⁶For a righteous man falls seven times, and rises again,
But the wicked stumble in *time of* disaster *and* collapse. [Job 5:19; Ps 34:19; 37:24; Mic 7:8]

¹⁷Do not rejoice *and* gloat when your enemy falls,
And do not let your heart be glad [in self-righteousness] when he stumbles,
¹⁸Or the Lord will see your gloating and be displeased,
And turn His anger away from your enemy.

¹⁹Do not get upset because of evildoers,
Or be envious of the wicked,
²⁰For there will be no future for the evil man;
The lamp of the wicked will be put out.

²¹My son, fear the Lord and the king;
And do not associate with those who are given to change [of allegiance, and are revolutionary],
²²For their tragedy will rise suddenly,
And who knows the punishment that both [the Lord and the king] will bring on the rebellious?

²³These also are sayings of the wise:

life point

Have people done you wrong and then later experienced problems in their own lives? Proverbs 24:17, 18 strongly warns us to keep a right heart attitude and not be happy about their afflictions. Basically these verses says that if we rejoice and think they deserve what they are getting, our offense becomes worse than theirs, and we will experience the wrath that would have come against them.

All of us will have to admit that when someone has done us wrong, it takes a lot of "heart work" for us not to be at least a little bit glad to see that person get what is coming to him or her. We may pretend we do not feel this way, but I believe we all have problems with spiteful attitudes from time to time.

We need to see that God is supremely concerned about our heart attitudes. It is so important for us not to be petty and small-minded about offenses against us. We simply need to keep a right heart attitude and let God take care of everybody else. We should always remember, "hurting people hurt people." Those who hurt us are usually hurting themselves, and their pain may be so strong that they are not even aware they are hurting us when they bring pain into our lives.

To show partiality in
judgment is not good.
²⁴He who says to the wicked,
"You are righteous,"
Peoples will curse him,
nations will denounce him;
²⁵But to those [honorable
judges] who rebuke the
wicked, it will go well with
them *and* they will find
delight,
And a good blessing will come
upon them.
²⁶He kisses the lips [and wins
the hearts of people]
Who gives a right *and*
straightforward answer.

²⁷Prepare your work outside
And get it ready for yourself
in the field;
Afterward build your house
and establish a home.

²⁸Do not be a witness against
your neighbor without
cause,
And do not deceive with your
lips [speak neither lies nor
half-truths]. [Eph 4:25]
²⁹Do not say, "I will do to him as
he has done to me;
I will pay the man back for
his deed." [Prov 20:22; Matt
5:39, 44; Rom 12:17, 19]

³⁰I went by the field of the lazy
man,
And by the vineyard of the
man lacking understanding
and common sense;
³¹And, behold, it was all
overgrown with thorns,
And nettles were covering its
surface,
And its stone wall was broken
down.

³²When I saw, I considered it
well;
I looked and received
instruction.
³³"Yet a little sleep, a little
slumber,
A little folding of the hands to
rest [and daydream],"
³⁴Then your poverty will come
as a robber,
And your want like an armed
man.

25 THESE ARE also the
proverbs of Solomon,
which the men of
Hezekiah king of Judah copied:
[1 Kin 4:32]

²It is the glory of God to
conceal a matter,
But the glory of kings is to
search out a matter. [Deut
29:29; Rom 11:33]
³As the heavens for height and
the earth for depth,
So the hearts *and* minds of
kings are unsearchable.
⁴Take away the dross from the
silver,
And there comes out [the pure
metal for] a vessel for the
silversmith [to shape]. [2 Tim
2:21]
⁵Take away the wicked from
before the king,
And his throne will
be established in
righteousness.
⁶Do not be boastfully ambitious
and claim honor in the
presence of the king,
And do not stand in the place
of great men;
⁷For it is better that it be said
to you, "Come up here,"

Than for you to be placed lower in the presence of the prince,
Whom your eyes have seen. [Luke 14:8–10]

8 Do not rush out to argue *your* case [before magistrates or judges];
Otherwise what will you do in the end [when your case is lost and]
When your neighbor (opponent) humiliates you? [Prov 17:14; Matt 5:25]

9 Argue your case with your neighbor himself [before you go to court];
And do not reveal another's secret, [Matt 18:15]

10 Or he who hears it will shame you
And the rumor about you [and your action in court] will have no end.

11 Like apples of gold in settings of silver
Is a word spoken at the right time. [Prov 15:23; Is 50:4]

12 Like an earring of gold and an ornament of fine gold
Is a wise reprover to an ear that listens *and* learns.

13 Like the cold of snow [brought from the mountains] in the time of harvest,
So is a faithful messenger to those who send him;
For he refreshes the life of his masters.

14 Like clouds and wind without rain
Is a man who boasts falsely of gifts [he does not give]. [Jude 12]

15 By patience *and* a calm spirit a ruler may be persuaded,
And a soft *and* gentle tongue breaks the bone [of resistance]. [Gen 32:4; 1 Sam 25:24; Prov 15:1; 16:14]

16 Have you found [pleasure sweet like] honey? Eat only as much as you need,
Otherwise, being filled excessively, you vomit it.

17 Let your foot seldom be in your neighbor's house,
Or he will become tired of you and hate you.

18 Like a club and a sword and a piercing arrow
Is a man who testifies falsely against his neighbor (acquaintance).

19 Like a broken tooth or an unsteady foot
Is confidence in an unfaithful man in time of trouble.

20 Like one who takes off a garment in cold weather, or like [a reactive, useless mixture of] vinegar on soda,
Is he who [thoughtlessly] sings [joyful] songs to a heavy heart. [Dan 6:18; Rom 12:15]

life point

Spending too much time with any one person or group of people is usually not a good idea. In fact, Proverbs 25:17 teaches us that people can get tired of us if we overdo it. We can appreciate one another more if we stay balanced in our relationships.

21 If your enemy is hungry, give
   him bread to eat;
And if he is thirsty, give him
   water to drink; [Matt 5:44;
   Rom 12:20]
22 For in doing so, you will heap
   coals of fire upon his head,
And the LORD will reward you.
23 The north wind brings forth
   rain,
And a backbiting tongue, an
   angry countenance.
24 It is better to live in a corner
   of the housetop [on the
   flat roof, exposed to the
   weather]
Than in a house shared with
   a quarrelsome (contentious)
   woman. [Prov 21:9]
25 Like cold water to a thirsty
   soul,
So is good news from a distant
   land.
26 Like a muddied fountain and
   a polluted spring
Is a righteous man who
   yields *and* compromises his
   integrity before the wicked.
27 It is not good to eat much
   honey,
Nor is it glorious to seek one's
   own glory.
28 Like a city that is broken
   down and without walls
   [leaving it unprotected]
Is a man who has no self-
   control over his spirit [and
   sets himself up for trouble].
   [Prov 16:32]

26 LIKE SNOW in
   summer and like rain
   in harvest,
So honor is not fitting for a
   [shortsighted] fool. [Is 32:6]

2 Like the sparrow in her
   wandering, like the swallow
   in her flying,
So the curse without cause
   does not come *and* alight
   [on the undeserving]. [Num
   23:8]
3 A whip for the horse, a bridle
   for the donkey,
And a rod for the backs of
   fools [who refuse to learn].
4 Do not answer [nor pretend
   to agree with the frivolous
   comments of] a [closed-
   minded] fool according to
   his folly,
Otherwise you, even you, will
   be like him.
5 Answer [and correct the
   erroneous concepts of] a
   fool according to his folly,
Otherwise he will be wise in
   his own eyes [if he thinks
   you agree with him]. [Matt
   16:1–4; 21:24–27]
6 He who sends a message by
   the hand of a fool
Cuts off *his own* feet
   (sabotages himself) and
   drinks the violence [it
   brings on himself as a
   consequence]. [Prov 13:17]
7 Like the legs which are
   useless to the lame,
So is a proverb in the mouth
   of a fool [who cannot learn
   from its wisdom].
8 Like one who [absurdly] binds
   a stone in a sling [making it
   impossible to throw],
So is he who [absurdly] gives
   honor to a fool.
9 Like a thorn that goes
   [without being felt] into the
   hand of a drunken man,

So is a proverb in the mouth
of a fool [who remains
unaffected by its wisdom].

¹⁰ Like a [careless] archer who
[shoots arrows wildly and]
wounds everyone,

So is he who hires a fool or
those who [by chance just]
pass by.

¹¹ Like a dog that returns to his
vomit

Is a fool who repeats his
foolishness.

¹² Do you see a man [who is
unteachable and] wise in
his own eyes *and* full of
self-conceit?

There is more hope for a fool
than for him. [Prov 29:20;
Luke 18:11; Rom 12:16; Rev
3:17]

¹³ The lazy person [who is
self-indulgent and relies on
lame excuses] says, "There
is a lion in the road!

A lion is in the open square
[and if I go outside to work I
will be killed]!" [Prov 22:13]

¹⁴ As the door turns on its hinges,
So does the lazy person on his
bed [never getting out of it].

¹⁵ The lazy person buries
his hand in the dish
[losing opportunity after
opportunity];

It wearies him to bring it back
to his mouth. [Prov 19:24]

¹⁶ The lazy person is wiser in
his own eyes

Than seven [sensible] men
who can give a discreet
answer.

¹⁷ Like one who grabs a dog by
the ears [and is likely to be
bitten]

Is he who, passing by, stops to
meddle with a dispute that
is none of his business.

¹⁸ Like a madman who throws
Firebrands, arrows, and death,

¹⁹ So is the man who deceives
his neighbor (acquaintance,
friend)

And then says, "Was I not
joking?" [Eph 5:4]

²⁰ For lack of wood the fire goes
out,

And where there is no
whisperer [who gossips],
contention quiets down.

²¹ Like charcoal to hot embers
and wood to fire,

So is a contentious man to
kindle strife. [Prov 15:18;
29:22]

²² The words of a whisperer
(gossip) are like dainty
morsels [to be greedily
eaten];

They go down into the
innermost chambers of the
body [to be remembered and
mused upon]. [Prov 18:8]

²³ Like a [common] clay vessel
covered with the silver
dross [making it appear
silver when it has no real
value]

Are burning lips [murmuring
manipulative words] and a
wicked heart.

²⁴ He who hates, disguises it
with his lips,

But he stores up deceit in his
heart.

²⁵ When he speaks graciously
and kindly [to conceal his
malice], do not trust him,

For seven abominations are in
his heart.

²⁶ *Though his* hatred covers itself with guile *and* deceit,
His malevolence will be revealed openly before the assembly.
²⁷ Whoever digs a pit [for another man's feet] will fall into it,
And he who rolls a stone [up a hill to do mischief], it will come back on him. [Ps 7:15, 16; 9:15; 10:2; 57:6; Prov 28:10; Eccl 10:8]
²⁸ A lying tongue hates those it wounds *and* crushes,
And a flattering mouth works ruin.

27

DO NOT boast about tomorrow,
For you do not know what a day may bring. [Luke 12:19, 20; James 4:13]
² Let another praise you, and not your own mouth;
A stranger, and not your own lips.
³ Stone is heavy and the sand weighty,
But a fool's [unreasonable] wrath is heavier *and* more burdensome than both of them.
⁴ Wrath is cruel and anger is an overwhelming flood,
But who is able to endure *and* stand before [the sin of] jealousy?
⁵ Better is an open reprimand [of loving correction]
Than love that is hidden. [Prov 28:23; Gal 2:14]
⁶ Faithful are the wounds of a friend [who corrects out of love and concern],

But the kisses of an enemy are deceitful [because they serve his hidden agenda].
⁷ He who is satisfied loathes honey,
But to the hungry soul any bitter thing is sweet.
⁸ Like a bird that wanders from her nest [with its comfort and safety],
So is a man who wanders from his home.
⁹ Oil and perfume make the heart glad;
So does the sweetness of a friend's counsel that comes from the heart.
¹⁰ Do not abandon your own friend and your father's friend,
And do not go to your brother's house in the day of your disaster.
Better is a neighbor who is near than a brother who is far away.
¹¹ My son, be wise, and make my heart glad,
That I may reply to him who reproaches (reprimands, criticizes) me. [Prov 10:1; 23:15, 24]
¹² A prudent man sees evil and hides himself *and* avoids it,
But the naive [who are easily misled] continue on and are punished [by suffering the consequences of sin]. [Prov 22:3]
¹³ [The judge tells the creditor,] "Take the garment of one who is surety (guarantees a loan) for a stranger;

bold as a lion

If we intend to succeed at being ourselves and truly enjoy our everyday lives, we must reach a point where we allow the Holy Spirit to lead us. Only God, through His Spirit, will lead us to succeed and be all we can be. Other people usually will not, the devil certainly will not, and we are not able to do it ourselves without God.

Being led by the Spirit does not mean we never make mistakes. The Holy Spirit does not make mistakes, but we do. Following the Spirit's leading is a process that can be learned only by doing. We start by stepping out into things we believe God is putting on our hearts, and we learn by wisdom and experience how to hear more clearly and definitely. I always say, "Step out and find out." That is one way to discover if what is in your heart is from God. If it works it is God, and if it doesn't work it is not, and there is no shame in stepping out to find out. Take little baby steps and see if the first one produces good fruit; if it does then take another step. If it does not, then back off and pray some more.

I say that boldness is required to be led by the Spirit because only boldness steps out and only boldness can survive making mistakes. We must remember that the "righteous are bold as a lion" (Proverbs 28:1). When insecure people make mistakes, often they will not try again. Bold people make many mistakes, but their attitude is, "I am going to keep trying until I learn to do this right."

Those who suffer from condemnation usually do not believe they can hear from God. Even if they think they may have heard from God and do step out, a minor failure is a major setback to them. Each time they make a mistake, they come under a new load of guilt and condemnation. They end up spending all their time in the cycle. They make a mistake, feel condemned, make another mistake, feel condemned, and on and on. Finally they become frozen with fear and never fulfill their destinies.

I encourage you to step out in faith and be all that God has called you to be. If you do step out and two weeks later discover you made a mistake, are you going to be bold enough to pray, wise enough to learn from your mistakes, and determined enough to go on—or are you going to feel condemned and go back to wasting your life? There is no point in learning to be led by the Holy Spirit if you do not understand that you will make some mistakes while on the journey.

Be as bold as a lion in your faith. Do not hide behind fears, insecurities, and mistakes any longer. If you have already made major blunders in your life and have been living under condemnation because of them, this is the time to forgive yourself and press on!

In Christ, you can be all God has planned for you to be. Do not be half of it or three-quarters of it, but be *all* that God designed you to be. Do all He wants you to do, and have all He wants you to have. You will not enjoy God's fullness without His boldness. Remember, condemnation destroys boldness, so do not stay under condemnation.

Proverbs 28:1 says that the wicked flee when no one is even pursuing them. The wicked are running all the time. They run from everything. But the uncompromisingly righteous are as bold as a lion. And whether you feel it or not, you are righteous!

And hold him in pledge when he is surety for an immoral woman [for it is unlikely the debt will be repaid]." [Prov 20:16]

14 He who blesses his neighbor with a loud voice early in the morning,
It will be counted as a curse to him [for it will either be annoying or his purpose will be suspect].

15 A constant dripping on a day of steady rain
And a contentious (quarrelsome) woman are alike; [Prov 19:13]

16 Whoever attempts to restrain her [criticism] might as well try to stop the wind,
And grasps oil with his right hand.

17 As iron sharpens iron,
So one man sharpens [and influences] another [through discussion].

18 He who tends the fig tree will eat its fruit,
And he who faithfully protects *and* cares for his master will be honored. [1 Cor 9:7, 13]

19 As in water face *reflects* face,

So the heart of man reflects man.

20 Sheol (the place of the dead) and Abaddon (the underworld) are never satisfied;
Nor are the eyes of man ever satisfied. [Prov 30:16; Hab 2:5]

21 The refining pot is for silver and the furnace for gold [to separate the impurities of the metal],
And each is tested by the praise given to him [and his response to it, whether humble or proud].

22 Even though you pound a [hardened, arrogant] fool [who rejects wisdom] in a mortar with a pestle like grain,
Yet his foolishness will not leave him.

23 Be diligent to know the condition of your flocks,
And pay attention to your herds;

24 For riches are not forever,
Nor does a crown *endure* to all generations.

25 When the grass is gone, the new growth is seen,

And herbs of the mountain
are gathered in,
26 The lambs will *supply wool* for
your clothing,
And the goats will bring the
price of a field.
27 And *there will be* enough
goats' milk for your food,
For the food of your household,
And for the maintenance of
your maids.

28 THE WICKED flee
when no one pursues
them,
But the righteous are as bold
as a lion. [Lev 26:17, 36;
Ps 53:5]
2 When a land does wrong, it
has many princes,
But when the ruler is a man
of understanding and
knowledge, its stability
endures.
3 A poor man who oppresses
and exploits the lowly
Is like a sweeping rain which
leaves no food. [Matt 18:28]
4 Those who set aside the law
[of God and man] praise the
wicked,
But those who keep the law
[of God and man] struggle
with them. [Prov 29:18]
5 Evil men do not understand
justice,
But they who long for *and*
seek the LORD understand it
fully. [John 7:17; 1 Cor 2:15;
1 John 2:20, 27]
6 Better is the poor who walks
in his integrity
Than he who is crooked *and*
two-faced though he is rich.
[Prov 19:1]

7 He who keeps the law [of
God and man] is a wise *and*
discerning son,
But he who is a companion
of gluttons humiliates his
father [and himself].
8 He who increases his wealth
by interest and usury
(excessive interest)
Gathers it for him who is
gracious to the poor. [Job
27:16, 17; Prov 13:22; Eccl 2:26]
9 He who turns his ear away
from listening to the law [of
God and man],
Even his prayer is repulsive
[to God]. [Ps 66:18; 109:7;
Prov 15:8; Zech 7:11]
10 He who leads the upright
astray on an evil path
Will himself fall into his own
pit,
But the blameless will inherit
good.
11 The rich man [who is
conceited and relies on his
wealth instead of God] is
wise in his own eyes,
But the poor man who has
understanding [because he
relies on God] is able to see
through him.
12 When the righteous triumph,
there is great glory *and*
celebration;
But when the wicked rise [to
prominence], men hide
themselves.
13 He who conceals his
transgressions will not
prosper,
But whoever confesses and
turns away from his sins will
find compassion *and* mercy.
[Ps 32:3, 5; 1 John 1:8–10]

14 Blessed *and* favored by God
is the man who fears [sin
and its consequence] at all
times,
But he who hardens his heart
[and is determined to sin]
will fall into disaster.
15 Like a roaring lion and a
charging bear
Is a wicked ruler over a poor
people.
16 A leader who is a great
oppressor lacks
understanding *and* common
sense [and his wickedness
shortens his days],
But he who hates unjust gain
will [be blessed and] prolong
his days.
17 A man who is burdened with
the guilt of human blood
(murder)
Will be a fugitive until death;
let no one support him *or*
give him refuge.
18 He who walks blamelessly *and*
uprightly will be kept safe,
But he who is crooked
(perverse) will suddenly
fall.
19 He who cultivates his land
will have plenty of bread,
But he who follows worthless
people *and* frivolous pursuits
will have plenty of poverty.

life point

A life of faithfully serving and obeying God allows Him to place us in a
position to be consistently blessed.
As we learn from Proverbs 28:20, a
person who is faithful abounds with
blessings.

20 A faithful (right-minded) man
will abound with blessings,
But he who hurries to be rich
will not go unpunished.
[Prov 13:11; 20:21; 23:4;
1 Tim 6:9]
21 To have regard for one person
over another *and* to show
favoritism is not good,
Because for a piece of bread a
man will transgress.
22 He who has an evil *and*
envious eye hurries to be
rich
And does not know that
poverty will come upon
him. [Prov 21:5; 28:20]
23 He who [appropriately]
reprimands a [wise] man
will afterward find more
favor
Than he who flatters with the
tongue.
24 He who robs his father or his
mother
And says, "This is no sin,"
Is [not only a thief but also]
the companion of a man
who destroys.
25 An arrogant *and* greedy man
stirs up strife,
But he who trusts in the Lord
will be blessed *and* prosper.
26 He who trusts confidently
in his own heart is a [dull,
thickheaded] fool,
But he who walks in [skillful
and godly] wisdom will be
rescued. [James 1:5]
27 He who gives to the poor will
never want,
But he who shuts his eyes
[from their need] will have
many curses. [Deut 15:7;
Prov 19:17; 22:9]

28 When the wicked rise [to power], men hide themselves;
But when the wicked perish, the [consistently] righteous increase *and* become great. [Prov 28:12]

29 HE WHO hardens his neck *and* refuses instruction after being often reproved (corrected, criticized),
Will suddenly be broken beyond repair.
2 When the righteous are in authority *and* become great, the people rejoice;
But when the wicked man rules, the people groan *and* sigh.
3 A man who loves [skillful and godly] wisdom makes his father joyful,
But he who associates with prostitutes wastes his wealth.
4 The king establishes (stabilizes) the land by justice,
But a man who takes bribes overthrows it.
5 A man who flatters his neighbor [with smooth words intending to do harm]
Is spreading a net for his own feet.
6 By his wicked plan an evil man is trapped,
But the righteous man sings and rejoices [for his plan brings good things to him].
7 The righteous man cares for the rights of the poor,
But the wicked man has no interest in such knowledge. [Job 29:16; 31:13; Ps 41:1]
8 Scoffers set a city afire [by stirring up trouble],
But wise men turn away anger [and restore order with their good judgment].
9 If a wise man has a controversy with a foolish *and* arrogant man,
The foolish man [ignores logic and fairness and] only rages or laughs, and there is no peace (rest, agreement).
10 The bloodthirsty hate the blameless [because of his integrity],
But the upright are concerned for his life. [Gen 4:5, 8; 1 John 3:12]
11 A [shortsighted] fool always loses his temper *and* displays his anger,
But a wise man [uses self-control and] holds it back.
12 If a ruler pays attention to lies [and encourages corruption],
All his officials *will become* wicked.
13 The poor man and the oppressor have this in common:
The LORD gives light to the eyes of both. [Prov 22:2]
14 If a king faithfully *and* truthfully judges the poor,
His throne shall be established forever.
15 The rod and reproof (godly instruction) give wisdom,
But a child who gets his own way brings shame to his mother.
16 When the wicked are in authority, transgression increases,
But the righteous will see the downfall of the wicked.

¹⁷Correct your son, and he will
   give you comfort;
 Yes, he will delight your soul.
¹⁸Where there is no vision
   [no revelation of God and
   His word], the people are
   unrestrained;
 But happy *and* blessed
   is he who keeps the law
   [of God]. [1 Sam 3:1;
   Amos 8:11, 12]
¹⁹A servant will not be
   corrected by words *alone;*
 For though he understands,
   he will not respond [nor pay
   attention].

²⁰Do you see a [conceited]
   man who speaks quickly
   [offering his opinions
   or answering without
   thinking]?
 There is more hope for a
   [thickheaded] fool than for
   him.
²¹He who pampers his slave
   from childhood
 Will find him to be a son in the
   end.
²²An angry man stirs up strife,
 And a hot-tempered *and*
   undisciplined man commits
   many transgressions.

the importance of vision

People who have a sad past need to be able to believe in a bright future. Proverbs 29:18 says that, "Where there is no vision [no revelation of God and His word], the people are unrestrained."

A vision is something we see in our minds, "a mental sight," as one definition puts it, or even an understanding of God and His Word. It may be something God plants in us supernaturally or something we see on purpose. It often involves the way we think about our past, our future, and ourselves.

Some people are afraid to believe God for a vision. They think they may be setting themselves up for disappointment. They have not realized they will be perpetually disappointed if they do not believe. If I am describing you, remember this truth: it *does not cost anything to believe*. I feel that if I believe for a lot and get even half of it, I am better off than I would be to believe for nothing and get all of nothing.

I challenge you to start believing that something good is going to happen to you. Ask God for a vision to pursue, and believe you can do whatever you need to do in life through Christ (see Philippians 4:13). Do not have a "give-up-easily" attitude. Let your faith soar. Be creative with your thoughts. Take an inventory and ask yourself, "What have I been believing lately?" An honest answer may help you understand why you have not been receiving what you have wanted. Allow God's redemptive revelation to lead you away from the dead ends of your life and give you vision for your future.

²³A man's pride *and* sense of self-importance will bring him down,
But he who has a humble spirit will obtain honor. [Prov 15:33; 18:12; Is 66:2; Dan 4:30; Matt 23:12; James 4:6, 10; 1 Pet 5:5]

²⁴Whoever is partner with a thief hates his own life;
He hears the curse [when swearing an oath to testify], but discloses nothing [and commits perjury by omission].

²⁵The fear of man brings a snare,
But whoever trusts in *and* puts his confidence in the LORD will be exalted *and* safe.

²⁶Many seek the ruler's favor,
But justice for man comes from the LORD.

²⁷An unjust man is repulsive to the righteous,
And he who is upright in the way [of the LORD] is repulsive to the wicked.

30

THE WORDS of Agur the son of Jakeh, the oracle:
The man says to Ithiel, to Ithiel and to Ucal:

²Surely I am more brutish *and* stupid than any man,
And I do not have the understanding of a man [for I do not know what I do not know].

³I have not learned [skillful and godly] wisdom,
Nor do I have knowledge of the Holy One [who is the source of wisdom].

⁴Who has ascended into heaven and descended?
Who has gathered the wind in His fists?
Who has bound the waters in His garment?
Who has established all the ends of the earth?
What is His name, and what is His Son's name?
Certainly you know! [John 3:13; Rev 19:12]

⁵Every word of God is tested *and* refined [like silver];
He is a shield to those who trust *and* take refuge in Him. [Ps 18:30; 84:11; 115:9–11]

⁶Do not add to His words,
Or He will reprove you, and you will be found a liar.

⁷Two things I have asked of You;
Do not deny them to me before I die:

⁸Keep deception and lies far from me;
Give me neither poverty nor riches;
Feed me with the food that is my portion,

⁹So that I will not be full and deny You and say, "Who is the LORD?"

speak the Word

God, every word of Yours is tested and refined like silver;
You are a shield to me because I trust and take refuge in You.
–ADAPTED FROM PROVERBS 30:5

Or that I will not be poor and steal,
And so profane the name of my God. [Deut 8:12, 14, 17; Neh 9:25, 26; Job 31:24; Hos 13:6]

10 Do not slander *or* malign a servant before his master [stay out of another's personal life],
Or he will curse you [for your interference], and you will be found guilty.

11 There is a generation (class of people) that curses its father
And does not bless its mother.
12 There is a generation (class of people) that is pure in its own eyes,
Yet is not washed from its filthiness.
13 There is a generation (class of people)—oh, how lofty are their eyes!
And their eyelids are raised *in arrogance.*
14 There is a generation (class of people) whose teeth are like swords
And whose jaw teeth are like knives,
To devour the afflicted from the earth
And the needy from among men.

15 The leech has two daughters, "Give, give!"
There are three things that are never satisfied,
Four that do not say, "It is enough":
16 Sheol, and the barren womb,
Earth that is never satisfied with water,

And fire that never says, "It is enough."
17 The eye that mocks a father
And scorns a mother,
The ravens of the valley will pick it out,
And the young vultures will devour it. [Lev 20:9; Prov 20:20; 23:22]

18 There are three things which are too astounding *and* unexpectedly wonderful for me,
Four which I do not understand:
19 The way of an eagle in the air,
The way of a serpent on a rock,
The way of a ship in the middle of the sea,
And the way of a man with a maid.
20 This is the way of an adulterous woman:
She eats and wipes her mouth
And says, "I have done no wrong."

21 Under three things the earth is disquieted *and* quakes,
And under four it cannot bear up:
22 Under a servant when he reigns,
Under a [spiritually blind] fool when he is filled with food,
23 Under an unloved woman when she gets married,
And *under* a maidservant when she supplants her mistress.

24 There are four things that are small on the earth,
But they are exceedingly wise:
25 The ants are not a strong people,

Yet they prepare their food in
the summer; [Prov 6:6]
26 The shephanim are not a
mighty folk,
Yet they make their houses in
the rocks; [Ps 104:18]
27 The locusts have no king,
Yet all of them go out in groups;
28 You may grasp the lizard with
your hands,

Yet it is in kings' palaces.
29 There are three things
which are stately
in step,
Even four which are stately in
their stride:
30 The lion, which is mighty
among beasts
And does not turn back before
any;

kindness on your lips

One of my biggest problems as I learned to control my anger and my words was the fact that I had been mistreated and abused in the earlier years of my life. As a result, I ended up with a harsh, hard spirit. I was determined that nobody was ever going to hurt me again, and that attitude influenced the things I said. Although I tried to say things that were right and pleasing to others, by the time my thoughts had passed through my soul and picked up the hardness and bitterness hidden there, my words came out harsh and hard.

No matter how right your heart may be before the Lord, if you have pride or anger or resentment in your spirit, you cannot open your mouth without expressing those negative traits and emotions. Why is that? Because, as Jesus told us, our mouths speak out of whatever fills our hearts (see Matthew 12:34).

I began to realize that the Lord had an important work to do in me. Gentleness became a key issue in my life. Part of what God revealed to me in His Word on this subject was in Proverbs 31, the chapter that speaks of the "spiritual, capable, intelligent, and virtuous" woman (verse 10). In verse 26 the writer says that on her tongue is the "teaching of kindness."

When I read that, I thought, *Oh, God, I've got anything in my mouth but the law of kindness!* It seemed to me that I was so hard inside that whenever I opened my mouth, out came a hammer.

You may relate to that situation. You may have been mistreated and abused as I was so that you are full of hatred, resentment, distrust, anger, and hostility. Instead of kindness and gentleness, you are filled with harshness and hardness.

Ask God to heal you from all the pain of your past and to help you develop the kindness and gentleness He wants you to possess. Let His healing words flow from your mouth and keep kindness on your lips.

31 The strutting rooster, the
     male goat also,
   And the king *when his* army is
     with him.

32 If you have foolishly exalted
     yourself,
   Or if you have plotted *evil, put
     your* hand on your mouth.
     [Job 21:5; 40:4]
33 Surely the churning of milk
     produces butter,
   And wringing the nose
     produces blood;
   So the churning of anger
     produces strife.

31

THE WORDS of King
Lemuel, the oracle,
which his mother taught
him:

2 What, O my son?
   And what, O son of my womb?
   And what [shall I advise you],
     O son of my vows?
3 Do not give your [generative]
     strength to women
     [neither foreign wives in
     marriages of alliances, nor
     concubines],
   Nor your ways to that which
     destroys kings.
4 It is not for kings, O Lemuel,
   It is not for kings to drink wine,
   Or for rulers to desire strong
     drink, [Eccl 10:17; Hos 4:11]
5 Otherwise they drink and
     forget the law *and* its decrees,
   And pervert the rights *and*
     justice of all the afflicted.
6 Give strong drink [as
     medicine] to him who is
     ready to pass away,
   And wine to him whose life is
     bitter.

7 Let him drink and forget his
     poverty
   And no longer remember his
     trouble.
8 Open your mouth for the
     mute,
   For the rights of all who
     are unfortunate *and*
     defenseless; [1 Sam 19:4;
     Esth 4:16;
     Job 29:15, 16]
9 Open your mouth, judge
     righteously,
   And administer justice for the
     afflicted and needy. [Lev
     19:15; Deut 1:16; Job 29:12; Is
     1:17; Jer 22:16]
10 An excellent woman [one
     who is spiritual, capable,
     intelligent, and virtuous],
     who is he who can find her?
   Her value is more precious
     than jewels *and* her worth
     is far above rubies *or* pearls.
     [Prov 12:4; 18:22; 19:14]
11 The heart of her husband
     trusts in her [with secure
     confidence],
   And he will have no lack of
     gain.
12 She comforts, encourages, *and*
     does him only good and not
     evil
   All the days of her life.
13 She looks for wool and flax
   And works with willing hands
     in delight.
14 She is like the merchant ships
     [abounding with treasure];
   She brings her [household's]
     food from far away.
15 She rises also while it is still
     night
   And gives food to her
     household

And assigns tasks to her
maids. [Job 23:12]
¹⁶ She considers a field before
she buys *or* accepts it
[expanding her business
prudently];
With her profits she plants
fruitful vines in her
vineyard.
¹⁷ She equips herself with
strength [spiritual, mental,
and physical fitness for her
God-given task]
And makes her arms strong.
¹⁸ She sees that her gain is good;
Her lamp does not go out, but
it burns continually through
the night [she is prepared
for whatever lies ahead].
¹⁹ She stretches out her hands to
the distaff,
And her hands hold the
spindle [as she spins wool
into thread for clothing].
²⁰ She opens *and* extends her
hand to the poor,
And she reaches out her filled
hands to the needy.
²¹ She does not fear the snow for
her household,
For all in her household are
clothed in [expensive]
scarlet [wool]. [Josh 2:18, 19;
Heb 9:19–22]
²² She makes for herself
coverlets, cushions, *and*
rugs of tapestry.
Her clothing is linen, pure
and fine, and purple [wool].
[Is 61:10; 1 Tim 2:9; Rev 3:5;
19:8, 14]
²³ Her husband is known in the
[city's] gates,
When he sits among the elders
of the land. [Prov 12:4]

²⁴ She makes [fine] linen
garments and sells them;
And supplies sashes to the
merchants.
²⁵ Strength and dignity are her
clothing *and* her position is
strong and secure;
And she smiles at the future
[knowing that she and her
family are prepared].
²⁶ She opens her mouth in
[skillful and godly]
wisdom,
And the teaching of kindness
is on her tongue [giving
counsel and instruction].
²⁷ She looks well to how things
go in her household,
And does not eat the bread of
idleness. [1 Tim 5:14; Titus
2:5]
²⁸ Her children rise up and
call her blessed (happy,
prosperous, to be admired);
Her husband also, and he
praises her, *saying,*
²⁹ "Many daughters have done
nobly, *and* well [with the
strength of character that is
steadfast in goodness],
But you excel them all."
³⁰ Charm *and* grace are
deceptive, and [superficial]
beauty is vain,
But a woman who fears
the Lord [reverently
worshiping, obeying,
serving, and trusting Him
with awe-filled respect],
she shall be praised.
³¹ Give her of the product of her
hands,
And let her own works praise
her in the gates [of the city].
[Phil 4:8]

How to Receive Jesus as Your Personal Lord and Savior

God loves you! He created you as a special, unique, one-of-a-kind individual, and He has a specific purpose and plan for your life. He wants you to live in victory. Through a personal relationship with your Creator—God—you can discover a way of life that will truly satisfy your soul.

No matter who you are, what you've done, or where you are in your life right now, God's love and grace are greater than your sin (your mistakes). Jesus willingly gave His life so you can receive forgiveness from God and have new life in Him. He's just waiting for you to invite Him to be your Savior and Lord.

If you are ready to commit your life to Jesus and follow Him, all you have to do is ask Him to forgive your sins and give you a fresh start in the life you are meant to live. You can begin right now by praying this prayer:

Lord Jesus, thank You for giving Your life for me and forgiving me of my sins so I can have a personal relationship with You. I am sincerely sorry for the mistakes I've made, and I know I need You to help me live right. Your Word says in Romans 10:9, "If you acknowledge and confess with your mouth that Jesus is Lord [recognizing His power, authority, and majesty as God], and believe in your heart that God raised Him from the dead, you will be saved." I believe You are the Son of God, and I confess You as my Savior and Lord. Take me just as I am, and work in my heart, making me the person You want me to be. I want to live for You, Jesus, and I am so grateful to You for giving me a fresh start in my new life with You today.
I love you, Jesus! Amen.

It's amazing to know that God loves us so much! He wants to have a deep, intimate relationship with us that grows every day as we spend time with Him in prayer and Bible study.

For more about your new life in Christ, visit www.joycemeyer.org/salvation to request at no cost the book *A New Way of Living*. At joycemeyer.org, you can also find other free resources to help you take your next steps toward everything God has for you.

Congratulations on your fresh start in your life in Christ!

Everyday Life Notes

I believe that God will do many things in your life as you read, study, and live according to His Word. For that reason, I wanted to provide the following pages as a place for you to write notes in this book. You may want to use them to record your prayer requests and answered prayers, to make a list of your favorite Scripture verses and passages, to jot down understanding or revelation God gives you through His Word, or to keep some sort of diary or journal of your walk with God. Just as this book of Psalms and Proverbs reflects many years of life lessons and ministry experience for me, I hope you will use these pages to write about all the lessons God is teaching you and the experiences you are having with Him during this time of your life.

—Joyce Meyer

....

....

....

....

....

....

....

....

....

....

....

....

....